# A NEW WRITING CLASSROOM

# A NEW WRITING CLASSROOM

*Listening, Motivation, and Habits of Mind*

**PATRICK SULLIVAN**

**UTAH STATE UNIVERSITY PRESS**
*Logan*

© 2014 by the University Press of Colorado

Published by Utah State University Press
An imprint of University Press of Colorado
5589 Arapahoe Avenue, Suite 206C
Boulder, Colorado 80303

 The University Press of Colorado is a proud member of
The Association of American University Presses.

The University Press of Colorado is a cooperative publishing enterprise supported,
in part, by Adams State College, Colorado State University, Fort Lewis College,
Metropolitan State College of Denver, Regis University, University of Colorado,
University of Northern Colorado, Utah State University, and Western State College of
Colorado.

ISBN: 978-0-87421-943-2 (paper)
ISBN: 978-0-87421-944-9 (e-book)

Library of Congress Cataloging-in-Publication Data

Sullivan, Patrick, 1956–
 A new writing classroom : listening, motivation, and habits of mind /
Patrick Sullivan.
     pages cm
 Includes bibliographical references and index.
 ISBN 978-0-87421-943-2 (pbk.) — ISBN 978-0-87421-944-9 (ebook)
 1. English language—Rhetoric—Study and teaching—United States. 2. Report writ-
ing—Study and teaching (Higher)—United States. 3. Listening—Study and teaching
(Higher)—United States. I. Title.
 PE1405.U6S85 2014
 808'.042071173—dc23
                              2013033545

Chapter 7 of this book appeared earlier in a somewhat different form as "'A Lifelong
    Aversion to Writing': What If Writing Courses Emphasized Motivation?" *Teaching
    English at the Two-Year College* 39.2 (2011): 118–140.
A portion of Chapter 8 originally appeared as "Essential Habits of Mind for College
    Readiness." *College English* 74.6 (2012): 547–553.
Chapters 9 and 10 originally appeared in a slightly modified form as "An Open Letter to
    Ninth Graders." *Academe* January/February 2009: 6–10.

Cover illustration: "Light," 2014 (acrylic on plastic), Susan Classen-Sullivan.

*To Susan*

*this sky, this sun,*
*this blessed home and these sacred children*
\*\*\*\*\*

*—and to Bonnie Rose and Nicholas*

# CONTENTS

*Midway on our life's journey, I found myself*
*In dark woods, the right road lost. To tell*
*About those woods is hard—so tangled and*
*rough*
*And savage that thinking of it now, I feel*
*The old fear stirring . . .*
—Dante, *Inferno* (Pinsky translation)

# INTRODUCTION
## Deep Structures

I cordially welcome readers to this exploration of the "deep structures" of our teaching practice (to borrow a phrase from learning theorist Robert Kegan). We will be examining foundational research from both within and outside our discipline, paying particular attention to classic learning theory and recent work outside of our discipline related to motivation, transfer of knowledge, and critical thinking. As I hope readers will see, there are a number of areas where our teaching practices are not congruent with this large body of important work. It is my goal here to help our discipline engage or reexamine this work and to begin building a pedagogy that is more responsive to this foundational scholarship and research, especially as it relates to everyday teaching practices in the classroom. We will be focusing on three major areas—listening, motivation, and habits of mind. Each of these areas is developmentally scaffolded and linked, and each is an interrelated part of the approach to composing that I am theorizing here. Good teaching and learning depend on three things: first, we have to design excellent curriculum; second, we have to motivate students to engage it; and finally, we have to think about transfer of knowledge to other contexts, disciplines, and knowledge domains. This book addresses each of these vitally important and interrelated elements of our teaching practice.

We begin our journey together by focusing on perhaps the most basic and most essential of subjects for teachers of writing—what we assign in our classrooms, why we assign what we do, and what such assignments actually ask students to do intellectually and cognitively. We will examine a very common type of assignment in the writing classroom, the simplistic argumentative essay, in light of classic learning theory. As I hope readers will see, much commonly-assigned argumentative writing traps students in lower order cognitive orientations and serves to support routine, automatic, and largely unexamined ways of looking at the world and engaging complex problems (see Bargh 1997; Bargh and Chartrand 1999; Willingham 2009). I propose, instead, the development of a different kind of pedagogy and teaching practice, one that is designed to be congruent with learning theory and privileges listening, empathy, and reflection as its primary values. A great deal of evidence supports a move to this kind of pedagogy.

We will then move on to consider motivation and the extensive body of research outside of our discipline about this subject. Motivation is a vitally important precondition for any kind of real learning and meaning-making, of course, but it is routinely ignored or undervalued when we theorize approaches to teaching and learning. We can have the best pedagogy and curriculum in the world, but if students are not engaged and motivated, our pedagogy and curriculum does us very little good. "Intrinsic motivation" is the key variable here, and if we can help nurture this kind of potent, indispensable, and transformative passion in our students, there may not be anything more important that we do.

Finally, we will look beyond our own classrooms and our own discipline to consider transfer of knowledge and the nature of writing expertise. What skills and dispositions actually transfer from one context to another? Research related to critical thinking, transfer of knowledge, and the development of writing expertise suggests that intellectual and dispositional "habits of mind" may be more valuable to students, especially in the long run, than knowledge about traditional subjects at the center of most writing instruction, including the thesis statement, MLA format, and even essays themselves. These "habits of mind" include curiosity, openness, engagement, creativity, persistence, responsibility, flexibility, and metacognition. Research suggests that these dispositional characteristics do, in fact, transfer and can be of great value to students across their entire life span—at home, at work, and in their communities.

## A PEDAGOGY OF LISTENING

This book attempts to begin building a foundation for a new kind of pedagogy, one focused around the art of listening. "Listening" is theorized here as an active, generative, constructive process that positions writers in an open, collaborative, and dialogical orientation toward the world and others. Following Levinas (2006) and Nussbaum (2001) (who we will discuss in more detail later in the book), listening is also theorized here as a philosophical orientation toward the world that is characterized by "a radical generosity" toward "the Other'" and is informed most essentially by empathy and compassion. I would like to move these values to the center of our pedagogical practice in the composition classroom.

James Berlin has famously noted that "in teaching writing we are tacitly teaching a version of reality and the student's place and mode of operation in it. . . . we are not simply offering training in a useful technical skill that is meant as a simple complement to the more important studies of other areas. We are teaching a way of experiencing the world, a way of ordering and making sense of it" (Berlin 1982, 766–76). If we are, indeed, teaching "a way of experiencing the world, a way of ordering and making sense of it," what better choices can we make than to build our curriculum around listening, empathy, and reflection?

## REFLECTIVE THINKING AND WRITING

Following King and Kitchener, Perry, Baxter Magolda, Levinas, Nussbaum, Dewey, Hillocks, Yancey, Fort, Zeiger, Meyer, Heilker, Qualley, Rogers, Elbow, and a variety of feminist scholars, the pedagogy I am theorizing here links listening with reflective thinking and a type of reflective writing activity that I believe has enormous potential for use in writing classrooms. I have been developing and field testing this particular version of reflective writing in my classrooms now for over ten years. I define this kind of writing activity in some unique and specific ways:

## REFLECTIVE WRITING DEFINED

1. The primary focus for student writers should be on "listening," defined here as an active, generative, constructive process that positions readers, writers, and thinkers in an open, collaborative, and dialogical orientation toward the world and others.

2. Reflective writing assignments should invite students to engage what learning theorists call "ill-structured problems"—complex kinds of questions that cannot be comfortably encountered intellectually or easily resolved. These ill-structured problems are often the kind of "big questions" that the Association of American Colleges and Universities recommends that we put at the center of our college curriculum (Association of American Colleges and Universities 2007, 26, "Principles of Excellence").

3. The privileged cognitive disposition should be reflection—that is to say, an openness to others and to new ideas and a willingness to acknowledge complexity and uncertainty. Unlike much current writing students are asked to do at school, the focus is not on closure and certainty. Here we are following King and Kitchener's important work on developing reflective judgment: "Judgments derived from the reflective

thinking process remain open to further scrutiny, evaluation, and re-formulation; as such, reflective judgments are open to self-correction" (King and Kitchener 1994, 8).

4. Assignments and classroom activities should be designed, following classic learning theory, with the primary purpose of "empowering individuals to know that the world is far more complex than it first appears" (King and Kitchener 1994, 1).

5. Reading should be situated at the center of this reflective writing activity. Here we follow Salvatori's foundational work on reading that asks students "to imagine a text's argument not as a position to be won and defended by one interlocutor at the expense of another, but rather as a 'topic' about which interlocutors generate critical questions that enable them to reflect on the meaning of knowledge and on different processes of knowledge formation" (Salvatori 1996, 440; see also Sullivan 2010).

6. Empathy should be modeled in the classroom and privileged as a key learning tool and an essential cognitive capacity.

## A CONVERSATION

This book is designed to be a conversation about the teaching of reading and writing, framed as a series of questions that I would like to explore collaboratively with my readers. These are essential questions for teachers of writing at all levels of instruction, questions that we will explore over the course of this book as we look at the current state of teaching reading and writing and survey current research and scholarship on this and related subjects:

1. What might we be able to say that we know for sure about learning how to read and write?

2. What do we know about the current state of teaching reading and writing in the United States?

3. How are students in the United States doing right now in terms of reading, writing, and college readiness?

4. What does a review of research and scholarship in our discipline tell us about what we should be doing in the writing classroom and how we might be able to do it most effectively?

5. Is there any scholarship *outside of our discipline* that we might need to consider and be familiar with as teachers of writing? Is any of this essential work that all writing teachers should be familiar with?

6. And what are the limits of our knowledge about these subjects? Philosopher Lorraine Code (1991) in her book, *What Can She Know?*

*Feminist Theory and the Construction of Knowledge,* suggests that knowing is always a matter of degree. Examining the limits of our knowledge and understanding will always be essential to any kind of informed engagement with the kind of large and important questions we are pursuing here. So it is important that we proceed with caution and humility.

There are good answers available to these questions, if we are willing to attend carefully to a wide variety of research and scholarship that can help inform our pedagogy and shape our curriculum. This book seeks to provide some direction toward providing these answers.

The problems facing our discipline, 6–13, are well known and diverse (see, for example, Beaufort 2007; Bowen, Kurzweil, and Tobin 2005; Darling-Hammond 2010; Friedman and Mandelbaum 2011; Koretz 2008; National 2007; Rothstein, Jacobsen, and Wilder 2008). Students in the United States are underachieving to an alarming degree, especially when compared to peer cohorts in other nations around the world (Sahlberg 2011; United States Department of Education 2014, 116–123; Wagner 2008). We are currently experiencing a "college readiness" crisis in the United States, and we obviously still have important work to do related to articulation and alignment across institutional boundaries (Achieve, Inc. 2007b; ACT 2010; ACT 2006; Association 2007; United States 2011). Not to put too fine a point on this, but many of our students don't write or read well. A large number of our students don't read for pleasure, and many don't read at all. A large number of students in our classrooms are also uninterested and unmotivated learners, and many would appear to prefer not to be there. We also have a transfer of knowledge problem—skills students currently learn in writing classes do not appear to transfer from one course to the next, one grade level to the next, or one discipline to the next. Increasing reliance on standardized testing at all levels of education has taken a great deal of control out of teachers' hands and have left many teachers almost powerless in their own classrooms.

Some excellent solutions to these problems are available to us, all supported by significant bodies of research. I invite readers to work collaboratively with me as we examine this work and think together how best to address these important problems facing our discipline. Although the issues we seek to address together are complex and multifaceted, research strongly supports the following solutions:

- Reduce our overreliance on argumentative writing, especially simplistic argumentative writing.
- Make listening, empathy, and reflection the primary skills we value in our classrooms.

- Develop curriculum with learning theory clearly in mind, especially landmark work by Perry, Kegan, King and Kitchener, and Baxter Magolda.
- Bring "ill-structured problems" to the center of our pedagogy.
- Teach reading.
- Theorize reading and writing as dual and essential elements of the same activity—thinking.
- Teach reading and writing together. Most writing that students do in writing classrooms should be linked to reading, and should require, following Hillocks, a rigorous "process of inquiry" (Hillocks 2010, 26).
- Construct and design learning activities and writing assignments very carefully and purposefully, targeting key areas identified by learning theory, cognitive psychology, and critical thinking scholarship.
- Move reflective, dialogic, exploratory writing to the center of our pedagogy and curriculum.
- Make transfer of knowledge an essential consideration in pedagogical and curricular design. Knowledge of the scholarship on this subject should be considered essential for anyone discussing curriculum for our discipline.
- Develop curriculum that acknowledges the powerful links between writing expertise and genre.
- Make improving student motivation a primary concern for teachers of writing. This should be an essential part of what it means to teach writing.
- Promote variety in the writing curriculum. Students should have to "write and write often in multigenres: stories, personal essays, critical essays, parodies, poems, freewrites, letters to teachers, journals, jingles, reader responses, lists" (Lujan 2010, 56).
- Find ways to bring choice into the classroom.
- Design creative activities that disguise repetitions of writing tasks.
- Develop policies and practices that require students to take responsibility for their own learning and their own development as readers, writers, and thinkers.
- Adopt an active learning pedagogy: reduce "teacher talk" (Hillocks 2002, 7–9) in the classroom so that teachers "teach less" and students "learn more" (Sahlberg 2011, 62–69). Active learning is widely acknowledged as an important component of good teaching, and conventional wisdom suggests it is widely practiced in our profession. Evidence provided by Hillocks and others, though, appears to suggest otherwise. In *The Testing Trap*, for example, Hillocks (2002, 5–33) still finds a great deal of "teacher talk" and reductive epistemologies driving much classroom practice.
- Intentionally and systematically nurture creativity and creative thinking, 6–13. Creativity is an extraordinarily important human capacity that has been routinely overlooked and undervalued in recent

discussions of academic rigor, curricular alignment, and articulation. As Ken Robinson notes, "Creativity is the greatest gift of human intelligence. The more complex the world becomes, the more creative we need to be to meet its challenges" (Robinson 2011, xiii).

- Attend carefully to critical thinking scholarship and the "habits of mind" identified in the WPA/NCTE/NWP document, "Framework for Success in Postsecondary Writing" (Council 2011). Dispositional characteristics like curiosity, open-mindedness, flexibility, as well as a "willingness to reconsider and revise views where honest reflection suggests that change is warranted" (Facione 1990, 25) are essential to good writing and good thinking. Furthermore, these are habits of mind that appear to transfer because these dispositions are not context-, discipline-, or field-dependent. These are habits of mind that all good thinkers and writers need to produce strong work, regardless of field, occupation, or discipline.

- Embrace recent work from neuroscience, especially "the revolutionary discovery that the human brain can change itself" (Doidge 2007, xvii). Active learning, a focus on questions, and a curriculum that nurtures curiosity should be key elements for all writing curriculum (see Healy 1999, 73).

- Attend carefully to international models that produce engaged students and quality learning.

There is much to consider here and important scholarship and research for us to assess. I invite readers to collaborate with me on this journey as we consider this important scholarship and research together.

## AUDIENCE AND ORGANIZATION

Finally, a word about audience and organization. The intended audience for this book is anyone who cares deeply about the teaching of reading and writing. But it is also my modest goal here to radicalize a new generation of writing teachers, to provide them with the means and the rationale to take back our classrooms and make writing the fascinating and essential subject it has always been—not the Dickensian Gradgrind experience it so often has now become, even in the best schools, 6–13 (Perlstein 2007; Ravitch 2010; Rothstein, Jacobsen, and Wilder 2008). So, for those of you getting certified to teach high school English, and for those of you who are in graduate school preparing to teach first-year composition, this book is perhaps most essentially for you.

The organization of this book has been inspired and made possible by Paul Heilker's (1996) work on the essay and his development of an organizational strategy he calls "chrono-logic," a form of writing that privileges an openness to diverse and nontraditional forms and organization.

This book does not have the classic symmetry that one might typically find in a traditional work of scholarship. Its final form, instead, is much more asymmetrical and organic. Part I, which focuses on listening, could be a book in itself, in fact. Parts II and III are much shorter, but they are equally important to my purposes here. It is my hope that readers will find a way to embrace these asymmetries.

Let us begin this journey together, shall we, following Sun Tzu's wise and immortal advice: "Know your enemy."

# PART I

*Listening*

# 1

# THE SIMPLISTIC ARGUMENTATIVE ESSAY

## ARGUMENTATIVE ESSAYS

Argument, of course, has long enjoyed a central place in our educational curriculum and in our rhetorical tradition. Founded on major works like Aristotle's *Rhetoric* and Cicero's *Orator*, our argumentative rhetorical tradition has helped shape the way we think and write now in the west for thousands of years. Argument has also played an important part in our democratic tradition, providing Americans with a means to assess truth and determine value in our grand "marketplace of ideas."

There are many different kinds of argument, however, and not all of them help us to assess truth and value in mature and useful ways, as we will see. What I propose that we examine together in this chapter is a particularly pernicious and detrimental strain of argument—the simplistic argumentative essay, ubiquitous and often highly valued in high school and first year composition classrooms.

The argumentative essay is currently at the very core of our curriculum, 6–13, and it has become the standard model for "writing" as it is taught in high school and first-year composition (FYC). We see it prominently positioned now at key threshold points across the academic environment (Lunsford and Lunsford 2008; see also Melzer 2009). The SAT Writing Test and the AP English Tests, for example, routinely require argumentative essays. Argumentative writing is also featured prominently in the Common Core Standards, beginning in the 6th grade:

> **Grade 6**: "Write arguments to support claims with clear reasons and relevant evidence."
> **Grades 11–12**: "Write arguments to support claims in an analysis of substantive topics or texts, using valid reasoning and relevant and sufficient evidence." (45)

Students demonstrate writing proficiency now almost exclusively by writing arguments.

DOI: 10.7330/9780874219449.c001

Furthermore, and in what I believe we should regard as related news, the National Commission on Writing has concluded in their report, *The Neglected "R,"* that 12th-grade students currently produce writing that is "relatively immature and unsophisticated" (National Commission 2003, 17). There is significant evidence to suggest this is, indeed, the case, and I would like to suggest here that this problem is directly related to simplistic argumentative writing.

High school students producing "immature and unsophisticated" writing is a significant problem for our profession, of course, especially as it relates to our ongoing work related to articulation and alignment. We have seen a number of recent high-profile reports addressing this issue, including Department of Education's *A Test of Leadership* (United States Department of Education 2006); the American Association of Colleges and Universities' (2007) *College Learning for the New Global Century*; Achieve, Inc.'s (2007b, 2013) *Closing the Expectations Gap*; and Stanford University's Bridge Project report, (Venezia, Kirst, and Antonio 2003) *Betraying the College Dream: How Disconnected K–12 and Postsecondary Education Systems Undermine Student Aspirations.* Articulation, alignment, and college readiness continue to be important concerns for our profession and probably will continue to be for many years to come.

Of particular importance for our purposes here is AACU's report, *College Learning for the New Global Century* (Association of American Colleges and Universities 2007). The authors of this report urge teachers across disciplines and institutional boundaries to focus more rigorously on developing skills in "inquiry and analysis" (3) and assessing "students' ability to apply learning to complex problems" (26). The writers of this report echo Robert Kegan's claim in his book, *In Over Our Heads*, about the cognitive challenges adults face in modern life, calling for a curriculum that invites students to engage "challenging questions": "In a world of daunting complexity, all students need practice in integrating and applying their learning to challenging questions and real-world problems" (Kegan 1994, 13). The writers of this report also call on educators to become more "intentional" about the kinds of learning students need:

> The council further calls on educators to help students become "intentional learners" who focus, across ascending levels of study and diverse academic programs, on achieving the essential learning outcomes. But to help students do this, educational communities will also have to become far more intentional themselves—both about the kinds of learning students need, and about effective educational practices that help students learn to integrate and apply their learning. (4)

What might such an "intentional" pedagogy look like? What kind of theory would inform its basic principles and practices? What kind of learning would students engage in? What kind of writing would they do in a composition class? And what does current scholarship and research tell us about these important questions?

In many places across the curricular landscape, rhetoric and the strategies of classical argumentation have been incorporated into the practice of teaching writing. The "WPA Outcomes Statement for First-Year Composition," for example, positions rhetorical knowledge at the center of first-year composition instruction:

### Rhetorical Knowledge
By the end of first year composition, students should
- Focus on a purpose
- Respond to the needs of different audiences
- Respond appropriately to different kinds of rhetorical situations
- Use conventions of format and structure appropriate to the rhetorical situation
- Adopt appropriate voice, tone, and level of formality
- Understand how genres shape reading and writing
- Write in several genres

Faculty in all programs and departments can build on this preparation by helping students learn
- The main features of writing in their fields
- The main uses of writing in their fields
- The expectations of readers in their fields (Council of Writing Program Administrators 2000)

Furthermore, many high schools now offer sophisticated instruction in rhetoric and argumentation in advanced-level English courses and in AP classes. Many first-year composition programs use rhetoric and classical argumentation as well. There is good work obviously being done here in high schools and in first-year composition programs in college.

## A BRIDGE TO NOWHERE

Unfortunately, however, we should probably not be surprised to learn that more simplistic types of argumentative writing are also being taught, especially at lower levels of curriculum in high schools and in basic writing classes in college. Workload issues come into play here (Mosley 2006), along with state-mandated testing programs that typically drive curriculum as well as teaching and learning (Koretz 2008; Perlstein 2007; Ravitch 2010; Rothstein, Jacobsen, and Wilder 2008; Sacks 1999). This type of simplified "argument," often using the five-paragraph theme format (Hillocks 2010; Seo 2007; Smith 2006; Tremmel 2011), is often the default writing assignment in high school and basic writing English classes. It is particularly common in circumstances where high stakes testing drives curriculum. The rationale for this approach is well known and seems, at least at first glance, commonsensical. This type of writing gives students a "place to begin." It is typically theorized and employed as a kind of "bridge" assignment—a kind of writing activity that is "challenging enough," until a student develops the skill to do something more sophisticated. But there are significant problems with this approach, as Ed White notes:

> Powerful formulas help students get going and often help them to pass tests—but at the cost of creativity or really thinking about what they say. I would like to argue here that formulas—and especially the five-paragraph essay formula—should be regarded by teachers as a way-station on the path to more real writing. This formula should only be used to meet short-term goals. Unfortunately, I think most students are happy to stop with the formula, so teachers should avoid it whenever possible. (White 2010, 213)

In an ideal world, we would have moved beyond this type of writing long ago, even for our most underprepared and unmotivated students. A good deal of evidence however, suggests that this type of writing is still very much with us—even though we know that in most important ways this is not real writing. How else to explain, for example, the extraordinary trove of material available online related to the five paragraph essay? A recent internet search using the phrase "the five-paragraph essay" returned 889,000 results. The size of that number suggests that this kind of writing is still stubbornly and unfortunately with us. This is a version of "writing" that is radically impoverished in a number of significant ways, as these guidelines for teachers available at About.com (and brought up from among the first of my 889,000 results) suggest:

*This simple step-by-step guide might make a great handout for your students!*
Difficulty: Average
Time Required: 45 minutes
Here's how:

1. Before you begin writing, decide on your answer to the question asked of you. This is your basic thesis.

2. Before you begin writing, decide on what three pieces of evidence/support you will use to prove your thesis.

3. Write your introductory paragraph. Place your thesis along with your three pieces of evidence in order of strength (least to most) at the end of this paragraph.

4. Write the first paragraph of your body. You should begin by restating your thesis, focusing on the support of your first piece of evidence.

5. End your first paragraph with a transitional sentence that leads to paragraph number two.

6. Write paragraph two of the body focusing on your second piece of evidence. Once again make the connection between your thesis and this piece of evidence.

7. End your second paragraph with a transitional sentence that leads to paragraph number three.

8. Repeat step #6 using your third piece of evidence.

9. Begin your concluding paragraph by restating your thesis. Include the three points you've used to prove your thesis.

*Tips:*

1. Never use I or you (Unless specifically told that it is allowed).

2. Do not use contractions in formal writing.
   Source: http://712educators.about.com/cs/englishlessons/ht/htwriteessay.htm

Completing an essay like this is not much different than filling out an activity sheet in a workbook. As Paul Heilker notes in his withering critique of our discipline's love affair with thesis and support writing in *The Essay: Theory and Pedagogy for an Active Form,*

> While the world is a complex and problematic web of perplexities, the thesis/support form keeps offering our students the same simple, straightforward, and insufficient answers. Our pedagogical reliance on this form suggests to students that they need only know how to use a single tool, that their mastery of one simple and easy procedure will allow them to "fix" the infinite variety of interconnected problems they will face in the world. (Heilker 1996, 6)

This is a crucially important point, and as we will see when we turn our attention to learning theory, one that has serious ramifications well beyond the writing classroom. One of Heilker's chapter titles summarizes his overall position (and mine, too, as it happens) eloquently and boldly: "The Need for an Alternative Form in Composition Instruction." I enthusiastically support Heilker's call for an alternate form of composition instruction, and I am in fact attempting to theorize such an alternate form here.

Unfortunately, simplistic argumentation continues to persist and flourish across our curriculum, and it is easy to find additional evidence of this problem. When George Hillocks examined a number of statewide writing assessment programs, for example, he found much writing that required only lower order thinking skills and simplistic kinds of argumentative writing, including the five-paragraph format (Hillocks 2002, 88–89, 108–10, 112–14, 116–17, 121–22). As he reports in *The Testing Trap*,

> It should be clear by now that writing assessments differ enormously, from the 40-minute assessments in Illinois to the portfolio assessments in Kentucky. Statements of standards lead people to believe that the stories of assessments are obvious in the standards, but they are not. As I have shown, it is imperative to examine the prompts, the criteria, and the benchmark papers to understand what the standards mean. Only upon such analysis can we discover the banal writing that assessments in Texas and Illinois not only encourage but hold up for admiration. Only then do we see that the Illinois criteria encourage the five-paragraph theme. Only then do we see that Texas and Illinois ignore the need for real evidence in making a case. Only then do we see that in Illinois narrative turns into exposition. Only then do we see that "in-depth analysis" in New York actually means relatively simple analysis. But at least it involves some analysis and requires actual evidence in some responses to the assessment. (Hillocks 2002, 189)

Importantly, Hillocks defines "writing" in this book as a way of *thinking*: "In the past 30 years, researchers and theorists have come to know that teaching writing entails teaching thinking" (6). He suggests here that students at most levels of instruction need to do much more "systematic thinking about difficult problems" (6–7).

Scherff and Piazza were also clearly disappointed by what they discovered from their survey of approximately two thousand high school students in Florida about the writing they did in school, as the title of their essay suggests: "The More Things Change, the More They Stay the Same: A Survey of High School Students' Writing Experiences." Scherff and Piazza note that despite advances in research and scholarship, little of this work appears to get translated effectively into classroom practices and pedagogy. "In spite of advances in writing research," they conclude, "little has changed in many high schools" (Scherff and Piazza 2005, 290). It is important to note here that Scherff and Piazza also found "an alarming trend in which writing was being used to achieve a narrow band of functions" (291) and that "much of the writing" taking place in Florida high schools was done solely to practice for standardized, high-stakes tests (285), most of which require simplistic types of argumentative writing. Like Hillocks, Scherff and Piazza did not find much evidence of higher-level cognitive engagement required of the students they surveyed or much call for "systematic thinking about difficult problems." Instead, it appears that most of the writing assignments were requiring students to "primarily use writing for the informative function" (291) and that much of the writing these students were doing appeared to consist of simple explanatory assignments requiring little higher level thinking or analysis.

There is also evidence in Anne Beaufort's important longitudinal study, *College Writing and Beyond*, that suggests this kind of simplistic argumentative writing is alive and well in writing classrooms in the United States. Tim, the student writer who is at the center of this study, appears to have had considerable exposure to this kind of simplistic argumentative writing in high school. In fact, he sums up his transition from high school to college writing this way:

> She [Carla, Tim's first-year composition instructor] basically came down on the five-paragraph essay and just said, "That's not what we're about here." That plucked a chord with me. I was like, I know this is right and I'm glad I'm finally hearing it and now I can begin to learn. Because I felt very frustrated with . . . the arbitrary kind of you have to have five sentences in every paragraph and five paragraphs in every essay. The only thing I did learn in that class in high school was the transition because you do have to transition from paragraph to paragraph. (Beaufort 2007, 56)

Like Hillocks, Beaufort recommends that student writers in high school and college spend more time engaging complex problems patiently and thoughtfully (something simplistic argumentative assignments often work against). One of her primary recommendations for writing program directors, in fact, is to "coach faculty to assign serious intellectual questions for exploration in writing courses and instantiate the inquiry in particular discourse communities" (Beaufort 2007, 158).

Both the SAT and the ACT writing tests also encourage this kind of thinking and writing. Recent sample essay prompts for both the SAT and the ACT (2013) suggest how central this kind of argument has become to the assessment of writing:

### ACT Writing Sample:

> Educators debate extending high school to five years because of increasing demands on students from employers and colleges to participate in extracurricular activities and community service in addition to having high grades. Some educators support extending high school to five years because they think students need more time to achieve all that is expected of them. Other educators do not support extending high school to five years because they think students would lose interest in school and

attendance would drop in the fifth year. In your opinion, should high school be extended to five years?

In your essay, take a position on this question. You may write about either one of the two points of view given, or you may present a different point of view on this question. Use specific reasons and examples to support your position.

Source: ACT Website (http://www.actstudent.org/writing/sample/)

## SAT Writing Sample:

Think carefully about the issue presented in the following excerpt and the assignment below.

Our cherished notions of what is equal and what is fair frequently conflict. Democracy presumes that we are all created equal; competition proves we are not, or else every contest would end in a tie. We talk about a level playing field, but it is difficult to make conditions equal for everyone without being unfair to some.

Adapted from Nancy Gibbs, "Cool Running"

**Assignment:** Is it possible for a society to be fair to everyone? Plan and write an essay in which you develop your point of view on this issue. Support your position with reasoning and examples taken from your reading, studies, experience, or observations.

Source: College Board Website (http://professionals.<br>collegeboard.com/testing/sat-reasoning/prep/essay-prompts)

Both these prompts require students to stake out "positions" or a "point of view" and then develop an argument without recourse to any kind of reading, data, or "listening." In these cases, writers are expected to produce positions without having read even a single page of writing or scholarship from a discipline or field of knowledge related to their subject. There are some examples of this kind of writing assignment that do involve readings, but they also often invite or require students to think almost as hastily and simplistically.

It is certainly possible to produce solid writing from prompts like this. The student writing sample that David Jolliffe discusses in his thoughtful essay, "Advanced Placement English and College Composition: 'Can't We All Get Along?'" certainly suggests this (Jolliffe 2010, 69–70). This student essay was developed in response to the 2008 AP English Language and Composition examination question related to corporate sponsorship and public schools. As Jolliffe notes,

Some readers might notice that this composition has five paragraphs and criticize it as just another stultifying, formulaic five-paragraph theme. It's not. As I have repeatedly taught my own writing classes, and as Cathy Birkenstein and Gerald Graff make clear in their co-authored *Chronicle of Higher Education* column, a student's composition is not stultifying and formulaic simply because it has five paragraphs. The bad five-paragraph theme is one in which the "arguments. . . are disengaged and decontextualized, severed from any social mission or context" (A40; see also Graff's *Clueless in Academe*). Such is certainly not the case with this sample composition, which engages with readers, anticipates and addresses their possible objections, fleshes out its evidence with appropriate detail, and amplifies and intensifies its argumentative reasoning. (Jolliffe 2010, 71)

It is important to keep in mind, however, that this essay was written by an AP student. How do less accomplished writers in high school and basic writing courses respond to this kind of assignment? And what does this kind of assignment tell them about the practice of writing and about the nature of mature meaning-making? These are vitally important questions for our profession to consider.

The writing samples provided in the NCEE report, *What Does It Really Mean to Be College and Work Ready?* (National Center on Education and the Economy 2013) are paradigmatic of the kind of problem we have identified here. This important and disturbing empirical study focusing on college readiness skills in math and English confirms the nature and scope of this problem. As the authors of this report note, we face serious problems both in terms of reading and writing:

### Reading

Our text complexity study noted that students who will be successful readers of information-rich texts written at the 11th or 12th grade level must possess the following capacities:

- The ability to read complex texts in unsupported environments;
- The capacity to process, retain and synthesize large amounts of new information;
- Significant reading experience in a wide range of content areas; and
- The ability to read and understand tables, charts, maps, lists and other documents that supplement the prose in many college texts.

Many students emerge from high school without these capacities and experiences because reading for in-depth subject matter comprehension is not formally taught in our high schools and the reading that is required more often than not demands little more than searching for basic facts as opposed to trying to make sense of complex or conflicting ideas or both. (National Center on Education and the Economy 2013, 2)

### Writing

Our analysis of the writing required to succeed in initial credit bearing courses in community college revealed that most introductory college classes demand very little writing; when writing is required, instructors tend to have very low expectations for grammatical accuracy, appropriate diction, clarity of expression, reasoning and the ability to present a logical argument or offer evidence in support of claims. (National Center on Education and the Economy 2013, 3)

This is disturbing news, indeed.

The writing samples included in this report are drawn from community colleges chosen randomly from across the nation, and they suggest a national curriculum that traps students in lower order cognitive orientations. Example 4, the Criminal Justice Final Exam Essay, for instance, asks students to "Give the pros and cons of the death penalty, after you give your opinion" (National Center on Education and the Economy 2013, 74). Although writers are instructed that they "may use" their textbook, professional journals, and educational movies, "only one reference is required" (74). The required length of the essay also seems designed to produce poor writing: "The content should be at least one page" (74). Given these instructions, it is not surprising that the sample essay (76–78) is simplistic and underdeveloped and does not engage this complex problem with college-level depth and thoughtfulness. The single quote that the student provides, presumably from the course textbook, suggests some idea of the complexity of this issue and what would have to be carefully considered to engage this issue responsibly: "The Icardi (2007) said, 'The death Penalty Debate, historically the arguments for or against capital punishment have revolved around issues of economics, retribution, public opinion, community projection, deterrence, irreversibility, discrimination, protection of the criminal justice system, brutalization, and cruel and unusual punishment' (p. 440)" (77). Unfortunately, this assignment does not provide students the opportunity to engage these questions thoughtfully. There would need to be much more familiarity with readings, data, research; much more "listening" and reflection; and much more "systematic thinking about difficult problems." This student essay (unsurprisingly) does not engage any of the morally complex questions at the heart of this issue effectively.

Example 5, the Argument Essay, poses similar problems. This prompt asks students to "brainstorm" about a very complex issue without recourse to any readings, research, or data—or any kind of "listening," inquiry, or reflection at all:

> Imagine that a congressman has introduced this new bill to Congress:
> "The United States government shall guarantee all American citizens a minimum income of $10,000 a year for a single person, $12,000 a year for a married couple, and $15,000–20,000 a year for

a family with children (depending on the number of children). Every adult citizen who makes less than the minimum income shall receive a refund from the government to bring their income up to the minimum."

In your essay, argue that the government should, or should not, pass this bill. In the columns below, brainstorm supporting arguments for your thesis, opposing viewpoints, and your rebuttals to the opposing argument. (National Center on Education and the Economy 2013, 80)

As George Hillocks suggests, "without analysis of any data (verbal and nonverbal texts, materials, surveys and samples), any thesis is likely to be no more than a preconception or assumption or clichéd popular belief that is unwarranted and, at worst, totally indefensible" (Hillocks 2010, 26). What this type of writing is missing, Hillocks suggests, is what he calls "the process of inquiry" (26). This lack of a "process of inquiry" manifests itself in very obvious ways in the student essay that accompanies this assignment. It is a traditional five-paragraph, thesis and support essay, and this artifact can be fairly described as, indeed, "relatively immature and unsophisticated." But it is difficult to imagine any kind of strong writing artifact produced in response to this assignment unless the student happens to have done a great deal of reading and thinking about this subject. Otherwise, the only thing we can really expect to see, as Hillocks suggests, is "preconception or assumption or clichéd popular belief that is unwarranted and, at worst, totally indefensible." Alas, this is, indeed, what we get. The general question the assignment is designed around is a good one, but students have been put in an impossible position with this assignment, being asked to comment authoritatively about a subject they probably know very little about. [I have developed an assignment that asks students to explore a similar question (related to economic inequality), but it is built around reading, listening, reflecting, and a rigorous process of inquiry (see the Rich Man, Poor Man assignment in Chapter 5.)]

To my mind, perhaps the most significant single piece of evidence that we have a problem with this type of simplistic argumentative writing, often rendered in the five-paragraph format, is Ed White's recent pastiche of this form, "My Five-Paragraph-Theme Theme," first published in *CCC* and later reprinted with commentary in *What Is "College-Level" Writing? Volume 2: Assignments, Readings, and Student Writing Samples* (Sullivan, Tinberg, and Blau 2010). White's critique is quite devastating:

Since the beginning of time, some college teachers have mocked the five paragraph theme. But I intend to show that they have been mistaken. There are three reasons why I always write five-paragraph themes. First, it gives me an organizational scheme: an introduction (like this one) setting out three subtopics, three paragraphs for my three subtopics, and a concluding paragraph reminding you what I have said, in case you weren't paying attention. Second, it focuses my topic, so I don't just go on and on when I don't have anything much to say. Three and only three subtopics force me to think in a limited way. And third, it lets me write pretty much the same essay on anything at all. So I do pretty well on essay tests. A lot of teachers actually like the five-paragraph theme as much as I do.

The first reason I always write five-paragraph themes is that it gives me an organizational scheme. It doesn't matter what the subject is, since there are three parts to everything you can think of. If you can't think of more than two, you just have to think harder or come up with something that might fit. An example will often work, like the three causes of the Civil War or abortion or reasons why the ridiculous twenty-one-year-old limit for drinking alcohol should be abolished. A worse problem is when you wind up with more than three subtopics, since sometimes you want to talk about all of them. But you can't. You have to pick the best three. That keeps you from thinking too much, which is a great time saver, especially on an essay test. (White 2010, 137)

The circumstances that led White to write this essay are significant as well, and they deserve to be carefully noted:

I wrote this little *jeu d'esprit* while flying back to Arizona from Florida after serving as a Table Leader for the 2007 Advanced Placement English test. I had been part of an army of readers scoring about 280,000 exams, each containing three impromptu essays, written by high school students— many of them trained to write five-paragraph essays in order to pass writing tests. I had been disheartened by how many good writers I saw writing badly. It was clear that this training in producing five-paragraph essays often had little to do with writing as a form of discovery and reflection, not to speak of developed argument. But what else can we expect of high school seniors writing an impromptu essay in 45 minutes? Many of these 280,000 students had obviously been trained to write 5-paragraph themes, and who can blame either the teachers or the students for that? Still, I was troubled: Why did so many of the AP essays show so little of what we teach in first-year writing courses, despite the obvious competence of the students in the techniques of essay production? (White 2010, 138–39)

We encounter two very telling sentences here: "I had been disheartened by how many good writers I saw writing badly. It was clear that this training in producing five-paragraph essays often had little to do with writing as a form of discovery and reflection, not to speak of developed argument." These are two sentences that all teachers of English should know well.

We see Professor White expressing here a very strong and clear sense that these students are struggling against a kind of writing task that traps or confines them in a lower order cognitive orientation. Surely it must be the design of this assignment that keeps these "good writers" from writing well, right? What is the problem, though, precisely? As I hope readers will see when we turn to our consideration of learning theory, we can identify the problem with considerable precision.

This type of simplified argument is not really an argument at all in any rigorous or perhaps even meaningful sense of that word, but in its outward form it does resemble an argument in some very basic ways: a "position" is established and defended. This kind of essay is, in fact, often simply a statement of opinion. It usually does not feature the various essential rhetorical elements of classical argumentative models, nor does it typically attempt the deep and meticulous engagement with a living body of data, research, and scholarship the way a mature academic argument typically does. Oftentimes, it involves no reading, engagement with others, or "listening" at all. Lunsford and Lunsford report, for example, that twenty-one percent of the papers they examined for their recent study of FYC were "argument" papers "with very few or no sources" (Lunsford and Lunsford 2008, 793).

I would like to suggest that this type of simplistic argumentative writing is not in any way a "bridge" to better types of writing. In fact, this kind of writing confines students to lower order cognitive orientations and serves to support routine, automatic, and cognitively unsophisticated ways of looking at the world and engaging complex problems. I think this is precisely the reason that the National Commission on Writing found that 12th grade students produce writing that is "relatively immature and unsophisticated" (National 2003, 17). These descriptors appear to be very well chosen. In very specific ways related to cognitive and emotional development, we are, indeed, currently asking students to engage ideas and complex problems in ways that are developmentally immature and unsophisticated. I would like to propose a different kind of "bridge" theory and assignment, one that privileges listening, empathy, and reflection.

## 2
# COGNITIVE DEVELOPMENT
# AND LEARNING THEORY

### "INTELLIGENT CONFUSION"

Learning theory can help us define precisely what is at stake here for our students. This is work that can also help us make good choices about assignment design, the writing we ask students to do in our classrooms, and the values we privilege in our pedagogy and curriculum. This is work that all compositionists should be familiar with. If this body of work is familiar to you, please forgive me for briefly reviewing it at this time. It is essential for our purposes as we map the cognitive landscape of the composition classroom and develop recommendations for redesigning our curriculum.

As many compositionists know, our discipline has had a long and fruitful engagement with learning theory, cognitive research, and theories of student development (Berlin 1987, 159–65; Berlin 2005; Evans, Forney, and Guido-DiBrito 1998, 3–30; Faigley 1986; Fulkerson 2005; Harris 1997; Pascarella and Terenzini 2005, 19–61; see also Ambrose et al. 2010). I would like to suggest here that a pedagogy focused on listening, empathy, and reflection has the potential to help students move toward thinking in more cognitively sophisticated ways about the world, their place in it, and the production of meaning and value.

Perhaps the best place to begin our examination of learning theory is with a brief discussion of King and Kitchener's three cognitive stages of development: "pre-reflective," "quasi-reflective," and "reflective." Along this continuum, King and Kitchener identify "seven distinct sets of assumptions about knowledge and how knowledge is acquired" (King and Kitchener 1994, 13) within these cognitive stages. These positions are theorized as part of a developmental progression (as they are for Perry, Kegan, and Baxter Magolda) that moves from a simplistic, absolutist orientation ("Knowledge is assumed to exist absolutely and concretely . . . It can be obtained with certainty by direct observation." [14]) to one that requires individuals to "hold the epistemic assumptions that

DOI: 10.7330/9780874219449.c002

allow them to understand and accept real uncertainty" (17). For King and Kitchener, the way students engage complexity and uncertainty is a key variable in terms of developing more sophisticated cognitive orientations:

> Recall that at Stage 4 [which is where King and Kitchener find many college seniors in their study (165–71)] comes the acknowledgement that uncertainty is not just a temporary condition of knowing. It is at this state, too, that students begin to use evidence systematically to support their judgment, a development of no small consequence. As Barry Knoll has described this type of development, students are abandoning "ignorant certainty" (characteristic of earlier stage reasoning) in favor of "intelligent confusion." While promoting student confusion is not a goal typically published in college mission statements, Knoll's observation serves to remind us that intelligent confusion is a developmental advance over ignorant, dogmatic certainty and that it paves the way for more thoughtful, reasoned judgments that may follow. (King and Kitchener 1994, 166–67)

A key marker for King and Kitchener in the process of developing more sophisticated cognitive orientations is how we employ evidence to support our judgments. Once students begin "to accept the concept that uncertainty may be an ongoing characteristic of the knowing process" (166), the use of evidence becomes crucial. This takes us to the heart of the problem with simplistic argumentative assignments like those we have surveyed. Many college students

> are at a loss when asked to defend their answers to ill-structured problems, for Stage 4 [reasoning] has as a major characteristic the assumption that, because there are many possible answers to every question and no absolutely certain way to adjudicate between competing answers, knowledge claims are simply idiosyncratic to the individual. In other words, an answer to an ill-structured problem is seen as merely an opinion. Further, many college students are not demonstrating an ability to articulate the role of evidence in making interpretations (Stage 5) or to defensibly critique their own judgments or explanations as being in some way better than or preferable to alternative explanations (Stage 7). (King and Kitchener 1994, 167)

Underlying all this is the assumption that "answers are contingent and knowledge is contextual" (168). An early report (1991) from the Association of American Colleges, "The Challenge of Connecting Learning," gets at precisely what's at stake here—and does so with noteworthy and memorable language:

> In the final analysis, the challenge of college, for students and faculty members alike, is empowering individuals to know that the world is far more complex than it first appears, and that they must make interpretive arguments and decisions—judgments that entail real consequences for

which they must take responsibility and from which they may not flee by disclaiming expertise (Association 1991, 16–17).

This is something that simplistic argumentative writing actively subverts. Such writing, unfortunately, typically rewards "ignorant certainty" at the expense of "intelligent confusion."

At the heart of King and Kitchener's pedagogical recommendations for promoting reflective judgment is the ill-structured problem. The type of problem we ask students to engage is obviously a key variable in any kind of writing pedagogy, so this distinction is vitally important for our discussion. Cognitive scientists typically identify two different types of problems: "well-structured" and "ill-structured." Well-structured problems, as King and Kitchener note, "have single correct answers that are ultimately available" and the "task for the problem solver is to find and apply a decision-making procedure to find, compute, or remember the solutions" (King and Kitchener 1994, 100). Ill-structured problems "cannot be resolved with a high degree of certainty" and "experts often disagree about the best solution, even when the problem can be considered solved" (11). In their recommendations for educators, King and Kitchener suggest that ill-structured problems have much to offer students:

> *Familiarize students with ill-structured problems within your own discipline or areas of expertise.* Do this even early in their educational experience. Such problems should not be viewed as the exclusive domain of seniors, senior seminars, or graduate courses. Students are usually attracted to a discipline because it promises a way of better understanding contemporary problems in a particular field, yet they are often asked to "cover the basics" for three or four years before they are permitted to wrestle with the compelling, unresolved issues of the day. Ill-structured problems should be viewed as essential aspects of undergraduate education. When the aim is to help students develop a more complex epistemological framework, opportunities to help students examine the evolution of knowledge itself are especially relevant. (King and Kitchener 1994, 233, 236)

The pedagogy I am theorizing here, which links a variety of activities, dispositions, and pedagogical strategies under the umbrella term "listening," seeks to bring the ill-structured problem and the idea that "uncertainty is not just a temporary condition of knowing" to the center of our curriculum.

Just a quick additional note about "ill-structured problems": Recent research on teaching and curriculum design also supports a focus on "ill-structured problems." Such problems are much more likely, following Ken Bain's (2004) formulation in *What the Best College Teachers Do,* to accomplish what excellent assignments do: "confront students with intriguing, beautiful, or important problems, authentic tasks that will challenge them to grapple with ideas, rethink their assumptions, and examine their mental models of reality" (18). A focus on "ill-structured problems" is also congruent with McTighe and Wiggins's (2005) call for a curricular focus on "essential questions"—that is, questions that are "open-ended," "thought-provoking" and "intellectually engaging," that call for "higher order thinking," point toward "important, transferable ideas," raise "additional questions," require "support and justification," and "recur over time" (the question can and should be revisited) (3). "Essential questions" are, in many ways, simply a different way to describe "ill-structured problems," as they also focus student attention on complex questions that cannot be easily resolved. As McTighe and Wiggins note, "essential questions"

> are not answerable with finality in a single lesson or a brief sentence—and that's the point. Their aim is to stimulate thought, to provoke inquiry, and to spark more questions, including thoughtful student questions, not just pat answers. They are provocative and generative. By tackling such questions, learners are engaged in *uncovering* the depth and richness of a topic that might otherwise be obscured by simply *covering* it. (McTighe and Wiggins 2005, 3)

A focus on "ill-structured problems" is also congruent with John Bean's work on integrating writing, critical thinking, and active learning in the classroom. Bean speaks eloquently in *Engaging Ideas* about the power of well-designed problems to "awaken and stimulate" even the "passive and unmotivated student" (Bean 2011, 3). The "problem-based" assignment—very similar to the kind of "ill-structured" problems we are discussing here—is at the heart of his pedagogy (89–145). Bean is following Joanne Kurfiss here, an important scholar of critical thinking, for whom "the prototypical academic problem is 'ill-structured'" (Bean 2011, 4). Kurfiss suggests, in fact, that "in critical thinking, all assumptions are open to question, divergent views are aggressively sought, and the inquiry is not biased in favor of a particular outcome" (Kurfiss 1988, 2). Critical thinking itself, suggests Kurfiss, is "a rational response to questions that cannot be answered definitively and for which all the relevant information may not be available" (Kurfiss 1988, 2). Specific and pragmatic curricular recommendations as well as what forms ill-structured problems might take in a writing classroom are provided in subsequent chapters.

William Perry's (1999) classic book, *Forms of Ethical and Intellectual Development in the College Years*, offers us additional clarity about developmental stages and what is at stake for our students in the writing classroom. King and Kitchener's research, like other studies on learning theory since Perry, draws on and updates the work Perry reports on in this important book. Perry identifies nine cognitive stages or "positions" in his scheme. The key positions for our purposes here are Positions 3, 4, 5, and 6:

> Position 3: The student accepts diversity and uncertainty as legitimate but still temporary in areas where Authority "hasn't found The Answer yet." He supposes Authority grades him in these areas on "good expression" but remains puzzled as to standards.
>
> Position 4: (a) The student perceives legitimate uncertainty (and therefore diversity of opinion) to be extensive and raises it to the status of an unstructured epistemological realm of its own in which "anyone has a right to his own opinion," a realm which he sets over against Authority's realm where right-wrong still prevails, or (b) the students discovers qualitative contextual relativistic reasoning as a special case of "what They want" within Authority's realm.
>
> Position 5: The student perceives all knowledge and values (including authority's) as contextual and relativistic and subordinates dualistic right-wrong functions to the status of a special case, in context.
>
> Position 6: The student apprehends the necessity of orienting himself in a relativistic world through some form of personal Commitment (as distinct from unquestioned or unconsidered commitment to simple belief in certainty). (Perry 1999, 10–11)

The significant qualitative difference between the 3rd and 5th positions in Perry's scheme—which is precisely where much of our work as writing teachers in high school, basic writing, and FYC classes should be focused—is the difference between simplistic, self-centered, absolutist ways of knowing the world and more contingent, situational, contextual ways of knowing the world and defining our relationship to knowledge and authority. Simplistic thesis and support argumentative writing, unfortunately, reinforces lower-order orientations, especially the idea that "anyone has a right to his own opinion" (Position 4). High school, basic writing, and FYC teachers should be actively engaged in helping students move *away* from this kind of simplistic thinking and *toward* the more cognitively sophisticated positions in Perry's scheme. Our focus should be less on certainty and closure, and more on exploration and reflection. Unfortunately, much simplistic argumentative writing actually *requires* premature, unearned, and in some cases even arbitrary certainty and closure. The key transition point at Position 5—"contextual relativism"—deserves careful attention from our discipline because it is a crucial developmental threshold for Perry, and it is associated in his work with the beginnings of mature adult thinking. Position 6 is also a crucial stage because it introduces students to Perry's important concept of "commitment" within a context in which there are few certainties or absolutes.

## COGNITIVE CHALLENGES OUTSIDE THE CLASSROOM

Robert Kegan's work helps clarify an important point here about the broad value of helping students move toward the more advanced positions in King and Kitchener's and Perry's developmental trajectories. Kegan's book, *In Over Our Heads*, systematically examines the imposing cognitive challenges adults encounter in daily life *outside the classroom*, including the domains of parenting, partnering, working, dealing with difference, and living as a citizen in the world. Most of the time, Kegan suggests, we are facing cognitive challenges that put us "in over our heads." One primary goal of Kegan's that has important implications for our discussion here is moving students beyond "an ultimate or absolute relationship" to one's own point of view (Kegan 1994, 24) and nurturing, instead, the ability to "internalize another's point of view in what becomes the co-construction of personal experience, thus creating a new capacity for empathy" (31). Kegan's book offers us compelling rationale for turning our attention as educators to student cognitive development. As Bizzell notes, it seems clear that "the kind of cultural literacy whose development is both chronicled and advocated in Perry's scheme [and I would add, in King and Kitchener's, Kegan's, and Baxter Magolda's work as well] is desirable for all students" (162). Following Kegan, it seems clear that there are broad applications here that could be of great value to students beyond the classroom and beyond the specialized discourse communities of the academy.

Kegan's example of the B' teacher (Kegan 1994, 48–56) provides a useful way of conceptualizing what can be gained by students from a pedagogical focus on learning theory and listening. Kegan compares two different pedagogical approaches, embodied by teachers B and B', responding to a common classroom problem: students in class are not listening to each other during discussions. Kegan is very specific about the nature of the problem he wishes to examine: students frequently "interrupt each other" and "even when they take turns, they seem to ignore completely or distort what the previous speaker has said in order to return to a point they favor" (53). Teacher B responds by establishing rules for class conduct and interrupting class to give a "sincere, eloquent, hortatory speech about the need for the students to treat each other better" (54). Teacher B', however, responds in a very different way—one designed to provide a bridge to more sophisticated cognitive orientations. Teacher B' "lets the conversation/debate proceed, but he institutes one new requirement: before any speaker may make her point, she must restate the preceding speaker's point with sufficient accuracy that the preceding speaker agrees it has been adequately restated" (Kegan 1994, 54).

This pedagogical strategy produces a number of positive outcomes, but perhaps foremost among these is the way that this new classroom protocol creates opportunities for the development of more sophisticated cognitive orientations. Teacher B' engages students "where they are," but he also invites them to "step beyond that limit":

> How? The rule that Teacher B' adds to the "game" of class conversation ingeniously transcends mere classroom management and joins the students' natural consciousness curriculum. Their categorical capacity to take another's perspective allows them to stand in a classmate's shoes and restate the classmate's position; but their incapacity either to hold multiple points of view simultaneously or integrate them means that when the student does stand in his classmate's shoes he experiences the temporary surrender of his own preferred view. . . . The trick is that this unwelcome route, first seen as a mere means to an end, has the promise of becoming an end in itself, since the continuous consideration of another's view in an uncooptive fashion, which requires a continuous stepping outside of one's own view, is a definitive move toward making one's own view object rather than subject and toward considering its relation to other views. (Kegan 1994, 55)

It is important to note here that at the heart of this strategy—the stepping-stone that makes progress toward more sophisticated cognitive orientations possible—is listening.

Marcia Baxter Magolda's (2001) important book, *Making Their Own Way: Narratives for Transforming Higher Education to Promote Self-Development*, which builds on King and Kitchener's, Perry's, and Kegan's research, supports this kind of pedagogical focus on listening, empathy, and reflection as well (see also Baxter Magolda 1992). Following conclusions drawn by Perry, Kegan, King and Kitchener, and others, Baxter Magolda has suggested here that real adult thinking becomes possible only when students embrace the idea that "knowledge is complex, ambiguous, and socially constructed in a context" (Baxter Magolda 2001, 195). For Baxter Magolda, "an internal sense of self" is essential to this mature process of meaning-making and "is central to effective participation in the social construction of knowledge" (195). This "internal sense of self," Magolda suggests, helps guide mature adults as they sift through competing "knowledge claims" (195) and assists them in essential ways as they participate in the construction of knowledge. For Baxter Magolda, developing this internal sense of self is part of a complex maturation process that theorizes authority and expertise as "shared in the mutual construction of knowledge among peers" (188). It is important for teachers of writing to find ways to nurture this "internal sense of self" and to make activities in writing classes more deliberately designed to address this important learning outcome. Bringing listening to the center of our curriculum can help us do this.

## WILLIAM PERRY AND COMPOSITION SCHOLARSHIP

It is important to note that among the learning theorists mentioned here, William Perry's work has proved to be especially influential in composition studies. As Toni-Lee Capossela (1993, 56) notes, "Given the strong affinities between holistic critical thinking and the upper positions of Perry's scheme, and given the connections between writing and thinking, it is not surprising that writing teachers have found Perry's findings applicable to their work in many ways." Bernard-Donals, Carroll and Hunt (2004), Patricia Bizzell (1984, 1986), Alice Brand (1987), Christopher Burnham (1986, 1992), Toni-Lee Capossela (1993), Curtis and Herrington (2003), Eubanks and Schaeffer (2008), Kay Halasek (1999), Douglas Hunt (2002), Donald Lazere (2009), Marcia Seabury (1991), Mary Soliday (2004), and Taczak and Thelin (2009) have all written about Perry or referenced his developmental scheme in significant ways in their work. Perhaps the most important recent work for our purposes here is Curtis and Herrington's recent essay, "Writing Development in the College Years: By Whose Definition?" Drawing on work from a variety of scholars and researchers in the field of student development (including Gilligan 1982; Haswell 1991, 2000; Sternglass 1997; Belenky et al. 1997; and Perry 1999), Curtis and Herrington suggest that writing teachers move beyond the "academic essay" and take "a broader view of writing development and a broader view of the kinds of self-reflection we want to urge for personal development" (Curtis and Herrington 2003, 86). Like many in our discipline, they are impatient with the reductive ways that standardized assessment practices have framed teaching and learning in the writing classroom: "We think many of us are frustrated by the way many assessment instruments and many statements of objectives narrow our view of what constitutes development for our students, narrow our view to focusing on grammar, syntax, and a limited range or single type of writing, primarily expository or argumentative writing" (85).

As I do here, Curtis and Herrington call for adding reflective writing to the undergraduate curriculum:

> An undergraduate liberal arts education should make room for the kind of overt self-focused reflection called for by Lawrence's spiritual autobiography course, as well as the kind of self- and cross-cultural reflection through empathic identification called for by Rachel's education and human services course. Rachel's claim that these writings "restructured the way I thought about things" is one a developmentalist has to love. (Curtis and Herrington 2003, 87)

## NEUROPLASTICITY

The field of neuroscience has provided us with fascinating new information about how the human brain develops and how it responds to its environment. This new research is incredibly important for how teachers of writing design curriculum and think about pedagogy. The old scientific model theorized a fixed, unchangeable brain capacity that was hardwired from birth. Current research reveals a brain with much more "plasticity," one that is deeply responsive to stimulus, activity, and environmental conditions. This news couldn't be more startling or encouraging for educators, and it reinforces the need for teachers of writing to attend carefully to learning theory. Taken in aggregate, this research suggests that "the brain can change its own structure and function though thought and activity" (Doidge 2007, xix).

Jane Healy first introduced teachers, parents, and the general reading public to the concept of "neuroplasticity," and to the role that activity, environment, and culture plays in shaping the way we think and the way that the neural pathways in our brains develop. The hypothesis advanced in her landmark book, *Endangered Minds: Why Children Don't Think and What We Can Do about It* (Healy 1999), has now been corroborated by hundreds of studies. As Healy notes in her new introduction to the book:

> I was pretty far out on a theoretical limb when I first presented the hypothesis that children's brains might be so significantly changed by contemporary culture as to be increasingly maladapted to our traditional notions of "school." In the intervening years, however, the concept of cortical plasticity—the process by which the brain shapes itself in response to various environmental stimuli—has become a staple of the mainstream press and has even sparked a White House conference.
>
> Given this understanding, the implication doesn't seem so far-fetched: Children surrounded by fast-paced visual stimuli (TV, videos, computer games) at the expense of face-to-face adult modeling, interactive

language, reflective problem solving, creative play, and sustained attention may be expected to arrive at school unprepared for academic learning—and to fall further behind and become increasingly "unmotivated" as the years go by. The current education scene attests to this misfit even more strongly than it did when this book was originally published. . . .

Neuroplasticity is now thought to include emotional/motivational as well as cognitive circuits. This would mean that a child's habits of motivation and attitudes toward learning don't all come with the package, but are physically formed in the brain by experience. Thus, if a child is discouraged, defeated, or emotionally abused by parents or teachers, she might develop physical "tracks" in the system or a negative pattern of neurochemical response that become increasingly resistant to change. When she enters a new learning situation, therefore, she brings a brain predisposed to apathy, negative response, and failure. (Healy 1999, 1–2)

Recent work in brain science now points teachers of all stripes, including those who teach writing, to attend carefully to "the revolutionary discovery that the human brain can change itself" (Doidge 2007, xvii; Bransford, Brown, and Cocking 2000). As Healy suggests, evidence from the hard sciences is now providing convincing support for the transformative value of interactive language use, reflective problem solving, creative play, sustained attention, the importance of reading and precise language use, and motivation (all key areas of concern for the pedagogy we are discussing here) (Healy 1999, 2). As Healy notes, "environment shapes intelligence" (66–82), and "the brain grows best when it is challenged, so high standards for children's learning are important" (69). Active learning, a focus on questions, and a curriculum that nurtures curiosity should be key pedagogical goals for teachers in all disciplines, according to Healy (1999, 73).

In *The Brain That Changes Itself: Stories of Personal Triumph from the Frontiers of Brain Science*, Norman Doidge provides a comprehensive review of this research and what we have learned about the brain and cognitive development. His book provides compelling support for Healy's claims. The key finding in this body of work is that "the brain can change its own structure and function through thought and activity" (Doidge 2007, xix). This is an incredibly important discovery for teachers and educators. Culture and activities like attending school "creates" and shapes the way the neural pathways in our brains develop over time. "The irony of this new discovery," Doidge notes,

is that for hundreds of years educators did seem to sense that children's brains had to be built up through exercises of increasing difficulty that strengthened brain functions. Up through the nineteenth and early twentieth centuries a classical education often include rote memorization of long poems in foreign languages, which strengthened the auditory memory (hence thinking in language) and an almost fanatical attention to handwriting, which probably helped strengthen motor capacities and thus not only helped handwriting but added speed and fluency to reading and speaking. Often a great deal of attention was paid to exact elocution and to perfecting the pronunciation of words. . . . But the loss of these drills has been costly; they may have been the only opportunity that many students had to systematically exercise the brain function that gives us fluency and grace with symbols. (Doidge 2007, 41–42)

As Doidge suggests, American popular culture and entertainment pose considerable problems for educators interested in helping students develop the ability to engage complex ideas thoughtfully because attention span, memory, and the ability to sustain focus are affected in problematic ways. Much of the harm from television and other electronic media, such as music videos and computer games, he suggests, "comes from their effect on attention":

It is the *form* of the television medium—cuts, edits, zooms, pans, and sudden noises—that alters the brain, by activating what Pavlov called the "orienting response," which occurs whenever we sense a sudden change in the world around us, especially a sudden movement. We instinctively interrupt whatever we are doing to turn, pay attention, and get our bearings. The orientation evolved, no doubt, because our forebears were both predators and prey and needed to react to situations that could be dangerous or could provide sudden opportunities for such things as food or sex, or simply to novel situations. The response is physiological: the heart rate decreases for four to six seconds. Television triggers this response at a far more rapid rate than we experience it in life, which is why we can't keep our eyes off the TV screen, even in the middle of an intimate conversation, and why people watch TV a lot longer than they intend. Because typical music videos, action sequences, and commercials trigger orienting responses at a rate of one per second, watching them puts us into continuous orienting response with no recovery. No wonder people report feeling drained from watching TV. Yet we acquire a taste for it and find slower changes boring. The cost is that such activities as reading, complex conversation, and listening to lectures become more difficult. (Doidge 2007, 309–10)

Clearly, this is vitally important research for teachers of writing because we are attempting to build curriculum around precisely these activities—reading, engaging in complex conversations, and listening.

This recent work in neuroscience confirms in some important ways Ruth Benedict's foundational ideas about the extraordinarily powerful role culture plays in our lives. Benedict famously suggested in her book, *Patterns of Culture*, that culture shapes everything about our lives, including our possibilities and our "impossibilities":

No man ever looks at the world with pristine eyes. He sees it edited by a definite set of customs and institutions and ways of thinking. Even in his philosophical probings he cannot go behind these stereotypes; his very concepts of the true and the false will still have reference to his particular traditional customs. . . .

The life history of the individual is first and foremost an accommodation to the patterns and standards traditionally handed down in his community. From the moment of his birth the customs into which he is born shape his experience and behavior. By the time he can talk, he is the little creature of his culture, and by the time he is grown and able to take part in its activities, its habits are his habits, its beliefs his beliefs, its impossibilities his impossibilities. (Benedict 2005, 2–3)

There is increasing evidence that this, indeed, is very much the case, and probably in ways that might have even surprised Benedict. And the more we learn about neuroplasticity and the effects of culture on the development of neural pathways, the more important the work we do as educators becomes. The pedagogy we are theorizing here has been designed with the goal of providing different—and better—kinds of "possibilities" for our students.

Carol Dweck's important work on "fixed" vs. "growth" mindsets (in the fields of developmental psychology, social psychology, and personality psychology) confirms these important findings from neuroscience and links this work in neuroscience to issues related to motivation and agency in the classroom (which we will be examining later in the book). Dweck has shown that different "mindsets" or beliefs about one's potential produce different kinds of experiences, futures, and lives: "For twenty years, my research has shown that *the view you adopt for yourself* profoundly affects the way you lead your life. It can determine whether you become the person you want to be and whether you accomplish the things you value" (Dweck 2007, 6).

People with fixed mindsets believe that their basic qualities like their intelligence or talent are "carved in stone"—that they are fixed and unalterable traits. People with "growth mindsets" believe that their basic qualities can be cultivated through their efforts (7). This work has very important implications for the classroom. One recent study conducted by Dweck and her colleagues, for example, found that "the belief that intelligence is malleable (incremental theory) predicted an upward trajectory in grades over two years of junior high school, while a belief that intelligence is fixed (entity theory) predicted a flat trajectory" (Blackwell, Trzesniewski, and Dweck 2007, 246).

## CURRICULUM DEVELOPMENT

As we can see, we have much to gain from helping students progress toward more sophisticated cognitive orientations. Do current practices in the writing classroom effectively nurture the development of mature cognitive orientations? Have we already responded effectively to this important body of research and scholarship? There is a considerable body of evidence that suggests that we have not. There clearly appears to be the need for a fresh approach to teaching writing, one informed by learning theory and congruent with what we know from the field of neuroscience and developmental psychology.

## 3

# "IT IS THE PRIVILEGE OF WISDOM TO LISTEN"

*It is the province of knowledge to speak,*
*and it is the privilege of wisdom to listen.*
—Oliver Wendell Holmes, Sr.

What might such a fresh approach to teaching composition look like? I would like to suggest developing a pedagogy that situates the practice of "listening" at the center of the intellectual work we do in the writing classroom. This pedagogy is designed to provide students with opportunities to engage required readings and complex ideas dialogically and collaboratively (and less simplistically and argumentatively). It is also designed to actively nurture the development of more mature cognitive orientations toward the world, toward others, and toward the production of knowledge and meaning. As I hope readers will see, this pedagogy would also provide students with a variety of skills and habits of mind that would transfer to writing and thinking tasks outside of the writing classroom. Any serious intellectual work, after all, must begin with listening, empathy, and reflection.

I situate this call for bringing listening to the center of our writing pedagogy within our ongoing scholarly conversation about learning and the teaching of writing. In this regard, I am especially indebted to Krista Ratcliffe's important work on rhetorical listening, Kay Halasek's work on Bakhtinian approaches to composition studies, and Mariolina Salvatori's work on reading in the composition classroom. I am positioning this new pedagogy at the place where recent scholarly work on listening converges with foundational work on learning theory, critical thinking, neuroplasticity, and the teaching of writing. This call to examine the value of listening in light of learning theory, critical thinking, and neuroscience introduces a variety of important new considerations into our conversation about writing pedagogy. One of our goals here is to replace argument and assertion as the primary focus in the composition classroom

DOI: 10.7330/9780874219449.c003

and to champion, instead, a teaching practice focused on listening, empathy, and reflection. Although argument is an important form of writing—and one we should continue to teach on a limited basis—I am calling here for a pedagogy that replaces argument as our primary focus in the writing classroom and embraces a new pedagogy that focuses instead on listening, empathy, and reflection, especially in grades 6–13.

We can begin theorizing the practice of listening on a continuum that begins with interpersonal communication skills like active and empathetic listening (Wolvin 2010; Wolvin and Coakley 1996, 279–84) and then moves outward toward more complex understandings of listening that include Krista Ratcliffe's (2005) work on "rhetorical listening" and Mariolina Salvatori's foundational work related to reading that theorizes the process of reading as carrying out "the tremendous responsibility of giving a voice, and therefore a sort of life, to the text's argument" (Salvatori 1996, 441). This continuum then ranges outward beyond the teaching of reading and writing toward more philosophically-informed approaches to the principled engagement of others. These include Emmanuel Levinas's (2006) important work developing an ethic of humanism defined by respect for the "humanity of the Other" in *The Humanism of the Other* and Martha Nussbaum's (2001) work on empathy and compassion in *Upheavals of Thought: The Intelligence of Emotions*. A focus on listening would situate students in very beneficial and sympathetic ways to "the other." Before moving on to discuss how this pedagogy might work in our classrooms on a practical, daily basis, let us first see how such a pedagogy might position itself in relation to the existing body of work related to listening and composition scholarship.

## LISTENING AND SILENCE AS A RHETORICAL ART

As Krista Ratcliffe has noted in *Rhetorical Listening*, "for more than two thousand years, the four rhetorical arts of reading, writing, speaking, and listening were cornerstones of Western rhetorical studies" (Ratcliffe 2005, 18). But in the early twentieth century, "these arts were separated from one another during the divorce of English studies from communication studies" and, "custody of these arts was awarded to different disciplines, with reading and writing relegated to English studies and speaking and listening relegated to communication studies. This divorce still haunts English studies" (Ratcliffe 2005, 18).

Ratcliffe identifies a number of reasons for the relative unimportance of listening in modern theory, scholarship, and curriculum development, including poststructuralist theory, a bias against listening brought about by our discipline's focus on the teaching of writing, and gender bias whereby "listening is gendered as feminine and valued negatively" (Ratcliffe 2005, 21). Ratcliffe's work seeks to return listening to a central place in our writing curriculum, something I seek to do as well. Ratcliffe defines listening much the way I do here: "as a stance of openness that a person may choose to assume in relation to any person, text, or culture" (25). Although her pedagogical recommendations are different than mine (see 133–71) and proceed from a different theoretical foundation, we are both attempting to have students engage others in more open, collegial, and collaborative ways.

Cheryl Glenn and Krista Ratcliffe's important work on listening and "silence" is also important to consider for our purposes here. As Glenn and Ratcliffe note in their introduction to *Silence and Listening as Rhetorical Art*, "Westerners have long forgotten (if we ever knew in the first place) the ancient Egyptian and Pythagorean beliefs about the value of silence and listening. The first canon of Egyptian rhetoric was silence, silence as a 'moral posture and rhetorical tactic'—not to be confused with 'passivity or quietism'" (Glenn and Ratcliffe 2011, 1).

A great deal can be gained for writing students by framing listening as a kind of "moral posture" that requires a principled engagement with others. Glenn and Ratcliffe suggest, for instance, that

> Individuals, as well as entire political parties, professions, communities, and nations, can more productively discern and implement actions that are more ethical, efficient and appropriate when all parties agree to engage in rhetorical situations that include not only respectful speaking, reading, and writing, but also productive silence and rhetorical listening, all of which help prepare a person for eloquence. (Glenn and Ratcliffe 2011, 3)

Both of these scholars champion listening and silence as valuable rhetorical tools in the writing classroom because they help develop a "judicious respect not just for the power of silence and listening but also for the spoken word" (2). Perhaps most importantly for our purposes here, as Gesa E. Kirsch notes, Glenn's work on silence invites us to examine "how contemplative practices can enrich a writing classroom and the intellectual life of students" (Kirsch 2009, W3; Glenn 2004). As I hope readers will see, we have much to gain, following Glenn and Ratcliffe, from embracing the idea that "the arts of silence and listening are as important to rhetoric and composition studies as the traditionally emphasized arts of reading, writing, and speaking" (Glenn and Ratcliffe 2011, 2).

Pat Belanoff's (2001) beautiful essay, "Silence: Reflection, Literacy, Learning, and Teaching," eloquently summons support from a variety of important thinkers and writers to champion the value of silence, reflection, and listening in the writing classroom. Drawing on the Old Testament, Augustine, Aquinas, medieval meditative practices, Bede, Keats, Tillie Olsen, and N. Scott Momaday, as well as the work of compositionists including Moffett, Birkerts, Berthoff, and Yancey and Spooner, Belanoff invites writing teachers to embrace silence as an essential pedagogical tool: "Silence (inhabited by meditation, reflection, contemplation, metacognition, and thoughtfulness) provides one lens through which to see the interlace of literacy; action (response, conversation) provides another lens, but both lenses are pointed at exactly the same object, which continuously turns on itself with no discernible beginning or ending" (Belanoff 2001, 422).

Belanoff, in fact, offers persuasive support in her essay for a pedagogy built around listening, empathy, and reflection. "I am arguing here," she says, "for another place of sanctuary that we as teachers can create for our students by valuing reflection and by creating reflective time and space in our classrooms and in our own and students' writing" (Belanoff 2001, 410). Like Glenn and Ratcliffe, Belanoff embraces silence as a rhetorical art, which for each of these scholars embodies a whole range of vital characteristics essential to good reading, writing, and thinking. These include, as Belanoff notes, meditation, reflection, contemplation, metacognition, and thoughtfulness. How is it possible that we have not fully embraced these noble foundational principles and moved them to the very center of our pedagogy? After all, in some ways, what we are seeking to do here is very simple. As Belanoff notes, "What I am campaigning for is space and time in our classrooms and in our scholarly lives for looking inward in silence" (420).

### LISTENING AND BAKHTIN

Kay Halasek's work on Bakhtinian approaches to teaching composition is also important for our discussion here. In *A Pedagogy of Possibility*, Halasek privileges a writing pedagogy that actively seeks to avoid "closure and opposition" (Halasek 1999, 18) and that replaces the dialectic with the dialogic. Of particular importance for our discussion here is the quality of engagement with others that Halasek embraces: "Through the concept of dialogism, Bakhtin establishes the critical need to sustain dialogue in the unending quest to maintain difference and diversity, hallmarks of intellectual growth and health, or what de

Man refers to as the 'heterogeneity of one voice with regard to any other'" (Halasek 1999, 8).

The phrase she uses here—"hallmarks of intellectual growth and health"—is a vitally important one, as it links our discussion of writing pedagogy to foundational ideas in learning theory. The critical need to "sustain" and privilege dialog rather than to seek the closure and finality of traditional argument is an important one for Halasek, and is one of the key elements of the pedagogy of listening, empathy, and reflection that we are developing here. It is important to note as well, that Halasek is defining the dialogical in opposition to the dialectical and the argumentative. Perhaps Halasek's most important statement about the value of emphasizing the dialogical in the classroom is this one, where she discusses and quotes from Don Bialostosky's work: "To read others dialogically, then, would be to read for an opening in the discussion or a provocation to further discourse. . . . Dialogic reading would not generally reduce others to consistent dialectical counterparts, or dwell on the inconsistencies in their positions, or transcend them in higher syntheses. Nor would it minimize others as rhetorical opponents by attempting to discredit them" (Halasek 1999, 18).

That last sentence contains a crucial phrase: "minimizing others as rhetorical opponents." This is something that is encouraged and perhaps even required by many kinds of simplistic argumentative writing done in high school and college. A pedagogy focused on listening would help promote the kind of "intellectual growth and health" that Halasek champions here, and also help develop the kind of "social and ideological self-awareness" (Halasek 1999, 170) that she seeks to promote with her "pedagogy of possibility."

We should also pause briefly here to note Halasek's reservations about the troublingly "static" nature of most academic writing assignments:

> Given that discussions in composition studies of the subject of discourse have remained essentially unchanged in recent years, it is perhaps not surprising that college essay forms, along with their objectified notions of the subject of discourses, have remained relatively static as well. If we are to believe Volosinov, who argues that cultural and social changes are reflected in discourse forms of a given community, then it follows that the changes in writing pedagogy and education in the past twenty years ought to be discernible in the discourse within the discipline. Still, a surprising standardization of form among college essay genres remains. Even some of the more progressive composition theorists promote prescriptive organizational formats. Why is it the case that college essay forms have not seen significant revision? Perhaps the changes in writing pedagogy are not as dramatic as we are led to believe, or perhaps the academy insulates

pedagogy from some of the conditions that may affect changes in generic forms. (Halasek 1999, 95)

We appear to have much to gain from moving beyond the minimizing of others as rhetorical opponents and opening up our curriculum to more dialogical and collaborative intellectual work.

## EMPATHY AND A "RADICAL GENEROSITY" TOWARD "THE OTHER"

Ratcliffe's ideas about listening, Glenn's work on silence, Halasek's work on Bakhtinian approaches to teaching composition, and Salvatori's work theorizing reading as a "hermeneutical conversation with a text" (Salvatori 1996, 440)—important work that we will be turning to in more detail later—all converge at a point that embraces a philosophically informed and principled engagement with others. This is the kind of ethic that has been championed perhaps most eloquently by Emmanuel Levinas and Martha Nussbaum, two thinkers who provide part of the philosophical foundation for the approach to teaching reading, writing, and thinking that we are theorizing here. Levinas is famous for promoting an ethic informed by an "absolute orientation toward the Other" (Levinas 2006, 27). His critique of the discipline of philosophy, for example, hinges on this quality of engagement: "Philosophy's itinerary still follows the path of Ulysses whose adventure in the world was but a return to his native island—complacency in the Same, misunderstanding of the Other" (Levinas 2006, 26).

Instead, Levinas champions "an orientation that goes freely from Same [or self] to Other is a Work" and that "the Work thought all the way through demands a radical generosity of movement in which the Same goes toward the Other" (26–27).

As we noted when we reviewed the work of learning theorists, this "radical generosity of movement" away from the self, the familiar, and the "Same" toward a principled engagement with the "Other" is precisely where learning theory suggests that mature meaning making and personal growth become possible. In fact, in some places in this book, Levinas sounds a great deal like King and Kitchener, Perry, Kegan, and Baxter Magolda. Consider this passage from *Humanism of the Other*, for example:

> "Turn to the truth with all one's soul"—Plato's recommendation is not simply a lesson in common sense, preaching effort and sincerity. Is it not aimed at the ultimate most underhand reticence of a soul that in the face of the Good, would persist in reflecting on Self, thereby arresting the movement toward Others? Is not the force of that "resistance of the

unreflected to reflection" the Will itself, anterior and posterior, alpha and omega to all Representation? Then is the will not thorough humility rather than will to power? Humility not to be confused with an ambiguous negation of Self, already prideful of its virtue which, on reflection, it immediately recognizes in itself. But humility of one who "has no time" to turn back to self, who takes no steps to "deny" the self, if not the abnegation of the Work's rectilinear movement toward the infinity of the other. (Levinas 2006, 34–5)

The distinction between "thorough humility" and "the will to power" captures one of the primary differences between simplistic argumentative essays and more reflective kinds of writing practices. A focus on listening, empathy, and reflection as a pedagogical practice is designed to promote this kind of humility by nurturing a more mature, productive, and open engagement with others. A philosophical orientation with a focus on listening can also help promote qualitatively better reading and thinking across grade levels and across institutional boundaries.

Martha Nussbaum's important work on empathy and compassion invites us to move in this pedagogical direction as well. In *Upheavals of Thought,* Nussbaum suggests that "a central part of developing an adequate ethical theory will be to develop an adequate theory of emotions" (Nussbaum 2001, 2). Nussbaum notes here that emotions are "intelligent responses to the perception of value" (1) and that "part of ethical thought itself will be omitted with the omission of emotions. Emotions are not just the fuel that powers the psychological mechanisms of a reasoning creature, they are parts, highly complex and messy parts, of this creature's reasoning itself" (3). At the center of this system of ethics are the related emotions of empathy and compassion (327–454). For Nussbaum, empathy is "a mental ability highly relevant to compassion" (333) and "is psychologically important as a guide" (359). Nussbaum places compassion at the center of her ethical system, and suggests that compassion "assists the personality in the struggle with ambivalence and helplessness" (351) and, particularly through encounters with art (especially tragedy), compassion can help "promote concern for someone different from oneself" (352).

Empathy and compassion, Nussbaum believes, help bring us to an "apprehension of a common humanity," a "delineation of the possibilities and weaknesses of human life," and the causes of "human difficulties" (Nussbaum 2001, 429). Furthermore, Nussbaum suggests that "compassion pushes the boundaries of the self further outward than many types of love" (300). Emotions, she notes, "involve judgments about important things, judgments in which, appraising an external object as salient for our own well being, we acknowledge our own nediness and incompleteness before parts of the world that we do not fully control" (Nussbaum 2001, 19).

This is a line of reasoning that parallels in some important ways ideas forwarded by the learning theorists we have discussed, and is also consistent with important recent work on intelligence. Both Howard Gardner and Daniel Goleman, for example, recognize and support the development of empathy and compassion as essential human qualities (Gardner 1993, 237–76; Goleman 2005, ix-xii, 96–110). This pedagogical focus is also supported by our discipline's growing interest in emotion and cognition (Brand 1987; Lindquist 2004; Robillard 2003; see also Damasio 1994; Damasio 2003). There is even international work that supports this kind of focus (Davidson and Harrington 2001). Listening is a gateway skill that can lead to the development of these vitally important characteristics. A pedagogy that focuses on listening, empathy, and reflection can help nurture better, more sophisticated, and ultimately more humane kinds of reading, writing, and thinking in our writing classroom and across the disciplines.

## LISTENING AND CRITICAL THINKING THEORY

Critical thinking theory lends additional support for developing the kind of pedagogy we are discussing. Considerable agreement has emerged among critical thinking scholars that the dispositional characteristics we are examining here—and can be included under the umbrella terms of listening, empathy, and reflection—are essential to mature critical thinking. (We will returning for a fuller discussion of these characteristics later in the book.) As the American Philosophical Association notes, for example, in its Delphi Report,

> The ideal critical thinker is habitually inquisitive, well-informed, trustful of reason, open-minded, flexible, fair-minded in evaluation, honest in facing personal biases, prudent in making judgments, willing to reconsider, clear about issues, orderly in complex matters, diligent in seeking relevant information, reasonable in the selection of criteria, focused in inquiry, and persistent in seeking results that are as precise as the subject and the circumstances of inquiry permit. (Facione 1990, 3)

Among the additional habits of mind that the American Philosophical Association identifies as important "affective dispositions of critical thinking" are the following:

- open-mindedness regarding divergent world views
- flexibility in considering alternatives and opinions

- understanding of the opinions of other people
- honesty in facing one's own biases, prejudices, stereotypes, egocentric or sociocentric tendencies
- prudence in suspending, making or altering judgments
- willingness to reconsider and revise views where honest reflection suggests that change is warranted (Facione 1990, 25)

In a more recent report, Facione et al. (1995) examine the growing consensus about dispositional qualities essential for critical thinking, and they develop in this report a fascinating "characterological profile" (2) of effective critical thinkers (see also Jones et al. 1995). Among the dispositional qualities that scholars now believe are essential to critical thinking are inquisitiveness and intellectual curiosity (4–5), open-mindedness (5), truth-seeking (5–6), and "maturity" (6–7). A pedagogy focused on listening, empathy, and reflection would actively support the development of each of these essential habits of mind. Open-mindedness, for example—"being tolerant of divergent views and sensitive to the possibility of one's own bias" (5)—is a foundational disposition in the pedagogy we are theorizing here, but it is often not valued very highly in classrooms focused on the development of thesis and support argumentative essays. The truth-seeking disposition is also foundational to our pedagogy. Critical thinking scholars define truth-seeking as

> the disposition of being eager to seek the best knowledge in a given context, courageous about asking questions, and honest and objective about pursuing inquiry even if the findings do not support one's self-interests or one's preconceived opinions. Once a liberally educated person acknowledges a given set of facts to be the case or a given set of reasons to be relevant and forceful, that person is inclined to adjust his or her beliefs in accord with those facts and reasons. The truth-seeker is one who remains receptive to giving serious consideration to additional facts, reasons, or perspectives even if this should necessitate changing one's mind on some issue. The truth-seeking professional (student, faculty member, scholar) continually evaluates new information and evidence. In contrast, being un-attuned to counter-evidence perpetuates professional practice which is unreflective and unresponsive to changes in its theory-base. (Facione et al. 1995, 5–6)

Simplistic types of argumentative writing actively enable this kind of "unreflective and unresponsive" thinking and writing, as we have seen.

The maturity disposition is also essential to good reading, writing, and thinking:

> The CT mature person can be characterized as one who approaches problems, inquiry, and decision making with a sense that some problems are necessarily ill-structured, some situations admit of more than one

plausible option, and many times judgments must be made based on standards, contexts and evidence which preclude certainty. This dispositional attribute has particular implications for responding to ill-structured problems and making complex decisions involving multiple stakeholders, such as policy-oriented and ethical decision-making, particularly in time-pressured environments. Cognitive maturity in CT would appear to be critical to the development of expertise as a clinician, administrator, educator, attorney, or a policymaker in any venue. (Facione et al. 1995, 6)

We see highlighted in this important description some of the foundational elements of the pedagogy we are theorizing here—the focus on ill-structured problems and a pedagogy that intentionally invites students to engage uncertainty with care and caution. As E.M. Glaser, a renowned critical thinking specialist, has suggested, listening must be at the heart of any kind of mature critical thinking: "One must be disposed to *listen* to another's presentation of opinion or argument, no matter whether he/she agrees with you or not. To *understand* the other person's point of view broadens one's ability to deal both with the differences in perception or values between one's self and others and with the emotional surcharge which is represented by the other's assertions" (Glaser 1985, 25).

The dispositions that are at the heart of mature critical thinking are precisely the dispositions that we are attempting to promote in a writing classroom built around listening, empathy, and reflection. It is important to note here that the pedagogy we are theorizing would create a classroom practice congruent with this foundational work on critical thinking.

## LISTENING: AN ACTIVE, GENERATIVE, CONSTRUCTIVE PROCESS

So how can we best define this essential term of listening? I propose that we theorize listening as an active, generative, constructive process that positions writers in an open, collaborative, and dialogical orientation toward the world and others. Following Levinas (2006) and Nussbaum (2001), we can also theorize listening as a philosophical orientation toward the world that is characterized by "a radical generosity" toward "the Other'" and informed most essentially by empathy and compassion. Listening can be defined as a practice that links a variety of activities, dispositions, and pedagogical strategies.

We can also theorize listening, following Arthur Costa and Bena Kallick's international, research-based work on "habits of mind," as a foundational "intellectual behavior that leads to productive actions"

(16). Costa and Kallick (2008) identify "listening with understanding and empathy" as one of their sixteen "habits of mind" essential for success in the classroom, the workplace, and life. These habits of mind have been widely embraced, and this work was instrumental in the development of the WPA/NCTE/NWP "Framework for Success in Postsecondary Writing" document (Council 2011; Johnson 2013; Summerfield and Anderson 2012). Costa and Kallick note that

> Some psychologists believe that the ability to listen to another person—to empathize with and to understand that person's point of view—is one of the highest forms of intelligent behavior. The ability to paraphrase another person's ideas; detect indicators (cues) of feelings or emotional states in oral and body language (empathy); and accurately express another person's concepts, emotions, and problems–all are indicators of listening behavior. (Piaget called it "overcoming egocentrism.") (Costa and Kallick 2008, 20).

Some of the key elements of our pedagogy are actively privileged here, including "listening," "empathy," "overcoming egocentrism," and learning theory represented by Paiget. Significantly, Costa and Kallick (2008) frame "listening with understanding and empathy" as a sophisticated cognitive capacity, as "one of the highest forms of intelligent behavior": "We want students to learn to hold in abeyance their own values, judgments, opinions, and prejudices so they can listen to and entertain another person's thoughts. This is a complex skill requiring the ability to monitor one's own thoughts while at the same time attending to a partner's words" (21). As we will see, other "habits of mind" identified by Costa and Kallick–including "thinking flexibly," "remaining open to continuous learning," and "thinking about thinking (metacognition)"— are learning outcomes that can be nurtured by a pedagogy built around listening, empathy, and reflection.

As I hope readers will see, students have the potential to benefit in a number of important ways from a pedagogy that privileges listening as its foundational skill and value. Furthermore, I would like to see our profession reconfigure the writing classroom so that the reflective essay, a kind of writing that intentionally privileges listening and the dialogical and collaborative engagement of others, moves to the center of our curriculum.

## THE GOAL OF FYC AND TRANSFER OF KNOWLEDGE

Finally, there has been much recent discussion about the purpose and goals of FYC that helps shed important light on the issues we are discussing here. What is this learning experience we call "First-Year Composition"? What should students be reading and writing about in this class? What should our goals be? What kind of writing and intellectual work should students be doing to prepare for the more advanced writing they will be doing in college and in their major areas of concentration? Here they will begin to work within the specialized communities of practice that define academic disciplines, each with a unique way of looking at the world and defining value, meaning, and knowledge (Hirst 1973). Students will also be asked to write in discipline-specific genres, each with complex and "naturally occurring rhetorical situations and exigencies" (Wardle 2009, 767). Students will be expected to theorize and situate this work within an ongoing professional conversation.

As we come to understand more fully the nature of expertise and how it is developed (Dreyfus and Dreyfus 1980; Dreyfus and Dreyfus 1992; Meyer, Land, and Baillie 2010; Scardamalia and Bereiter 2006; Sommers 1980; Sommers 1982), and as we come to understand more fully the nature of writing expertise and how closely this is linked to genre proficiency (Bazerman 1988; Beaufort 2007; Carter 1990; Freedman and Adam 1996; Russell 2002; Smit 2004; Soliday 2011; Sommers and Saltz 2004; Winsor 2000), the traditional stand-alone first-year writing course that "prepares students to write at college" and purports to develop skills that will transfer to their other courses across the curriculum becomes increasingly problematic (Freedman 1995; Petraglia 1995; Wardle 2009; Yancey, Robertson, and Taczak 2014). This is a difference, theoretically, between seeing writing as "a single elementary skill, a transparent recording of speech or thought or physical reality" vs. "writing as a complex rhetorical activity, embedded in the differentiated practices of academic discourse communities" (Russell 2002, 9). Elizabeth Wardle has described what is at stake here very memorably:

> The gist of the critiques against FYC as a general writing skills course is this: the goal of teaching students to write across the university in other academic courses assumes that students in FYC can be taught ways of writing (genre and genre knowledge) that they can then transfer to the writing they do in other courses across the university. This goal and its underlying assumption, however, are complicated by the fact that the activity system of FYC is radically different from other academic activity systems in its use of writing as the object of primary attention rather than as a tool for acting on other objects of attention. Because of this difference in primary focus, the rhetorical situations of FYC courses around the country do not mirror the multiple, diverse, and complex rhetorical situations found across the university in even the most basic ways. Transfer to such varied situations is not easily accomplished. (Wardle 2009, 766)

Wardle goes on to suggest that "we should no longer ask FYC to teach students *to write* in the university" but should, instead, "construct FYC to teach students *about writing* in the university" (Wardle 2009, 767). So a great deal is at stake here in terms of the entire enterprise of teaching writing to students and using scholarship and research to guide our practices.

While we often can't control what happens in courses across the disciplines, at the very least writing teachers, grades 6–13, can attempt to equip students with skills, habits of mind, and orientations toward the world that will help them productively engage new discourses, genres, and fields of knowledge. A curricular emphasis on listening, empathy, and reflection, and a pedagogy that embraces openness and dialog is an approach to teaching writing that offers students transferable skills as well as habits of mind that will be of great value to them across a wide variety of disciplines and in many areas of their lives outside the classroom.

What should the purpose of FYC be? And what should students be doing in writing classes in high school? Developing an ability to listen, experiencing the power of empathy and reflection, and learning to value dialogic intellectual work are excellent goals for writing courses in high school and FYC. Given what we are beginning to understand about transfer of knowledge (Beaufort 2007; Brent 2012; Perkins and Salomon 2012), these appear to be transferable skills as well. As Doug Brent has noted in regard to research related to transfer of knowledge, there is growing interest in dispositions and habits of mind that may turn out to be more important than most other traditional subjects and skillsets currently at the center of many writing classes:

> An even broader view of transfer underlies literature on transfer of dispositions. Researchers in this school of thought such as Carl Bereiter suggest that although it may be difficult to transfer discrete bundles of skills from one context to another, it may be more possible (and ultimately more important) to transfer dispositions or "habits of mind." Dispositions in this sense, such as scientific thinking and moral reasoning (we might add rhetorical thinking) more closely resemble character traits than bundles of skills. Studies in this tradition are often as frustratingly equivocal as other studies of transfer. However, the most encouraging ones emphasize long-term immersion in contexts that nurture the desired disposition in complex ways. Frequently, these studies involve entire classrooms (Campione, Shapiro, and Brown) and even entire programs (Pressley et al.), which become microcultures that nurture particular learning dispositions. Shari Tishman, Eileen Jay, and David N. Perkins see the goal of such programs as "enculturation" rather than simply teaching for transfer. (Brent 2012, 563)

The pedagogy we are discussing here is designed to provide students with this kind of "immersion in contexts that nurture the desired disposition in complex ways." The "desired disposition," in our case, involves listening, empathy, and reflection, as well as the habits of mind identified in the WPA/NCTE/NWP document, "A Framework for College Success." These include curiosity, openness, engagement, creativity, persistence, responsibility, flexibility, and metacognition. This pedagogy is also designed to nurture the dispositional characteristics outlined in critical thinking scholarship: open-mindedness regarding divergent world views; flexibility in considering alternatives and opinions; understanding of the opinions of other people; honesty in facing one's own biases, prejudices, stereotypes, egocentric or sociocentric tendencies; prudence in suspending, making or altering judgments; and a willingness to reconsider and revise views where honest reflection suggests that change is warranted. (See Appendix 5 for a sample student artifact where these qualities are highlighted in a FYC essay.) Following findings from neuroscience research and important work done by scholars like Ruth Benedict and Jane Healy, our goal is, indeed, one of "enculturation"—that is, inviting students to see the tremendous power of listening, empathy, and reflection by an immersion process, 6–13, whereby these dispositions and habits of mind are actively, purposefully, and intentionally promoted and developed over the course of many years. We will return to examine this subject in more detail later in the book when we discuss habits of mind, but I would like to pause briefly here to offer readers a brief overview of important recent work on transfer of knowledge from outside of our discipline. This work will be of considerable value to us as we move forward with our discussion, especially when we turn our attention to motivation and habits of mind. Both motivation and dispositional characteristics have become increasingly important in discussions of teaching and learning.

David N. Perkins and Gavriel Salomon, in a recent summative essay about transfer of knowledge research and scholarship, "Knowledge to Go: A Motivational and Dispositional View of Transfer," make a number of important points that will be of concern for us as we move forward discussing pedagogy and the teaching of writing. First, Perkins and Salomon note that much current research related to transfer of knowledge tends to

> obscure the role of motivations and dispositions "in the wild," even as they disclose the role of deep structure or related constructs. In virtually all the foregoing cases [which Perkins and Salomon review in this essay], learners are directly asked to undertake tasks, motivated by compliance

and rewards such as subject fees or course-completion credits. Emphasis falls on learners' ability to make the desired connections rather than their motivation or disposition to do so. (Perkins and Salomon 2012, 261)

In addition, Perkins and Salomon suggest that "reflection" can be used as an effective pedagogical tool for teachers to address the problem of "previously ingrained responses and other motives hijacking the desired transfer. Rehearsal techniques with reflection are one way of coping with this . . ." (Perkins and Salomon 2012, 263). Much thinking that we do, as a number of researchers have suggested, is done automatically (Bargh 1997; Bargh and Chartrand 1999; Willingham 2009) and is "thinking" only in the most limited sense of that term. Such thinking, Perkins and Salomon note, is often a function of bias, entrenched ways of looking at the world, "overlearned routines" (Perkins and Salomon 2012, 261), and "mindlessly treating new problems as if they are familiar ones" (261). The pedagogy we are theorizing here actively seeks to address this problem by seeking to challenge these kinds of entrenched ways of looking at the world and these "overlearned routines." A focus on reflection is how we can begin nurturing better kinds of student thinking.

Perkins and Salomon sum up their recommendations for teachers by contrasting what they see as the current "culture of demand" with an alternative "culture of opportunity." A "culture of demand" theorizes learning as a rather mechanical, circumscribed, and "passive" activity. A "culture of opportunity" asks much more of students both cognitively and dispositionally:

> Recalling the familiar distinction between passive and active vocabulary, a culture of demand can build a passive "vocabulary" of skills, information, and understandings. Moreover, a culture of demand simplifies the logistics of education in ways reinforced by the current emphasis on high-stakes standardized exams. Exercises and tests can be relatively direct rather than open-ended. Courses and units can be relatively encapsulated rather than richly cross-connected—bounded rather than expansive framing in terms of Engle et al. Finally, notice that a culture of demand does not exclude some degree of learning for understanding. For instance, one can teach the law of supply and demand with plenty of interpretive exercises in response to varied problems.
>
> However, for many of the roles educators envision for knowledge in learners' lives, a passive vocabulary is not enough. The environment does not strongly cue up the knowledge. Also, use is more discretionary and often in the face of contrary habits, intuitions, motives, and expectations from oneself or others. Most students participating in a straightforward unit on the law of supply and demand probably would not make spontaneous links later to love or the price of oranges. One needs to

be motivated to do so or have a general mindful disposition to look for possible bridges.

What's needed rather than a learning culture of demand is a *learning culture of opportunity* with the expansive framing Engle et al. suggest. Such a culture would not constantly organize students' work as a series of highly targeted demands. It would often engage learners in farther ranging and more open-ended experiences where supports are "faded" over time. Learners would more often need to grope for potentially relevant prior knowledge (detect) and use judgment to decide on its relevance and how to proceed (elect). Such a culture would anticipate likely counterhabits and countermotivations undermining later opportunities and prepare learners to face them. Indeed, such a culture would not limit its activities strictly to the classroom, but reach beyond the walls, for instance through reflective diary keeping about facets of everyday life or participation in social and intellectual initiatives in the home and community. (Perkins and Salomon 2012, 257)

Developing a "general mindful disposition" is one of the primary goals of the pedagogy we are discussing here. A focus on reflection and openness (rather than certainty and closure) and the priority we place on encouraging students to stay "open to further scrutiny, evaluation, and reformulation" and self-correction actively seeks to help students overcome "likely counterhabits and countermotivations" undermining opportunities for mature meaning making and transfer of knowledge. The "culture of opportunity" Perkins and Salomon recommend is also built around "open-ended" questions, the kind of ill-structured problems that we have already discussed and recommend positioning at the center of intellectual work in the writing classroom.

Perkins and Salomon cite Randi Engle's important scholarship, work that has important implications for teachers of writing. Engle and her colleagues have examined the powerful ways that "framing" strategies affect learning. Engle's work suggests that the way teachers "frame" instruction in their classrooms determines the kinds of things students learn—and the way they move forward applying or not applying that knowledge to other situations both in and beyond the classroom. The crucial difference for Engle is between "expansive" and "bounded" frames. "Expansive" framing encourages and enables transfer of knowledge, while "bounded" framing typically does not:

Here we investigate the idea that otherwise physically similar contexts can be framed as quite different social realities that may encourage or discourage transfer (Engle 2006). As Pea (1987, 647) explained, "contexts [that matter for transfer] are not defined in terms of physical features of settings, but in terms of the meanings of these settings constructed by the people present."

We use the term framing to refer to the communicative processes of establishing these social realities (Bateson 1972; Goffman 1974; Goodwin and Duranti 1992; Hammer et al.; Tannen 1993). Contextual framing is usually initiated in social interactions through meta-communicative signals about the context itself (Gumperz 1982, 1992; Hammer et al. 2005; Tannen 1993). For example, through organizing the desks in a classroom in particular ways and making certain kinds of directives, a teacher can work to frame a classroom as one in which students learn by quietly listening or by collaboratively engaging in knowledge construction with each other.

For purposes of understanding transfer, we focus on different ways that the boundaries of learning and transfer contexts can be framed, as this framing affects which contexts students orient to as being relevant sites for using what they have learned. For example, a teacher can introduce a lesson as an opportunity for students to begin taking on knowledgeable roles within communities they plan to participate in throughout their lives. Doing so expands the social boundary of the lesson temporally, spatially, and socially to encompass additional times, locations, and people for which each student's understanding of the lesson will be relevant. In contrast, the same teacher could have introduced the same lesson as only relevant to the next day's quiz, framing it much more narrowly as divorced from other contexts. By making links between the classroom and other contexts, the teacher's first framing created what is referred to as "intercontextuality" between contexts while the second framing did not (Bloome et al. 2005; Floriani 1994; Gee and Green 1998; Leander 2001; Putney et al. 2000). The creation of intercontextuality is thought to give learners the message that they are allowed, encouraged, and even responsible for transferring what they know from one context to all others linked with it (Brown 1989; Engle 2006; Greeno et al. 1993; Pea 1987). (Engle, Nguyen, and Mendelson 2011, 604–5)

To maximize opportunities for transfer, it appears that students should optimally be framed as active meaning-makers. As Perkins and Salomon note,

> Expansive framing emphasizes the meaningfulness and usefulness of what's being learned and its potential to relate to a range of other circumstances. Bounded framing treats what's being learned as for the unit, for the class, for the quiz. The broad teaching/learning moves that characterize expansive framing plainly put learners in a better position to detect opportunities for transfer. They include: cultivating expectations that what's being learned will speak to related settings, treating previous learning as continuously relevant, treating the use of prior learning as desired socially, and, broadly speaking, encouraging students to see themselves as the agents of their own learning and use of knowledge. (Perkins and Salomon 2012, 254)

A pedagogy focused on listening, empathy, and reflection is designed to be "expansive" in nature, framing learning in ways that have direct and important applications to many areas of a student's life and career, not just writing classes. This pedagogy is also designed to position student writers as "agents of their own learning and use of knowledge." In sum, a pedagogy that privileges listening, empathy, and reflection is a pedagogy that is congruent not only with learning theory, neuroscience, cognitive psychology, and composition and critical thinking scholarship, but also congruent with important recent work being done on transfer of knowledge.

# 4

# TOWARD A PEDAGOGY OF LISTENING

## "FALSELY AUTHORITATIVE PAPERS"

How might a pedagogical approach informed by listening, empathy, and reflection, and responsive to foundational work on learning theory, critical thinking, neuroscience, and transfer of knowledge actually work in a high school writing classroom, basic writing course, or first-year composition? To give readers a sense of the crucial "deep structures" of our teaching practices, I would like to offer readers the following case studies—featuring two very different types of writing assignments and two very different types of pedagogies. It is my hope that these case studies will provide some clarity about what is at stake in the writing classroom. It is also my hope that this dialog will help guide us to make informed, thoughtful decisions about how we can develop more effective curriculum and writing assignments for our students, especially for grades 6–13. One pedagogy I will be discussing is traditional and focused on argumentation. This is a pedagogical approach that employs what Gary Olson has called "the rhetoric of assertion":

> In one way or another, composing (at least the way it is often taught) has always seemed to be associated with asserting something to be true. Students are instructed to write an essay, which usually meant to take a position on a subject (often stated in a "strong," "clear" thesis statement, which is itself expressed in the form of an assertion), and to construct a piece of discourse that then "supports" the position. Passages in an essay that do not support the position are judged irrelevant, and the essay is evaluated accordingly. (Olson 1999, 9)

The problem with this kind of writing for scholars like Olson, Lyotard, and others is that it "pretends to be complete," that it presumes to "build a system of total knowledge about something," and that it undervalues dialog, inquiry, and the exploration of complex ideas and feelings in favor of a certain kind of closure and certainty (Olson 1999, 12–15). These are the kinds of "falsely authoritative papers" that Richard Marius rightly criticizes in his essay in *Redrawing the Boundaries* (Marius

DOI: 10.7330/9780874219449.c004

1992, 476). Olson, following Lyotard, has called this kind of writing "the discourse of mastery" (Lyotard 1988; Olson 1995, 169–72).

The other pedagogy I will be examining (and recommending instead of a pedagogy that privileges simplistic thesis and support argumentative writing) focuses instead on establishing listening, empathy, and reflection as the primary values in the classroom, embracing respect for uncertainty and complexity, and requiring students to engage assigned readings and ideas dialogically and collaboratively (and not argumentatively). For purposes of comparison, I identify this kind of writing as "the discourse of mindfulness." Here we are following Curtis and Herrington (2003), Nussbaum (2001), Perkins and Salomon (2012), as well as the important work of psychologist Ellen Langer on mindfulness. Langer's research, as readers may know, examines routine, automatic, and "mindless" ways of thinking. During the course of our lives, she notes, "we routinely engage in a great deal of complex behavior without consciously paying attention to it" (Langer 1989, 13). Much of what appears to be "thinking," in fact, actually isn't. Langer champions, instead, a quality of thought she calls *mindfulness*, a habit of mind characterized by flexibility, an embrace of "creative uncertainty" as a way to "stay open to experience" (Langer 1989, 117), creation of new categories ("once distinctions are created, they take on a life of their own" [1989, 11]), openness to new information, and awareness of more than one perspective (see also Langer 1997). These are all important characteristics of the pedagogy we are theorizing here. As we move forward with these two case studies, we will be paying particular attention to the kinds of learning opportunities that each approach provides for student cognitive development.

## CASE STUDY #1: THE DISCOURSE OF MASTERY

Let us look carefully now at the kind of thinking that is encouraged by simplistic argumentative writing, often embodied by the five-paragraph essay. Accomplished writers can often transcend the limitations of this kind of writing assignment because they are typically working from a more advanced cognitive orientation than their less accomplished peers, but as we will see, this kind of writing assignment doesn't benefit less accomplished writers either.

First of all, this pedagogy sends a very clear message to students about what it means to "think" about a subject. Since the approach of this pedagogy is clearly focused on individual "opinion" and thesis formulation, the cognitive focus of this classroom is necessarily self-centered in a very particular way. There is a great deal of status and attention given to the opinions of individual students, particularly their positions—that is to say, their opinion in response to a prompt, a reading, or group of readings. Simply developing a thesis and stating it in a single sentence is therefore considered a kind of triumph.

Despite whatever good things might happen in class as students discuss the prompt or the assigned readings together, such a pedagogy also ultimately endorses the idea that "Everyone has a right to their own opinion." After all, students see the entire classroom enterprise focused on this primary outcome—developing a thesis and then writing an essay to support that thesis. Functionally, and despite our best efforts to promote "critical thinking" (a common but very slippery term that is defined in all sorts of ways in our scholarship), this classroom orientation makes it very difficult for students to engage the "chaos" of mature meaning-making (Berthoff 1981; see also Melzer 2009; Sommers 1980; Sommers and Saltz 2004; Yancey 2009).

Why is this the case? Well, this kind of simple argument-driven assignment (which is often very different from the kind of argument that develops in classes where the focus is on rhetorical strategies or classical argumentation) requires students to cultivate an artificial sense of authority and "mastery" concerning subjects they typically know very little about. For example, how can a student who has been assigned to read two short essays about economic inequality, gender roles, or popular culture write with any kind of authority about any of these subjects? How can a student given nothing to read at all—and therefore forced to proceed as a writer and a thinker without any kind of process of inquiry—be expected to write in any meaningful or authoritative way about a complicated subject like economic inequality? And yet, this kind of absolute sureness is what a basic argumentative essay requires. The pedagogy that drives this kind of assignment invites students to take positions on morally and intellectually complex subjects in ways that effectively require students to simplify and distort these complex subjects. This kind of pedagogy also requires that students adopt an artificial position of authority that ultimately subverts their ability to engage complexity with thoughtfulness, patience, and—crucially here for our purposes—respect for uncertainty. It also sends an unfortunate message to students about what it means to think critically about a subject.

Different, more cognitively sophisticated ways of thinking about knowledge formation and meaning-making that would challenge this orientation are typically left unexplored. Students also are not typically asked to consider metacognitive questions about their own thinking and learning, such as "What can I say that I know for sure about this subject?"

and "What has this reading taught me about the way that I think and look at the world?" These are important questions that would help promote significant cognitive development, for example, beyond Perry's 3rd or 4th positions, by asking students to, in his words, "think about their thinking" (Perry 1999). Furthermore, questions related to the production of knowledge and meaning are also often left unexplored in this pedagogical approach. Such questions might include the following:

- What does it mean to "know" a subject?
- What can I say that I know for sure about the subject I am writing about now?
- What are the limits of my knowledge and understanding of this subject?
- What is my opinion, at this moment, worth?
- What has my reading taught me about the way that I think and look at the world?

If we go back to Perry's developmental scheme, we find that this pedagogy requires students to operate primarily within a Position 4 orientation:

> Position 4: (a) The student perceives legitimate uncertainty (and therefore diversity of opinion) to be extensive and raises it to the status of an unstructured epistemological realm of its own in which "anyone has a right to his own opinion," a realm which he sets over against Authority's realm where right-wrong still prevails, or (b) the student discovers qualitative contextual relativistic reasoning as a special case of "what They want" within Authority's realm. (Perry 1999, 11)

Unfortunately, this is still at least one important cognitive step away from what Perry regards as the beginning of mature adult thinking. For Perry, this begins with an acknowledgment of "legitimate human uncertainty" (Perry 1999, 99) and moves toward a way of knowing the world that is based on "contextual relativism." By "contextual relativism" Perry means that thinkers "assume complexity as a general state" (126) and that this way of thinking "becomes habitual" (124). The disposition to think primarily in terms of simple binaries like either/or and pro/con is left behind, as is one's sense that solutions to complex problems can be resolved simply by individual opinion.

## "REFLECTIVE JUDGMENT"

On King and Kitchener's "Reflective Judgment Scale," this kind of thinking falls roughly between Stage 3, "pre-reflective" thinking—"Knowledge is assumed to be absolutely certain or temporarily uncertain" (King and Kitchener 1994, 14)—and Stage 4, "quasi-reflective" thinking— "Knowledge is uncertain and knowledge claims are idiosyncratic to the individual since situational variables (such as incorrect reporting of data, data lost over time, or disparities in access to information) dictate that knowing always involves an element of ambiguity" (14–15). As King and Kitchener note,

> Stage 4 has as a major characteristic the assumption that, because there are many possible answers to every question and no absolutely certain way to adjudicate between competing answers, knowledge claims are simply idiosyncratic to the individual. In other words, an answer to an ill-structured problem is seen merely as opinion. Further, many college students are not demonstrating an ability to articulate the role of evidence in making interpretations (Stage 5) or to defensibly critique their own judgments or explanations as being in some way better than or preferable to alternative explanations (Stage 7). (King and Kitchener 1994, 167)

King and Kitchener have found that first-year college students "typically scored just above 3.5 on the Reflective Judgment Interview" (King and Kitchener 1994, 224). Furthermore, they note that "the prevalence of Stage 3 reasoning means that a sizable proportion of the freshmen tested expressed the belief that absolute truth is only temporarily inaccessible, that knowing is limited to one's personal impressions about the topic (uninformed by evidence), and that most if not all problems are well structured (defined with a high degree of certainty and completeness)" (224).

What does this all mean in practical terms? Well, since this is an orientation that many students already bring with them to high school and college classrooms, most students feel very comfortable in this world, with its positions and opinions that can be rather easily (if superficially) defended and discussed. The pedagogical practice at work in this classroom therefore actively entrenches or traps students at this cognitive stage. There are no opportunities provided for students to move beyond the conceptual boundaries, frontiers, and cognitive limitations of this position. In terms of learning theory, this practice does not seek to move students out of an already completed developmental cycle and into a "zone of proximal development" (Vygotsky 1978, 84–91; see also Baxter Magolda 2001, 193–237), a crucial concern for teachers who wish to provide students with learning experiences that can lead to real personal and cognitive growth.

The crucial variable here might be described as "listening." In this case, of primary concern for us is the quality of a student's engagement with data, research, and assigned readings. In many cases, there is no process of inquiry required or modeled for students at all. Students are simply asked to state and support a position without recourse to any data, research, reading, or listening. Even if readings are assigned, this type of writing assignment still creates complications. If an assignment is framed most essentially as argument-driven, for example, students typically read with this in mind, looking not necessarily to engage a reading or issue carefully and patiently, but instead looking for bold, obvious ideas that they can strongly agree or disagree with and then use in their essays. Opportunities to read for nuance and subtlety and to listen carefully to writers they are reading and to fellow classmates in class discussions—preconditions for mature reading, writing, and thinking—are often compromised (see Achieve, Inc. 2007a; ACT 2006; Association of American Colleges and Universities 2007; Board of Directors of the Association of American Colleges and Universities 2004; Jolliffe and Harl 2008; McCormick 1994; Roberts and Roberts 2008; Weimer 2013, 30–32). Furthermore, assigned readings selected by teachers for use in classrooms that privilege this pedagogy are often selected for precisely this reason as well—teachers often select readings that make claims that provoke strong responses and generate a certain kind of lively class discussion, often at the expense of subtlety, nuance, and acknowledgment of complexity and uncertainty. Listening—that is to say, an open, collaborative, dialogical engagement with others—is often actively hindered by this pedagogy and this kind of writing assignment.

## CASE STUDY #2: THE DISCOURSE OF MINDFULNESS

Let us turn our attention now to another type of pedagogy, one that privileges listening, empathy, and reflection. This is a pedagogy that puts ill-structured problems at the center of student intellectual work and that actively seeks to have students engage legitimate complexity and uncertainty. It is also a pedagogy, following Langer (1989), founded on *mindfulness,* a habit of mind characterized by flexibility, an embrace of "creative uncertainty," creation of new categories, openness to new information, and awareness of more than one perspective. This pedagogy is drawn from my own teaching practice, and it is the result of many years of reading, research, scholarship, and field testing. This is a pedagogy that embraces listening as its primary value and orientation, and the writing assignments we will be discussing here have been designed specifically with learning theory, cognitive development, critical thinking theory, and transfer of knowledge in mind. In order to be as clear as possible about the kind of opportunities for cognitive development that this pedagogy offers students, I would like to share with readers a specific assignment that I use in one of my basic writing classes, English 93. This class is an ideal site from which to draw an assignment and writing sample, as it bridges both high school–level and college-level writing skills and will therefore provide a large range of readers with a practical, pragmatic example of the kind of pedagogy we are theorizing together here.

Before proceeding, a word about demographics. My college serves a demographically diverse student population and enrolls over 15,000 students in credit and credit-free classes each year. We are located in a small city in central Connecticut, and draw students from suburban as well as urban districts. The average age of our students is 25, and 54 percent of our students are women. 48.5 percent of our students attend full time (the system average in Connecticut is 35 percent). Approximately 33 percent of students enrolled at our college in credit-bearing classes self-report as minorities.

Here is the reading sequence for this assignment, which focuses on family and culture:

**"Us and Them"**
**Reading Sequence:**
1. Alice Hoffman, "The Perfect Family"
2. David Sedaris, "Us and Them" from *Dress Your Family in Corduroy and Denim*
3. E. Mavis Hetherington and John Kelly, from *For Better or for Worse: Divorce Reconsidered* (Chapters 1, 2, 11, 12, and 13)

I have selected these readings because they offer students an opportunity to think and write about a familiar topic, the family. The reading sequence has been designed so that students find themselves on comfortable conceptual ground at the beginning of this assignment. Students typically have a rich history of lived and observed experience with families on which to draw, and they are often naturally interested in this subject. This unit has also been designed, however, to encourage students to move beyond this comfortable ground by providing them with a complex, ill-structured problem to consider. It is a problem that will require careful listening, engagement of multiple perspectives, and an appreciation of complexity and uncertainty.

## THE READINGS

Each reading in this unit offers students cognitive and conceptual challenges, but the first two readings are used to give students a degree of solid, familiar, conceptual ground to stand on. By the end of this unit, however, the question about what children might "need" in order to grow up healthy and whole will be examined, and students will be invited to engage this issue in ways that require an appreciation of relativity, contextual variables, and, ultimately, uncertainty. It is important to note here that these readings have not been selected to promote an argumentative, pro/con discussion.

"The Perfect Family" (Hoffman 2006) appeared at an historical moment when discussions of the American family were very much in the news and popular media. The traditional nuclear family was regarded by many as threatened, and Hoffman's piece is written at least in some ways to defend nontraditional family configurations, especially families with single mothers. Hoffmann herself, as she tells us in the essay, grew up with a single mother, and this essay is a meditation on "the nature of love" and its role in the family. Although this essay clearly emerges from a particular historical moment, Hoffman skillfully explores issues here that may be timeless (the nature of love and family, the human impulse to judge others, the variety of influences that shape the way we look at the world). This essay certainly continues to resonate powerfully with my students.

Hoffman is a thoughtful and careful writer, and she begins by discussing popular 1950 television programs that present an idealized, idyllic view of the American family. She quickly moves on to challenge this "simple view of the world," however, and suggests that such a view has its costs: "There was only one small bargain we had to make to exist in this world: we were never to ask questions, never to think about people who didn't have as much or who were different in any way" (Hoffman 1992, 135).

She also discusses the destructive power of passing judgment on others, and draws attention to issues related to class, poverty, difference, and "otherness": "But back then, there were good citizens who were only too ready to set their standards for women and children, factoring out poverty or exhaustion or simply a different set of beliefs" (Hoffman 1992, 136).

Hoffman also acknowledges in this essay historical and situational factors in her life that were beyond her control, and she introduces students to a way of thinking about life that requires a least some acknowledgment of "contextual relativism":

> If my father had not sent the child support checks on time, if my mother hadn't been white and college educated, it could have easily been us in one of those apartments she visited, where the heat didn't work on the coldest days, and the dirt was so encrusted you could mop all day and

still be called a poor housekeeper, and there was often nothing more for dinner than Frosted Flakes and milk, or, if it was toward the end of the month, the cereal might be served with tap water. Would this have meant that my mother loved her children any less, that we were less of a family? (Hoffman 1992, 135–6).

This essay offers students solid conceptual ground to stand on (a defense of single mothers), but it also invites students to begin seeing the world in ways that are more contextual, relative, and cognitively complex. Where does one get the moral authority, for example, to pass judgment on others? If popular television shows present a "simple view of the world," what would be a more accurate and less "simple" view of the world? What can we say we know for sure about "love"?

These questions are taken up again in the next reading by David Sedaris (2004). "Us and Them" is a humorous personal essay about family, culture, difference, and how we engage difference and "the other," and it complements Hoffman's essay in some important ways. Like Hoffman's essay, "Us and Them" also offers students solid conceptual ground to stand on (on one level, this is simply a humorous story about an "eccentric" neighborhood family), but it also invites students to begin thinking about the world in more cognitively sophisticated ways.

At the center of the story are two families: "Us" (the narrator's traditional, TV-loving, suburban American family) and "Them" (the Tomkeys, a nontraditional neighborhood family that does not watch TV and is "different" in other significant ways as well). Sedaris's family embodies precisely the kind of dominant social values that Hoffman critiques in her essay—particularly the conservative impulse of dominant cultural groups to judge difference and "otherness" harshly. As Raymond Williams has noted, dominant social values will almost always be in conflict with residual or emergent cultural values (Williams 1977, 121–27). Dominant social values are also transmitted largely unconsciously, of course, and this is why students typically have trouble seeing them. This essay thus provides a bridge to a different way of seeing and thinking, as it invites students to move from concrete narrative content (a funny story about two families) toward more abstract thought (a consideration of the way culture works).

The adolescent boy at the center of this essay is enthralled and intrigued by the Tomkey family, a family that "does not believe in television." The TV is at the very center of his own family's life, and the absence of TV from the life of the Tomkeys makes them virtually unfathomable to him. The narrator cannot find a way to understand the Tomkeys using his current way of knowing the world:

> Because they had no TV, the Tomkeys were forced to talk during dinner. They had no idea how puny their lives were, and so they were not ashamed that a camera would have found them uninteresting. They did not know what attractive was or what dinner was supposed to look like or even what time people were supposed to eat. Sometimes they wouldn't sit down until eight o'clock, long after everyone else had finished doing the dishes. (Sedaris 2004, 5)

During the course of the essay, we see the narrator study this family much like an anthropologist might. He is fascinated by what they do and why they do it, how they live their lives and why they make the choices they make. He is given the opportunity to begin to move toward a more sophisticated cognitive orientation that would include the Tomkeys, but he ultimately chooses instead the safety of what he already knows and thinks about the world. The moment of choice is a humorous and poignant one, which has developed because of some unfortunate behavior involving Halloween candy. The Tomkey family is at the front door and, nontraditionalists that they are, they have come trick-or-treating the day after Halloween. The narrator has been asked by his mother to get up and give some of his own Halloween candy to the Tomkeys, while his family watches a TV Western:

> For months I had protected and watched over these people, but now, with one stupid act, they had turned my pity into something hard and ugly. The shift wasn't gradual, but immediate, and it provoked an uncomfortable feeling of loss. We hadn't been friends, the Tomkeys and I, but still I had given them the gift of my curiosity. Wondering about the Tomkey family had made me feel generous, but now I would have to shift gears and find pleasure in hating them. The only alternative was to do as my mother had instructed and take a good look at myself. This was an old trick, designed to turn one's hatred inward, and while I was determined not to fall for it, it was hard to shake the mental picture snapped by her suggestion: here is a boy sitting on a bed, his mouth smeared with chocolate. He's a human being, but also he's a pig, surrounded by trash and gorging himself so that others may be denied. Were this the only image in the world, you'd be forced to give it your full attention, but fortunately there were others. This stagecoach, for instance, coming round the bend with a cargo of gold. This shiny new Mustang convertible. This teenage girl, her hair a beautiful mane, sipping Pepsi through a straw, one picture after another, on and on until the news, and whatever came on after the news. (Sedaris 2004, 11–12)

In some important ways, the young narrator in this story is dramatizing the primary features of the journey I am inviting my students to take and choice is involved at every step along the way. One can choose to move away from "self," away from thinking that is dependent on "durable categories" (to borrow a phrase from Kegan), and away from looking at knowledge and values as fixed and rigid. One can also choose, as Perry notes in his scheme, to retreat, temporize, or escape. Or one can move away from comfortable, familiar, self-focused ways of thinking and open oneself up to more contingent, more contextual ways of thinking about the world and the people in it. The young man in this essay, unfortunately, chooses retreat. I believe that students have a great deal to gain by examining the costs and benefits of this retreat.

The final reading in this unit is a selection from Hetherington and Kelly's (2002) landmark book, *For Better or for Worse: Divorce Reconsidered,* and it is a key text in this sequence because it offers students an opportunity to engage the world in ways that are more relative and contextual. Like the previous two readings in this unit, this selection focuses on family issues, particularly the effect of divorce on children and divorced adult men and women.

*For Better or for Worse* reports findings from a long-term longitudinal study of fourteen hundred families over the course of almost forty-five years. Hetherington and Kelly report a number of significant findings related to divorce, but perhaps the most significant for our purposes here is their comment about "diversity":

> What are the lessons my research colleagues and I have learned in over forty-five years of studying families over time? What have we learned about what sustains families and nurtures family members' well-being or leads to conflict, distress, and marital breakup? What helps or hurts adults and children as they deal with the changes and stresses in their lives associated with divorce, life in a single-parent household, and remarriage?
>
> *Lesson One: The Diversity Lesson*
>
> Be suspicious of averages and focus on diversity. Averages conceal the great variability in how individual men and women, boys and girls, function in intimate relationships, and how they cope when these relationships alter or break down and they have to build a new life. It is the diversity rather than the predictability or inevitability of pathways in intimate relationships over the course of life that is striking. (Hetherington and Kelly 2002, 275)

Hetherington and Kelly also present an imposing array of variables related to the effects of divorce on families and children. These variables are discussed in great detail in the book. Hetherington and Kelly conclude, for example, that "[d]ivorce is too complex a process to produce just winners and losers. People adjust in many different ways, and these patterns of adjusting change over time" (Hetherington and Kelly 2002, 5).

They also conclude that "[m]arital failure cannot be understood as a single event; it is part of a series of interconnected transitions in a pathway of life experiences that lead to and issue from divorce" (Hetherington and Kelly 2002, 4).

Should parents stay together for the sake of their children? Is divorce always a bad thing for a child? What can we say for sure about any individual family? Hetherington and Kelly make it very difficult to establish any categorical answers to these kinds of questions. Absolutes must now be questioned and contextual variables must be acknowledged and discussed. The readings in this unit have been chosen and sequenced in order to invite students to begin "trying on" new ways of thinking about complex issues and ill-structured problems—ways of thinking that will necessarily require them to think more relatively and more contextually.

Of course, finding the right readings and subjects, and sequencing materials and activities effectively has a lot to do with the success of any writing assignment, and this is especially true for assignments designed around ill-structured problems. The pedagogy we are discussing here sets a premium on assignment design, a complex and vitally important aspect of our work. As compositionists, we should be able to link every one of our writing assignments to the scholarship, research, and learning theory that inform them, as we are doing here. Without such patent linkages, we run many risks, including irrelevance, sloppy or misguided connectivity between classroom activities and desired outcomes, and supporting routine, automatic, and largely unexamined ways of looking at the world and engaging complex problems. There are few things that writing instructors do that are more important than designing assignments and selecting readings. This must be done with great care and attention to learning theory, to composition scholarship, and to a whole range of other research and scholarship inside and outside of our discipline. Ideally, our goal should be to create assignments that "produce or create a kind of 'existential crisis'" for students. (Caldwell et al. 2011, 375). This is not easy to do, of course, and it requires time, care, patience, imagination, and creativity. Assignment design is currently undervalued as a professional activity in our discipline, and we must work together to begin building a professional culture that values this kind of work as the indispensable art form that it is.

### THE WRITING ASSIGNMENT: A REFLECTIVE ESSAY

Once my class has completed our discussion of these readings, I ask students to write a reflective essay about how these readings speak to each other. Here is the assignment:

### Us and Them Essay Assignment

*The readings in this unit invite you to explore a number of issues related to culture, difference, and modern American family life.*

*Please note that it is not our goal here to arrive at any definitive or final answer to the questions these writers explore. Instead, our goal is simply to "listen" carefully to these writers and then to engage these readings in ways that are exploratory, thoughtful, and collaborative.*

*Here are some questions that I invite you to consider as you work on your essay. I also invite you to generate your own questions for these readings.*

- Do some popular television shows present a "simple view of the world," as Hoffman suggests? If so, in what ways are they "simple"? What would be a more accurate view of the world?

- Who are the "good citizens" that Hoffman talks about "who were only too ready to set their standards for women and children, factoring out poverty or exhaustion or simply a different set of beliefs"? Why should we care if they set the standards or "factor out poverty or exhaustion or simply a different set of beliefs"? What would a "different set of beliefs" look like?

- Hoffman says at one point, "This may be the only thing we need to know about love." What is this thing we need to know about love? Is she right?

- Why is the young boy in "Us and Them" so fascinated by the Tomkey family?

- What causes conflict in this story?

- What do Hetherington and Kelly have to tell us about marriage, divorce, and family?

- Is there anything that you found personally meaningful in this group of readings?

*You may organize your essay however you wish, and I invite you to reflect on and discuss any issue in these readings that you think is important. Feel free to be creative and to use personal experience and observation if you wish.*

*Essays should be approximately 1250 words in length. Please quote at least once from each of these three readings in your essay.*

By design, students are not required here to produce thinking that "pretends to be complete," "builds a system of total knowledge about something," (Olson 1999, 12–15) or achieves artificial or easy closure and certainty about a very complex issue. Instead, this assignment design invites students to put their own ideas and argumentative positions aside and to focus on engaging others with empathy and patience. This practice frees students from having to pronounce definitely and argumentatively on a subject and allows them to concentrate their energies on developing a more exploratory, collaborative, and dialogical engagement with each author and each reading. This assignment has been designed with that purpose in mind—to promote listening, empathy, and reflection.

This pedagogy is informed in some important ways by Mariolina Salvatori's landmark work on reading in the composition classroom (particularly her essay, "Conversations with Texts: Reading in the Teaching of Composition") and Kenneth Bruffee's work on collaborative learning. Following Gadamer, Salvatori theorizes reading as a "'hermeneutical conversation with a text'—a conversation that can only begin and be sustained if and when the reader/interlocutor reconstructs and critically engages the 'question,' or the argument, that the text itself might have been occasioned by or be an answer to" (Salvatori 1996, 440; see also Salvatori and Donahue 2005). This view of reading, Salvatori suggests, "enables us to imagine a text's argument not as a position to be won and defended by one interlocutor at the expense of another, but rather as a 'topic' about which interlocutors generate critical questions that enable them to reflect on the meaning of knowledge and on different processes of knowledge formation" (Salvatori 1996, 440).

The focus of student intellectual work in writing classrooms, Salvatori suggests, should not be on debate-style argumentation, using readings to support sometimes arbitrary positions, and imposing one's "will to power" over a text (to borrow a phrase from Kenneth Bruffee [1984, 645]; see also Bruffee 1999)—but on a more collaborative and conversational engagement with assigned readings that Salvatori, Bruffee, and Nancy Morrow advocate (see also Yancey and Spooner 1998). We can use "conversational" as a pedagogical term here not in the sense of an "informal" discussion but in the way Bruffee uses the term in "Collaborative Learning and the 'Conversation of Mankind'"—as a way to describe a theory of knowledge in which "thought" is regarded not as an "essential attribute of the human mind but that it is instead an artifact created by social interaction" (Bruffee 1984, 640). That is to say, a theory of knowledge deeply and fundamentally informed by listening, empathy, and reflection.

Theoretical principles are crucial here because so much depends on how we choose to conceptualize and theorize both the act of reading and the role of reading in the process of inquiry and practice in the writing classroom. Nancy Morrow articulates what is at stake here eloquently:

> Most composition textbooks have presented students with a definition of reading that emphasizes the reader's mastery and control over the text.

Kurt Spellmeyer has argued, for example, that even though most widely-used composition textbooks encourage "active" reading, most textbooks still define reading as a linear, acontextual, monological process (56). As composition studies has emerged as a distinct discipline, some scholars have tried to define reading in more complex and useful ways. For example, David Bartholomae and Anthony Petrosky, in *Facts and Counterfacts: Theory and Method for a Reading and Writing Course* (1986), offer a description of reading as a transformative and constructive process. . . . For Bartholomae and Petrosky, reading is part of a complex process of finding ways to respond to ideas and to construct ideas. (Morrow 1997)

Although it would no doubt make many of us very happy to hear that students in high school, basic writing courses, and FYC classes could write well in response to the kinds of challenging assignments focused on ill-structured problems that we are discussing here, most students will probably find this kind of writing, these kinds of reading assignments, and this kind of intellectual work demanding. Fortunately, we don't need to expect students to produce definitive readings of the texts we assign. In fact, it would be a significant achievement for most students if they could produce writing that *begins working toward a provisional understanding or reading of them.* Students' written work would therefore have to be much more tentative and exploratory, and it would no doubt lack some of the order and tidiness that we have come to expect from simplistic argumentative essays. To me, that would be a good thing. I know from my own reading and listening experience as a reader, that it has sometimes taken me years to be able to read or hear complex texts with the full depth and understanding they deserve. (And, of course, there are some great texts that I will always continue to reread, engage, and be challenged by in new ways, no matter how many times I may read them. I will never "finish" reading them.) We could regard it as a success if students simply began this exploratory process. Here we would be following Bartholomae and Petrosky's suggestion in *Ways of Reading* that students focus on "opening a subject up rather than closing one down" (Bartholomae and Petrosky 2005, 19).

## WRITING SAMPLE

So that readers can get a concrete sense of the kind of student writing that I would like to put at the center of our pedagogy, let us turn our attention now to an essay written by one of my students in response to the assignment we have been discussing here. This writing sample is the final draft of an essay and was completed in a process-oriented classroom. Our class spent approximately four weeks on this project, writing four hundred-word journal responses for each reading; discussing the readings in whole class discussions and also in small groups and pairs; and then working together on drafts of this essay with peer editing teams. In addition, I met with each student in this class at least twice during this time to offer feedback and guidance as students developed their essays. In terms of more specific kinds of pedagogical practices that guide my approach in this classroom, I invite students in this class to theorize writing expertise in terms of Anne Beaufort's "five knowledge domains" (Beaufort 2007, 5–27):

1. Discourse Community Knowledge

2. Writing Process Knowledge

3. Subject Matter Knowledge

4. Genre Knowledge

5. Rhetorical Knowledge

I also spend time with the class discussing what a reflective essay is. Most students are familiar with only one kind of writing assignment—argument—so they are all almost always at a loss if they are not able to assert something and then develop an argument for it. I typically work in a different direction: I stress caution, restraint, dialog, and exploration. I provide students with an example of an excellent reflective essay (an essay written by a student from a previous semester), and I spend time explaining to my class that I want them to focus on the ideas in the readings and the key questions that this group of readings raises—not on constructing an argument or necessarily coming to any final conclusion about these complex questions. My goal here is to focus attention on listening, empathy, and reflection, and then let their essays take whatever shape that attention brings them. My approach here parallels Donna Qualley's use of reflexive inquiry and the "essayistic stance," a way of "thinking about ideas that is dialogic and reflective": "Along with a number of scholars writing about the essay, I believe that what distinguishes the essay as a genre is not the form in which it appears on the page, but rather, the stance or approach the writer/reader adopts toward his or her subject and/or audience" (Qualley 1997, 3).

For Qualley, this "essayistic stance" is "receptive, deferent, exploratory, tentative" (Qualley 1997, 141). The pedagogy we are theorizing here seeks to nurture a similar kind of open, dialogic, collaborative, empathetic, and reflective stance in student writers.

One of our primary goals is to liberate students from having to construct an argument and to give them more freedom in terms of the things they can choose to pay attention to and think about. This single change means everything. As Langer and Applebee note in *How Writing Shapes Thinking,* "different kinds of writing activities lead students to focus on different kinds of information, think about that information in different ways, and in turn, to take quantitatively and qualitatively different kinds of knowledge away from their writing experiences" (Langer and Applebee 1988, 135). This is what we are trying to accomplish here—for students to take "quantitatively and qualitatively different kinds of knowledge away from their writing experiences." Generally, I am not too prescriptive about how students achieve this kind of open, collaborative stance toward what they read, as long as they engage the readings attentively.

Because an ill-structured problem has been positioned at the heart of this writing assignment, there are no easy or obvious answers available to student thinkers responding to this assignment. Students have to focus carefully and thoughtfully on the readings, and on the complexity, nuance, and subtlety that is built into the assignment. This provides us with the opportunity to frame reading and writing as methods and tools for thinking, learning, and inquiry, and not just as vehicles to communicate often readymade assertions and beliefs.

In terms of how students apply these orientations to drafting and revising their work, I encourage students to resist as much as possible the need to create work that "pretends to be complete" or that presumes to "build a system of total knowledge about something" (Olson 1999, 12–15). We can invite students to engage the ideas as they understand them, and we can remind them throughout this process that closure and definitive answers will probably be difficult to find. Students are all familiar with basic essay format, and that is the format we use to shape and present these responses.

The artifact we will be examining here was written by Rose Moriarty, a student in one of my English 93 classes. There are areas of strength and weakness here, and no doubt a student who was writing from a more advanced position in our writing curriculum would have been able to do more with this assignment. Nonetheless, the quality of the listening, empathy, and reflection is promising. Furthermore, Rose's essay embodies precisely the kind of engagement with readings, ideas, and with others that we want to encourage in the writing classroom. I would like to thank Rose for allowing me to use her essay in this book. Rose wrote this essay for me in her second semester in college after graduating from high school.

## Families

*After reading "Us and Them," "The Perfect Family," and sections of "For Better or For Worse," I learned many things about divorces and how it can affect each person in a family. My opinion on what the perfect family is has also changed. I used to think that everything had to be perfect and no one could ever fight, and that would be a perfect family. After reading all of these writings, I no longer believe that is what a perfect family is.*

*Television shows usually try to present a "simple view of the world" as Hoffman would say. In most television shows, everything seems to be perfect. If there is a problem, it is usually solved in the thirty minutes that the show is on. This is definitely not what real life is like. The "simple view of the world" is related to the story, "The Perfect Family" because the Hoffman family noticed that other families were concerned with trying to be perfect; and they judged the Hoffman family and other families like them. During this time period, the 1950's, families passed judgment on the Hoffmans because they were divorced. In my opinion, it seemed as if most of the families during this time period relied on husbands or fathers; and thought that they knew what was best. If a father was absent from a family, other families would judge the family for not having a father and think less of them. Even though in the "Perfect Family" many people did not get divorced, I still think that many people were unhappy with their marriages. I believe that during this time period, many women were afraid to get divorced because they did not want to be judged, and they were afraid to be on their own without their husbands. An example of this is shown in Hoffman's story when one of her friends couldn't come over and play at her house because her parents wouldn't let her. The reason why the parents wouldn't let her is that they knew that Hoffman's parents were divorced and didn't want their daughter in that environment. Yet her friend's father was abusing his children and no one would do anything about it. In this case, divorce would have been a better option for this family than having the children get abused by the father. I do not understand how someone in this position could judge anyone else.*

*Also, in the 1950's, getting a divorce wasn't possible. Even if someone wanted to get a divorce the law said that they could not. Divorces were socially unacceptable. All of these barriers demonstrate how it was hard to get divorced during the 1950's. In "For Better or For Worse," the author talks about social changes. "In a blink of an eye, the entire country seemed to jump from the paternal certainties of "Father Knows Best" to the postmodern chaos of "the Brady Bunch." This author is telling us that divorce was starting to become more acceptable in the view of society. "America was in the midst of an unprecedented social change— one that would be played out for decades to come in the nation's living rooms, bedrooms, courtrooms, and legislatures." It seems to me that the American culture was changing rapidly and some people didn't like or were afraid of all the changes that were being made.*

*In most television shows the "perfect family" consists of men working while the wife is usually staying home to clean the house, take care of the children and cook meals for the family. Television shows don't really show the men helping out around the house. In the real view of the world today, fathers or males aren't usually the only ones that are working. More often then not, the wife or female also has to have a full time job in order to make enough money for their family. This means that not only does the wife have to do the household chores; but the men also have to pitch in to help get the work done. Not everyone is safe or happy all the time in real life, especially because of how hard it is today to find work or a job.*

*"In the Perfect Family," Hoffman talks about the different types of mothers that her mother had to visit while working at the Department of Social Services. Part of her mother's job was to visit apartments of single women. She said the following about what she found sometimes: "where the heat wouldn't be working on the coldest days and the dirt on the floor was so encrusted that you could mop all day and still be called a bad housekeeper." After seeing one of these dirty apartments, most people would assume that the mother of the family is doing a poor job at being a mother. People would say that the mother shouldn't be raising her children in that kind of environment; and the children will not turn out okay because of it. In "For Better or for Worse," the author stated, "Most of our divorced women managed to provide the support, sensitivity, and engagement their children needed for normal development." The author's statement demonstrates that even though people might misjudge divorced mothers on how they are raising their children, they usually are doing a good job because their children turn out to have normal development. Hoffman compares her mother to the mothers that were living in these apartments and wonders if she were living in one of the dirty apartments, would it mean her mother loved her less. "Would that have meant my mother loved her children any less, that we were less than a family?" Hoffman is saying that it doesn't matter what your living conditions are. All that matters is the love from your mother. Hoffman goes on to say, "This may be the only thing we need to know about love." She is saying that there is no such thing as a perfect family. It should not matter whether parents are divorced or not; divorce does not mean that the parents don't love or care about their children the same way as when they were married.*

*Hoffman's father left her mother. During that time period, that was really unusual and frowned upon. Even though she did not have a father growing up, her mother made up for it by working hard and taking care of her family. The author talks about how she didn't feel deprived or neglected when she was growing up. The only time she did was when her family was "measured against some notion of what we were supposed to be." I don't understand why people would compare families to one another because each family is different. Just because families are different does not mean that one way is right compared to another.*

*All that really matters in a family is the love that they have for one another and that they are always there for each other. I felt it was terrible that the children in this family knew that people were judging them and measuring them against a social standard which belittled children of divorce.*

*At the end of "The Perfect Family," the author admits that she sometimes struggles while raising her own children and wonders how women have a family without a husband to help. She says, "That they do it, in spite of everything, is a simple fact. They rise from sleep in the middle of the night when their children call out to them. They rush for the cough syrup and cold washcloths and keep watch till dawn. These are real family values." This quote captures what love and family values really mean. To the author, it means being there when your children need you even if you are exhausted and tired from working all day. I agree with Hoffman. It's the little things that a mother does for her children that shows how much she loves them. To me, it doesn't matter how many or how few parents are around to make up the "perfect family." Instead, it is about how the family treats, loves and cares for one another. I believe that a single mom can do almost anything that two parents can.*

*I think that the "Perfect Family" relates to "For Better or For Worse" because children usually live with their mother when their parents get divorced. In "For Better or For Worse" Hetherington and Kelly say "If someone creates a Nobel Prize for Unsung Hero, my nominee will be the divorced mother. Even when the world was collapsing around them, many divorced mothers found the courage and resiliency to do what had to be done." This quote proves to me that a single mother can do just about anything, especially when it comes to the love and care for their children. They would drop everything for them. After reading these two stories and learning that divorce is not as uncommon as I thought, I think sometimes divorce is the best option for the entire family. I also learned that it is okay to only have a mother in some children's lives. The mother can take care and love the children as much as two parents would.*

*In the story "Us and Them," the young boy's family is very different from another family in the neighborhood whose name is Tomkeys. The main reason that the Tomkeys are thought of as different is that they don't own a television. I thought that the Tomkeys spent a lot of quality family time together because they did not spend any time watching television. While I was reading the story, I tried to imagine what it would be like to not have a television; and it almost seemed impossible! The other boy in the story didn't have as much family time as the Tomkeys. When the Tomkeys family decided to go trick or treating after the holiday has already past, I was a little confused. The boy living in the house did not want the Tomkeys children getting any of the candy, even the ones that he does not like! I think the boy might have been jealous of the Tomkeys and the types of family things that they did together and how close they were. "We hadn't been best friends, the Tomkey's and I, but still I had given them the gift of my curiosity. Wondering about the Tomkey's family made me feel generous, but now I would have to shift gears and find pleasure in hating them."* This seemed so harsh to me that the only explanation has to be that the boy was incredibly jealous. This story is similar to "The Perfect Family" because it seemed like people were judging other families again for not being exactly similar to one another.

I think that Sedaris is trying to tell us that we should cherish the life that we have because it is a gift. We shouldn't spend so much time watching television because that's an unhealthy way of living. The average American watches four hours of television a day. That's a really long time to be doing something, especially watching television. There are so many other things that you could be doing instead. For example, people could spend more family time together. People could socialize more with friends that they haven't talked to in a while. People can also just go outside and enjoy some fresh air. Those are some things that you can do rather then spending the whole day watching television. Life is too short for that.

In "For Better or For Worse," I learned about the many affects that divorce has on families. I did not realize how people are affected by going through a divorce. The author showed us how unique each divorce situation can be. Even though a divorce can be a painful process, I believe that it is the best way for some people to live because of how unhappy they were in their marriage. I never realized that divorce usually affects men more than women. "The emotional climate of a marriage influences the emotional climate of a divorce and the role that men and women play in a marriage, the habits that they develop, affect their ability to adjust to post divorce life." This quote explained to me that the way men and women act in a marriage is usually the way that they will act through a divorce. There are many reasons for different couples to get a divorce. It is usually not one big thing, but many little things that add up over the years of their marriage. I could not believe that violence was such a big issue. This is something that is never seen on television shows.

After reading, "The Perfect Family," "For Better or For Worse," and "Dress Your Family in Corduroy and Denim," I learned many things about relationships, families and marriage that I never thought about or realized before. There is no such thing as a perfect family or the best family. Many people judge each other based on minor things. I also learned that a family may seem "perfect" on the outside because the parents are still married; but what is going on inside the house, the part that no one sees, could be a disaster. [Word count: 2,225]

## DISCUSSION OF WRITING SAMPLE

Rose struggles a little with her introduction and with getting herself situated and under way, and this writing sample is obviously the work of a writer who is just beginning to show an emerging sense of fluency and skill. But her discussion of Alice Hoffman's "The Perfect Family" is solid, and she demonstrates a willingness to engage complexity and uncertainty throughout the essay. For example, she addresses one of the key themes in "The Perfect Family"—the idea that certain kinds of television shows back in the 1950s offered viewers a "simple view of the world." She engages that question with care and thoughtfulness:

> Television shows usually try to present a "simple view of the world" as Hoffman would say. In most television shows, everything seems to be perfect. If there is a problem, it is usually solved in the thirty minutes that the show is on. This is definitely not what real life is like. The "simple view of the world" is related to the story, "The Perfect Family" because the Hoffman family noticed that other families were concerned with trying to be perfect; and they judged the Hoffman family and other families like them. During this time period, the 1950's, families passed judgment on the Hoffmans because they were divorced. In my opinion, it seemed as if most of the families during this time period relied on husbands or fathers; and thought that they knew what was best. If a father was absent from a family, other families would judge the family for not having a father and think less of them.

There is more to say about this question, of course, but Rose has clearly made an effort to engage this question thoughtfully.

Rose does simplify some of the ideas in the readings here, especially when she turns to the Sedaris essay. I think there are important ideas here that Rose leaves unexplored, and I'm not quite sure that I would say that Sedaris is trying to tell us that "we should cherish the life that we have because it is a gift." But Rose does display at least an emerging sense of historical contingency in this essay ("During this time period, the 1950's, families passed judgment on the Hoffmans because they were divorced."). She also seems willing to "assume complexity as a general state" (Perry 1999, 126), one of the key threshold measures for so many of the learning theorists we've discussed ("The author showed us how unique each divorce situation can be" and "There are many reasons for different couples to get a divorce.") In fact, the whole essay could be said to focus on that important idea.

What we should note here is that this essay is much more of a "conversation" in the way Bruffee defines that term ("thought" is regarded not as an "essential attribute of the human mind but that it is instead an artifact created by social interaction" [Bruffee 1984, 640]) than an argument—and that is a good thing. Rose is free to focus her attention on listening and reflecting on these readings and on the questions she finds important. She is not compelled by the assignment to construct an argument or to engage the readings looking for things to strongly agree or disagree with. Nor is she required by the assignment to pronounce definitively and imperially on complex subjects she has limited knowledge about. Instead, she is free to listen to what each author is saying, and this puts engagement with the readings and the ideas in these readings at the center of this writing assignment, which is precisely where they should be. The detail that Rose provides for many of the ideas she discusses here is also noteworthy. She uses quotes well, and she doesn't appear to be hurrying through this process to get to the end and finish her essay.

Overall, Rose engages these readings patiently and thoughtfully—something this assignment design encourages and requires. A more experienced or accomplished reader and writer might have been able to do more with these readings, but as a teacher in a basic writing class I was happy with how closely and carefully Rose engaged these texts. Particularly noteworthy for me were the connections between the readings that deepen Rose's understanding of family and culture. For example, there is a nice moment where Rose connects Hetherington and Kelly's research to Hoffman's mother's observations about poor single mothers:

> "In the Perfect Family," Hoffman talks about the different types of mothers that her mother had to visit while working at the Department of Social Services. Part of her mother's job was to visit apartments of single women. She said the following about what she found sometimes, "where the heat wouldn't be working on the coldest days and the dirt on the floor was so encrusted that you could mop all day and still be called a bad housekeeper." After seeing one of these dirty apartments, most people would assume that the mother of the family is doing a poor job at being a mother. People would say that the mother shouldn't be raising her children in that kind of environment; and the children will not turn out okay because of it. In "For Better or for Worse," the author stated, "Most of our divorced women managed to provide the support, sensitivity, and engagement their children needed for normal development." The author's statement demonstrates that even though people might misjudge divorced mothers on how they are raising their children, they usually are doing a good job because their children turn out to have normal development.

There is nice attention here to these two writings and what they have to say to each other. Rose has been a careful reader and picked up on some of these important connections. Students in this class often struggle with Hetherington and Kelly (see Sullivan 2010), but Rose has identified and understood the major conclusions reported in this landmark study as well as some of the important nuances of these conclusions.

Rose makes another nice connection between these two readings when she talks about single mothers:

I think that the "Perfect Family" relates to "For Better or For Worse" because children usually live with their mother when their parents get divorced. In "For Better or For Worse" Hetherington and Kelly say "If someone creates a Nobel Prize for Unsung Hero, my nominee will be the divorced mother. Even when the world was collapsing around them, many divorced mothers found the courage and resiliency to do what had to be done." This quote proves to me that a single mother can do just about anything, especially when it comes to the love and care for their children. They would drop everything for them. After reading these two stories and learning that divorce is not as uncommon as I thought, I think sometimes divorce is the best option for the entire family. I also learned that it is okay to only have a mother in some children's lives. The mother can take care and love the children as much as two parents would.

The quality of the listening, empathy, and reflection here is encouraging.

If the way that students engage complexity and "uncertainty" is a key variable in terms of developing more sophisticated cognitive orientations, as Perry, Kegan, King and Kitchener, and Baxter Magolda all suggest, then this writing assignment would appear to have been successful because we see Rose moving however imperfectly here toward embracing "complexity as a general state." In fact, I believe that there is evidence in this artifact to suggest that this assignment has ushered Rose into a zone of proximal development, for in some important ways we see her confronting exactly the same decision that the young man in "Us and Them" faces—choosing to retreat, temporize, and escape or to move away from comfortable, familiar, self-focused ways of thinking and opening oneself up to more contingent, more contextual ways of thinking about the world and the people in it. Rose is tempted to retreat and escape ("While I was reading the story, I tried to imagine what it would be like to not have a television; and it almost seemed impossible!"), but she presses boldly and perhaps courageously on ("I used to think that everything had to be perfect and no one could ever fight, and that would be a perfect family. After reading all of these writings, I no longer believe that is what a perfect family is.")

This essay is also mindful in some important ways. Rose demonstrates in this essay a willingness to be flexible, openness to new information, and awareness of more than one perspective. She also appears to be embracing uncertainty as a way to "stay open to experience" (Langer 1989, 117). She also appears to be in the process of rethinking old categories and creating new ones ("My opinion on what the perfect family is has also changed.")

A pedagogy focused on listening—that is to say, an active, generative, constructive process that positions writers in an open, collaborative, and dialogical orientation toward the world and others—is also much more likely than a pedagogy focused on argument, with its focus on closure and opposition, to lead to this kind of development. A pedagogy focused on listening can also nurture the "internal sense of self" that Baxter Magolda believes is essential to intellectual and emotional maturity, especially for students in high school and the first years of college. We see evidence of that emerging sense of self-authorship here in Rose's writing. Her patience, openness, and empathy are especially encouraging in this regard. A pedagogy with a focus on listening, empathy, and reflection is also likely to nurture the kind of mindfulness Langer celebrates in her work.

## 5
# TEACHING LISTENING AND THE REFLECTIVE ESSAY

**"YES, BUT WHAT ARE WE GOING TO DO ON MONDAY?"**

Discussions about theory and scholarship are all well and good, of course, but the real question that teachers want answered is much more immediate and pragmatic: "How does this translate into classroom practice?" Or, to put the question more bluntly, in its most indispensable form for teachers of writing: "I hear what you're saying, but what do I do on Monday, when I meet my classes?"

How might a pedagogy structured around listening, empathy, and reflection be realized in high school, basic writing classes, and FYC? I have been teaching writing with this focus now for the last ten years, and I have developed a variety of teaching practices designed to help promote listening, empathy, and reflection, and to help nurture more advanced cognitive orientations in the classroom. Here are the pragmatic classroom strategies that can help us translate this theory into practice:

### 1. Foreground Listening, Reflection, and Mindfulness

It's important for students to know the primary values that we are privileging in our classrooms. I talk at considerable length at the beginning of each of my classes about "openness" and the value of listening, empathy, and reflection. Much of this has to do with how I teach reading and how I encourage students to engage ideas when they write. I do not assign argumentative essays in my classes, and all of the written work students complete in my classes is reflective in nature. Also, following Salvatori, Bruffee, and Morrow, I encourage students to position themselves dialogically and collaboratively, rather than argumentatively, as they engage ideas and readings. This can be done in a variety of ways. For example, all of my directions for reflective journal responses and reflective essays include the following statement:

DOI: 10.7330/9780874219449.c005

Please focus your response on "listening" carefully to each assigned reading and then reflecting on what these writers have to tell us. Please note that it is not our goal here to arrive at any definitive or final answer to the questions these readings explore. Instead, our goal is simply to encounter and engage these readings and the questions they raise in a way that is exploratory, thoughtful, and collaborative. I am not interested in having you formulate a thesis and supporting it.

I also incorporate what I want students to learn from each assignment in other ways in the written material I provide them. Here, for example, is the material I give my students for their first major assignment. My goal here is to foreground listening:

### Educational Best Practices

"Your teacher explains in advance what he or she wants you TO LEARN." (National Survey of Student Engagement)

What do I want you to learn from this assignment?

Well, remember that the special focus for this first major assignment is on Listening!

I want you to learn how to read and "listen to" complex, college-level texts effectively.

The idea is not just to get to the end and say, "I did it! I'm done!"

The idea is for you not just to finish the reading, but to understand what you've read and be able to talk and write about it. That's what we're after here.

So you may have to reread (maybe a few passages more than twice), underline, read out loud, and perhaps even talk over the readings with a tutor or come to visit me during my office hours.

You are going to have to focus, reread, bear down, and not give up until you get it and it's clear.

You will need to use the kind of "strategic focused attention" that Jonah Lehrer talks about in his essay on Walter Mischel that we've discussed.

So: No guessing, no superficial, no simplified, no hit or miss, no "whatever"!

Without a good reading of this text, there is no way that you can produce a good essay.

So spend some time really reading and getting things clear. Don't clip off a corner; go for the heart!

I also want to make sure that you can select some great quotations and talk about what they mean. That's really where college-level writing can be said to begin.

## 2. Provide Students with a Rationale for This Approach

It's common practice for teachers of writing to theorize their approach to composition for their students at the beginning of each semester, and

I think this is a very valuable practice for both teachers and students. I always devote a considerable amount of time at the beginning of the semester reviewing research on learning theory and writing scholarship to frame the approach I am using and to talk about why I conduct each class the way I do. My students typically find this very interesting and worthwhile. Much of what I discuss is related to the work I have done on listening, empathy, reflection, and learning theory. I find students benefit a great deal from having our class assignments and activities framed and theorized in this way.

### 3. Design Reading and Writing Assignments with "the End in Mind": Engaging Legitimate Complexity

Writing assignments in high school, basic writing courses, and FYC classes must be very carefully crafted and scaffolded with learning theory in mind. If our goal is "empowering individuals to know that the world is far more complex than it first appears" (King and Kitchener 1994, 1), then our assignments must be designed with such outcomes as their primary focus. "Beginning with the end in mind," to borrow a phrase from Stephen Covey (1990, 95–144), can help us design assignments that nurture listening, empathy, and reflection, and can help students begin to encounter and engage complexity in cognitively mature ways.

I have developed the following sequence of assignments for the writing class I have been discussing in this book. All of these units have been classroom tested and have proven to challenge, engage, and interest students in all the ways we have been discussing here. The units toward the beginning of this assignment sequence are designed to pose moderate cognitive challenges, while the units toward the end of the sequence are designed to pose more demanding kinds of challenges (the ideas are more abstract and the readings are more demanding and difficult [see Salvatori and Donahue 2005 for a discussion of "difficulty"]). As I build my reading and assignment list each semester, I typically am able to work through three of these units.

**Sample Student Assignments**
Assignments Designed with Learning Theory in Mind

### 1. Introduction
1. Are You Ready for College? A Discussion of "College Readiness" and a Personal College-Readiness Checklist!

2. "Don't" by Jonah Lehrer (*New Yorker,* May 18, 2009): Walter Mischel, the art of self-control, and "strategically allocated attention" (vs. constant fractured attention)

3. Geoffrey Colvin's (2008) *Talent Is Overrated* (Chapters 2, 4, and 11)

## 2. Listening

1. James Baldwin, "Sonny's Blues"

## 3. "Where I Live and What I Live For": Developing a System of Personal Values

1. Shirley Jackson, "The Lottery"

2. David Foster Wallace, *This Is Water* (Kenyon College Commencement Address, 2005)

3. Jonathan Haidt, from *The Happiness Hypothesis* (Chapters 5 and 7: "The Pursuit of Happiness" and "The Uses of Adversity")

## 4. Us and Them

1. Alice Hoffman, "Perfect Family"

2. David Sedaris, "Us and Them" from *Dress Your Family in Corduroy and Denim*

3. E. Mavis Hetherington and John Kelly, from *For Better or for Worse: Divorce Reconsidered* (Chapters 1, 2, 11, 12, and 13)

## 5. Intelligence

1. Alfred W. Munzert, Kim Muzert, and Alfred Munzert, from *Test Your IQ* (a timed, self-scoring IQ test)

2. Howard Gardner, *Multiple Intelligences: New Horizons* (Chapters 1, 2, and 3)

3. Daniel Goleman, from *Emotional Intelligence* (Chapters 3, 4, 5, 6, and 12)

## 6. Mindfulness

1. Dana Mrkich, "Do You Choose your Identity or is it Chosen for You?"

2. Alice Walker, "Everyday Use"

3. Ellen Langer, from *Mindfulness* (Chapter 1, 2, 3, 4, 5, and 7)

## 7. Bowling Alone: Exploring the Value of "Social Capital"

1. Shaun Tan, *The Arrival* (graphic novel)

2. Robert Putnam, from *Bowling Alone* (Chapter 1: Thinking about Social Change in America; browse through pages 31–133, looking mostly at the graphs (what kind of story do these graphs tell?); Chapter 8: Reciprocity, Honesty, and Trust, and the "So What?" section: Chapters 16 through 21 (pages 288–349).

## 8. Happy Endings

1. Margaret Atwood, "Happy Endings"

2. Aaron T. Beck, from *Love Is Never Enough* (Chapter 2: The Light and the Darkness)

3. Elaine Hatfield and Richard Rapson, from *Love and Sex: Cross Cultural Perspectives* (Chapters 1 and 2)

## 9. Patterns of Culture

1. Ruth Benedict, from *Patterns of Culture* (Chapter One: The Science of Custom)

2. Kathryn Edin and Maria Kefalas, from *Promises I Can Keep: Why Poor Women Put Motherhood before Marriage* (Introduction, Chapters 1, 2, 3, 4, 6, and Conclusion)

## 10. Creativity

"Imagination is more important than knowledge."

—Albert Einstein

1. We complete a variety of creative activities in class for this unit.
2. Tomaz Salamun, "I Have a Horse"
3. Amanda Holzer, "Love and Other Catastrophes: A Mix Tape"
4. Jamica Kincaid, "Girl"
5. Jonathan Safran Foer, "A Primer for the Punctuation of Heart Disease"
6. Ken Robinson, *Out of Our Minds: Learning to Be Creative* (Preface, Chapter 1, 3, 6, 7, and 10)

## 11. Meeting Thomas Jefferson: Readings from Three Biographies

1. Dumas Malone, *Thomas Jefferson: A Brief Biography*
2. Andrew Burstein, from *Jefferson's Secrets: Death and Desire at Monticello* (Chapter 5: The Continuing Debate: Jefferson and Slavery, pp. 113–150)
3. Annette Gordon-Reed, from *Thomas Jefferson and Sally Hemings: An American Controversy* (Chapters 4, 5, 6, 7 and Appendix B: The Memoirs of Madison Hemings and Appendix C: The Memoirs of Israel Jefferson)

## 12. Rich Man, Poor Man

1. Milton and Rose Friedman, from *Free to Choose* (Chapter 1: The Power of the Market)
2. Herbert J. Gans, "The Uses of Poverty: The Poor Pay All." *Social Policy* July/August 1971: 20–24
3. John Cassidy, "Relatively Deprived: How Poor is Poor?" (*The New Yorker*, April 3, 2006)
4. David Shipler, from *The Working Poor: Invisible in America* (Preface, Introduction, Chapters 2, 3 and 11).
5. Dr. Martin Luther King, from the Nobel Lecture (December 11, 1964): "Why should there be hunger and privation in any land, in any city, at any table when man has the resources and the scientific know-how to provide all mankind with the basic necessities of life?"

## 13. The Shadow

"It is well that war is so terrible, lest we should grow too fond of it."

—Robert E. Lee

1. Karl Marlantes, *What It Is Like to Go to War* (Chapters 1, 2, 3, 5, and 11)
2. Mark Twain, "The War Prayer"
3. Sigmund Freud, from *Civilization and Its Discontents* (Chapter 5: "The clue may be supplied by one of the ideal demands, as we have called them, of civilized society. It runs: 'Thou shalt love thy neighbor as thyself.'")

   4. Hannah Arendt, from *Eichmann in Jerusalem: A Report on the Banality of Evil* (Chapter VI: The Final Solution; Chapter XV: Judgment, Appeal, and Execution; Epilogue)
   5. The listing of wars throughout human history on Wikipedia: http://en.wikipedia.org/wiki/Lists_of_wars
   6. Introduction to *Meeting the Shadow* by Connie Zweig and Jeremiah Abrams
   7. Carl Jung, "The Shadow" (excerpts from a variety of sources, including *Psychology and Religion: West and East* and *Two Essays on Analytical Psychology*)

## 14. Freedom
   1. Albert Camus, "The Guest"
   2. Milan Kundera, from *The Unbearable Lightness of Being* (Chapter 15: "What happens but once might as well not have happened at all.")

Assigned readings must be chosen carefully, with cognitive challenge and complexity being key variables in this selection process. Readings for a pedagogy focused on ill-structured problems must be selected and sequenced very differently than the way we typically select and group readings for argumentative assignments.

## 4. Teach Reading

As David Jolliffe has suggested, teaching reading must be considered is an essential part of teaching writing, but this is something composition-ists appear to do only reluctantly and haphazardly: "At every college and university where I have taught in the past twenty-five years—and this list includes four state universities, a private liberal arts college, and a large Catholic university—the talk about student reading is like the weather: everybody complains about it, but nobody does anything about it" (Jolliffe 2007, 470). Unfortunately, as Jolliffe notes, formal reading instruction for most students usually ends by the eighth grade. After that, students are expected to simply "know how to read." College-level texts, however, appear to be posing significant challenges for many college students because reading has been theorized as a skill set that is based on information capture and data mining, and as a skill that is learned early in one's academic career and then simply used and applied. Advanced reading skills are often left for individual students to nurture and develop on their own. Furthermore, reading instruction is something that has been systematically ignored in our writing pedagogy, as Jolliffe suggests:

> A quirky wrinkle in the traditional secondary school curriculum makes it difficult even for high school teachers to accept that they ought to teach reading, let alone college-level instructors. By the time students are

graduating from high school, the course called "reading" has been absent from the curriculum for at least three or four years, having usually made its last appearance in the eighth grade, at the latest. By the time they come to college, then, students haven't had a course called "reading" for five or six years. Oh, to be sure, some of their high school teachers might have tucked something resembling reading instruction into courses or units labeled "critical thinking" or "study skills," and college students may have a class called "first-year seminar" or "first-year experience" that takes a stab at helping students cope with the reading demands of college. But by the time students come to college, it's been a long time since students have had any instructor say to them, "Okay, let's work on how to read this text."

Moreover, while the notion of taking a "reading class" has dropped off the radar screen for most first-year college students, the very thought of what a "reading class" might be at the post-secondary level has never quite coalesced. To put it starkly: reading as a concept is largely absent from the theory and practice of college composition. The program of the 2005 Conference on College Composition and Communication, for example, mentions the word *reading* only thirty times in the titles of papers given in the four-hundred-odd concurrent panels and special sessions. In the opening chapter of a book I'll return to later in this essay, Marguerite Helmers claims that "the act of reading is not part of the common professional discourse in composition studies" (4). In other words, no clear, salient theory of what reading is or does prevails in college composition, even though an anthology of readings sits at the center of many, if not most, college writing courses. Students have to read in college composition, but rarely does anyone tell them why or how they should read. As a result of this ill-defined perspective on reading, when college composition instructors (and administrators and textbook authors) actually do take up reading as a curricular or pedagogical focus, they often do so at diametrically opposite ends of a continuum of complexity. (Jolliffe 2007, 473–74)

A pedagogical and curricular focus on listening, empathy, and reflection can actively help aid the teaching of reading in high school and basic writing classes.

## 5. Provide High School Students, Basic Writers, and First-Year Composition Students with Reading Guides that Highlight Key Passages in Assigned Readings and Ask Questions about These Passages

In my advanced, 200-level classes, students are generally sophisticated enough to generate key questions about assigned readings on their own. This is one important mark of intellectual maturity, of course, but it is something that is very challenging to unskilled readers, as anyone who has taught a basic writing or reading class knows. As accomplished readers ourselves, this kind of internalized, reflective, inquiry-based reading and questioning process is something we do naturally and effortlessly, but this is because most of us have many years of practice at it and this way of engaging written work has become second nature to us. Many students, however, struggle with assigned readings—especially if they have been selected because they are challenging in one way or another—and many students often need help understanding what kinds of questions one can ask and what kinds of questions are worth asking about a reading. The ideal is to strike an equitable balance between support and challenge—to give students enough help as they engage complex texts so that they don't get overwhelmed and give up, while at the same time not "giving away the store," as the saying goes (providing them with answers or preferred readings or doing all the important work for them). This is why a focus on ill-structured problems is so important. In most cases, instructors cannot give answers to students even if they wanted to because such answers are not available and they must be developed in response to complex situational and contextual variables as well as other voices and competing ideas in an ongoing conversation.

As I have suggested elsewhere (Sullivan 2010, 246–48), on those dark days when my class discussions don't go particularly well—or when my students seem to miss the most important parts of assigned readings when they discuss them in their essays—I sometimes wonder if it's just not a matter of *effort*. "Why can't they try harder?" I think. "Why don't they reread? Why don't they get help at the Writing Center with reading material they don't understand? Why don't they visit me during my office hours?"

But this also appears to clearly be a matter of *skill development* as well. Reading skills are an often invisible and overlooked variable in many discussions of college-level writing skills and overall college readiness. Reading ability is probably the single most essential skill for both predicting and achieving success in college. Unfortunately, these skills are in decline. A recent NEA report, "To Read or Not to Read: A Question of National Consequence" (National Endowment for the Arts 2007), paints a dire picture:

> When one assembles data from disparate sources, the results often present contradictions. This is not the case with *To Read or Not To Read*. Here the results are startling in their consistency. All of the data combine to tell the same story about American reading.
>
> The story the data tell is simple, consistent, and alarming. Although there has been measurable progress in recent years in reading ability at the elementary school level, all progress appears to halt as children enter their teenage years. There is a general decline in reading among teenage

and adult Americans. Most alarming, both reading ability and the habit of regular reading have greatly declined among college graduates. These negative trends have more than literary importance. As this report makes clear, the declines have demonstrable social, economic, cultural, and civic implications. (National 2007, 5)

What this might mean operationally in a classroom is defined in rather disturbing specificity by a report from the American College Testing Program (ACT) entitled "Reading between the Lines—What the ACT Reveals about College Readiness in Reading" (ACT 2006). This report indicates that many high school graduates lack the reading skills they need to be successful at college. This study is based on approximately 1.2 million high school students who took the ACT and indicated that they would graduate from high school in 2005. Unfortunately, as the editors of the report note, only 51 percent of these students appear ready to be successful college-level readers:

> Just over half of our students are able to meet the demands of college-level reading, based on ACT's national readiness indicator. Only 51 percent of ACT-tested high school graduates met ACT's College Readiness Benchmark for Reading, demonstrating their readiness to handle the reading requirements for typical credit-bearing first-year college coursework, based on the 2004–2005 results of the ACT. (ACT 2006, 1)
>
> ACT's College Readiness Benchmark for Reading represents the level of achievement required for students to have a high probability of success (a 75 percent chance of earning a course grade of C or better, a 50 percent chance of earning a B or better) in such credit-bearing college courses as Psychology and U.S. History—first-year courses generally considered to be typically reading dependent. The benchmark corresponds to a score of 21 on the ACT Reading Test. (ACT 2006, 1)

These worrisome results are reflected in international assessment measures as well. For example, the 2012 Program for International Student Assessment (PISA) indicates that the international standing of U.S. students in terms of reading literacy is, alas, quite average. Among fifteen-year-old students, nineteen education systems had higher average scores in reading literacy:

> In reading literacy, average scores ranged from 384 in Peru to 570 in Shanghai-CHN. The U.S. average score (498) was not measurably different from the OECD average (496). Nineteen education systems and 2 U.S. states had higher average reading scores and 11 education systems and 1 U.S. state had scores that were not measurably different. The 19 education systems with higher average scores than the United States in reading literacy were Shanghai-CHN, Hong Kong-CHN, Singapore, Japan, the Republic of Korea, Finland, Ireland, Chinese Taipei-CHN,

Canada, Poland, Estonia, Liechtenstein, New Zealand, Australia, the Netherlands, Switzerland, Macao-CHN, Belgium, and Germany. (United States Department of Education 2014, 122)

Recent data from the US Department of Education, National Center for Education Statistics confirms that college-level readiness in terms of reading is a major problem in America. *The Condition of Education 2011*, for example, reports that in 2009, 26 percent of 12-grade students read at "below basic" level, 36 percent read at a "basic" level," and 33 percent read at a "proficient" level (Figure 10.2) (United States Department of Education 2011, 43). Only 5 percent of 12-graders read at an "advanced" level. The US Department of Education defines its "basic" reading level this way: "Basic: This level denotes partial mastery of prerequisite knowledge and skills that are fundamental for proficient work at each grade assessed" (United States Department of Education 2011, 333). So if we combine the numbers for "below basic" and "basic" readers, we have 62 percent of 12-graders in America reading with only "partial mastery of prerequisite knowledge and skills that are fundamental for proficient work." Put another way, this report indicates that only 38 percent of 12-grade students are ready to be successful college-level readers. This is discouraging news, indeed. Unpreparedness in terms of reading (and what this suggests about student ability to think reflectively, dialogically, and maturely) is at the heart of most writing problems we encounter in our composition classrooms (see Hassel and Giordano 2009; Jolliffe and Harl 2008; National 2007; Rothstein 2004). There are few things more important to academic success than reading ability and, perhaps most importantly, a disposition to find reading interesting and enjoyable (see Rothstein 2004, 19–26).

Furthermore, it is difficult to say precisely what a reading score on Accuplacer or ACT might mean in terms of college-level proficiency. We know, for example, thanks to the work Achieve has done examining college placement and admissions tests, that placement instruments like Accuplacer and Compass test certain kinds of reading and thinking skills—and not others. Unfortunately, these are mostly lower level reading skills like "literal recall," "low inference," and "high inference" (Achieve Inc. 2007a, 13–18). As the editors note, "Very few items on either test [Accuplacer or Compass] require analysis, which is regarded as the most demanding performance and is cited as an important skill by college professors" (16). In terms of "cognitive demand" or "cognitive challenge," only 1 percent of the questions on the Accuplacer test, for example, require "analysis" (Achieve Inc. 2007a, 16). As Dana Gioia notes in his Preface of *To Read or Not to Read: A Question of National Consequence*, a great deal is at stake here:

> All of the data suggest how powerfully reading transforms the lives of individuals—whatever their social circumstances. Regular reading not only boosts the likelihood of an individual's academic and economic success—facts that are not especially surprising—but it also seems to awaken a person's social and civic sense. Reading correlates with almost every measurement of positive personal and social behavior surveyed. It is reassuring, though hardly amazing, that readers attend more concerts and theater than non-readers, but it is surprising that they exercise more and play more sports—no matter what their educational level. The cold statistics confirm something that most readers know but have mostly been reluctant to declare as fact—books change lives for the better. . . .
>
> *To Read or Not To Read* confirms—without any serious qualification—the central importance of reading for a prosperous, free society. The data here demonstrate that reading is an irreplaceable activity in developing productive and active adults as well as healthy communities. Whatever the benefits of newer electronic media, they provide no measurable substitute for the intellectual and personal development initiated and sustained by frequent reading. (Gioia 2007, 6)

This is a report that all teachers of writing should be familiar with. The modern world has become increasingly complex, dynamic, interconnected across institutional and national boundaries, and dangerous. Writing teachers build a stronger democracy and a better, safer, more just world by helping students become more enthusiastic, skilled, and reflective readers and thinkers. These are essential twenty-first century skills.

### "Interrogative Mood"

To help address this problem and to engage the teaching of reading in the writing classroom, I have developed a teaching strategy that has proved very successful. Here I am following the advice of David Jolliffe:

> In a workshop I conducted recently, a very good high school teacher claimed that "the days of simply saying to your students 'Read this for Friday' are long gone." I would make the same claim about reading in college composition. We need to do considerably more to teach students *how* to read the new, challenging kinds of texts they encounter in their college courses. (Jolliffe 2007, 493)

Instead of the questions that traditionally follow readings in textbooks or that teachers ask on assignment sheets, I provide students with a "guided reading" for key assigned texts each semester. I don't do this for every assignment, but I do provide these guides for more challenging and complex readings. My goal here is to focus attention on key passages within each text—to point them out, to ask questions about them, and to initiate conversation and thinking about them. Again, my focus is on promoting listening, empathy, and reflection and the thoughtful engagement of legitimate complexity.

It is important to note here that I only ask questions. I don't provide answers or preferred readings. I think of this as establishing an "interrogative mood" in the classroom, following Maynard Mack's famous observation about *Hamlet*: "Hamlet's world is preeminently in the interrogative mood. It reverberates with questions . . ." (Mack 1993, 109). My goal is to make everything in this class "reverberate with questions." Such an approach is consistent with teaching strategies and best practices outlined by Ken Bain in *What the Best College Teachers Do*. This approach is informed by a belief in the power of questions to spur growth, exploration, and learning:

> In the learning literature and in the thinking of the best teachers, questions play an essential role in the process of learning and modifying mental models. Questions help us construct knowledge. They point to holes in our memory structures and are critical for indexing the information that we attain when we develop an answer for that inquiry. Some cognitive scientists think that questions are so important that we cannot learn until the right one has been asked . . . (Bain 2004, 31)

As Eugene Ionesco once famously observed, "It is not the answer that enlightens, but the question." Our students' classroom experience should be reverberating with interesting and challenging questions. It is important to let our students find their own way to whatever "answers" and conclusions they can find or make, however humble or imperfect these may be.

I also seek to have students do most of the talking and exploring in my classroom. Following Hillocks, this is one way I seek to reduce the amount of "teacher talk" in the classroom and bring student thinking and exploration to the center of my pedagogy:

> In my over 40 years in education, I have spent thousands of hours visiting classrooms, as a colleague of teachers, as a secondary school English department chair, as a director of freshman English, and as a researcher in secondary, community college, and university classrooms. The vast majority of the classes I have observed in these capacities have been as Goodlad and Nystrand describe them [lots of "teacher talk"]. They have consisted mostly of teacher talk. When students do talk, it is more often to answer questions that may be answered in a single word or short phrase that bears little or no relationship to the preceding answer. That is to say, the classroom discourse is largely disconnected and serves mainly to let teachers

know if students know bits and pieces of information about whatever is being studied. (Hillocks 2002, 7)

The questions I ask are designed to help students understand how to listen to a reading and how to engage assigned readings productively, collaboratively, and thoughtfully. In this way, I am attempting to model what good listening, good reading, and good thinking look like (Tishman, Perkins, and Jay 1994).

These reading guides are also extremely useful if students miss a class discussion or are just struggling with a particular reading and need a more guided experience through the text. My goal here is to take students through this process—engaging a text that asks thought-provoking and challenging questions and leading students through a critical thinking process that ultimately makes them better readers and writers. It seems to me there is great value in this kind of guided reading experience.

I have provided in an appendix some samples of the kind of guided reading handouts I provide to students. The first is for an assignment that focuses on James Baldwin's "Sonny's Blues," a story that I think offers readers of all levels important questions to consider. I often begin my semester in English 93 with this reading for our first major writing assignment because it is a richly complex and beautifully realized work of art that students find fascinating and powerful and because at its most essential, it is a story about listening. The second sample is an assignment for a paired group of readings related to culture. Both of the readings in this unit pose significant challenges for students. Generally, students in my classes have found these guided reading handouts extremely useful as they have worked to read, understand, and engage challenging work.

I have also developed guides for students that ask no questions at all but simply focus their attention on key passages and quotations from the readings. I have included a sample of this kind of "quotations reading guide" in an appendix as well. It is a guide I developed for a unit on readings related to economic inequality, poverty, and the distribution of wealth. I don't ask questions, but I do give students some key passages to consider and reflect on. I have found this kind of "highlighting" helps students engage more challenging readings and provides them with an effective way to begin grappling with a challenging text.

As I hope readers will see, all of the assignments I have developed for this approach to teaching writing have been developed in order to provide students with real college-level complexity and real college-level reading, writing, and thinking challenges. These reading guides will help readers of this book see what kind of cognitive challenges I am privileging here. On a pragmatic note, I have found that about ten pages of single-spaced material for reading guides is about the maximum I can expect students to manage (even though most of this material is quoted material from the readings). Most students report that the current length of these reading guides (between seven and ten pages) is "just right."

## 6. Assign at Least One Writing Assignment that Focuses on *Rereading*

English teachers often do a great job of *talking about* the value of reread-ing to students, but we seldom devote class time to actually *allowing students to experience for themselves* what happens when they reread. This can be an especially transformative activity if the text students are reading is one that is rich and complex. Helping students understand and nurture this crucial reading skill—rereading—is something we must make time for and emphasize in our teaching practice. And it needs to be experi-ential. Students can't be expected to just take our word for it. They have to experience what happens when they reread on their own.

I assign a rereading assignment for the first major assignment in all of my writing classes. In my English 93 class, for example, my unit on "Sonny's Blues" begins in the traditional way, asking students to read the story and then write a reflective journal response to it. We discuss the story in class, and for the next class meeting I ask them to reread the story and then write about what happened when they reread it. The assignment is very simple:

> **Homework:** 1. Reread "Sonny's Blues" and write a response about what you learned about reading and rereading from this experience.

The majority of students get a great deal out of this assignment, and student comments about the value of rereading are often precisely what we hope for and expect. These new insights about reading and reread-ing have the additional advantage of having been earned, active, and experienced—and for this reason, they are more likely be remembered and retained more deeply and reused and applied in other situations and contexts. My goal here is to set in students' minds a model for the kind of deeper understanding that rereading provides, and to put that at the center of how they define "reading." For many students, reading is simply getting to the end of whatever text may have been assigned. With this assignment, I seek to replace that with a more sophisticated understanding of what reading is. "You're not finished reading some-thing until you understand it," I tell them. This is often a key moment for basic writers. At the heart of this experience, of course, is the ability to listen and reflect.

## 7. Provide Models of Reflective Writing

Students are so accustomed to writing arguments that they often feel uncomfortable at first writing anything that does not have a thesis and an argumentative structure. Students often ask me, "How do I write something without a thesis?" Especially at the beginning of the semester, students often need help understanding what listening, empathy, and reflection are, what such practices can offer them as readers, writers, and thinkers, and what a reflective journal response or reflective essay might look like. It's important to provide models of this kind of writing so that students can see the kinds of things writers focus on when they bring listening, empathy, and reflection to the center of their intellectual work. For example, in addition to providing students with an excellent reflective essay written by a student from a previous semester, I always take at least one of the best journal responses I get from my first major journal assignment and distribute this to the class. We read and discuss this artifact together. This writing sample provides students with an inspiring concrete example of what good reflective writing looks like.

## 8. Following Baxter Magolda, Consider Assigning at Least One Assignment Each Semester Designed to Nurture "Self-Authorship"

As we noted above, Baxter Magolda has suggested that "an internal sense of self" is essential to mature meaning making. This internal sense of self, Baxter Magolda suggests, helps guide mature adults as they sift through competing "knowledge claims" and assists them in essential ways as they participate in the "social construction of knowledge" (Baxter Magolda 2001, 195). Students can benefit greatly from assignments that assist them in this important process of self-authorship, and assignments in writing classes can easily be designed with this essential learning outcome in mind. I try to have at least one major assignment each semester that provides students with the opportunity for this kind of personal reflection, exploration, and self-authorship. If these assignments are also carefully designed with the learning outcomes we are discussing here in mind, they will provide powerful cognitive growth opportunities for students.

These assignments are qualitatively different in one crucial way than the assignments I have previously discussed because they provide students with an opportunity to focus on their own life experience and the development of their personal values within a larger context and intellectual framework. A good example of this kind of activity from my teaching practice is the following assignment, which is designed with the work of Baxter Magolda in mind. This assignment, which I have used successfully now for a number of years, provides students with an opportunity to review thousands of years of wisdom literature related to "happiness" and living a meaningful life, and then invites students to discuss, develop, refine, and articulate their own personal value system:

### *"Where I Live and What I Live for"*: Developing a System of Personal Values

For this essay, we will be examining work that invites you to think about your values and where they come from. The purpose of this project is to provide you with an opportunity to reflect carefully on your own core values, and to think carefully about what you want your values to be. Our third reading surveys recent research about what makes a "happy" and fulfilling life.

Reading Sequence:

1. Shirley Jackson, "The Lottery"
2. David Foster Wallace, *This Is Water* (Kenyon College Commencement Address, 2005)
3. Jonathan Haidt, from *The Happiness Hypothesis* (Chapter 5: The Pursuit of Happiness and Chapter 7: The Uses of Adversity)

Once we have completed our class discussion, I would like you to write a reflective essay that carefully and thoughtfully engages the ideas and research presented in these readings. I would then like you to move on to discuss your own core values and where they come from. As you do this, please include quotations from the texts we've read and discussed.

Here are some questions to consider as you move forward:

- Why do the people in the village in "The Lottery" conduct the lottery?
- What does David Foster Wallace mean by "default settings"?
- What does research and ancient wisdom tell us about what leads to happiness?

You may organize your essay in whatever way you wish. Feel free to be creative and to use personal experience and observation. Please quote at least once from each of our three readings.

Please focus your response on "listening" carefully to each writer and then reflecting on what they have to tell us. Please note that it is not our goal here to arrive at any definitive or final answer to the questions these readings explore. Instead, our goal is simply to encounter and engage these readings and the questions they raise in a way that is exploratory, thoughtful, and collaborative. I am not interested in having you formulate a thesis and support it.

Essays should be approximately 1250 words in length.

This assignment is designed to do a number of important things: (1) Like all the assignments I am theorizing here for writing classes, it provides students with a complex, ill-structured problem to consider; and (2) It also allows students to engage this complex problem in a personal, meaningful way linked to landmark learning theory. I have included a sample student response to this assignment in Appendix 4.

### 9. Bring Learning Theory into the Classroom and Build It into Assignments

Here's an example of how I foreground learning theory in one of my assignments:

**Essay #2: Rich Man, Poor Man**
Reading Sequence:

1. Milton and Rose Friedman, from *Free to Choose*

2. Herbert J. Gans, "The Uses of Poverty: The Poor Pay All." *Social Policy* July/August 1971: 20–24

3. John Cassidy, "Relatively Deprived: How Poor is Poor?" (*The New Yorker*, April 3, 2006)

4. David Shipler, from *The Working Poor: Invisible in America* (Preface, Introduction, Chapters 2, 3 and 11).

5. Dr. Martin Luther King, from the Nobel Lecture (December 11, 1964): "Why should there be hunger and privation in any land, in any city, at any table when man has the resources and the scientific know-how to provide all mankind with the basic necessities of life?"

This unit is designed to provide you with the opportunity to encounter a number of very different theories seeking to explain poverty, class, and economic inequality.

Please note here that our goal is not to read and then select among these theories the "best" one. Nor am I interested in having you develop a thesis and then support that thesis in your essay.

Instead, I am primarily interested here in providing you with the opportunity to encounter "legitimate human uncertainty" and the opportunity to engage it thoughtfully. As I built this unit, I had in mind an important passage at the beginning of William Perry's (1999) famous book, *Forms of Ethical and Intellectual Development in the College Years*, where he discusses different kinds of student responses to a lecture. The lecturer is introducing students to competing theoretical models, and Perry notes that these students can respond to this lecture in a variety of different ways. As Perry suggests, each of these responses reflects a specific cognitive orientation:

Let us suppose that a lecturer announces that today he will consider three theories explanatory of _____ (whatever his topic may be).

Student A has always taken it for granted that knowledge consists of correct answers, that there is one right answer per problem, and that teachers explain these answers for students to learn.

Student B makes the same general assumptions but with an elaboration to the effect that teachers sometimes present problems and procedures, rather than answers, "so that we can learn to find the right answer on our own." He therefore perceives the lecture as a kind of guessing game in which he is to "figure out" which theory is correct, a game that is fair enough if the lecturer does not carry it so far as to hide things too obscurely.

Student C assumes that an answer can be called "right" only in the light of its context, and that contexts or "frames of reference" differ. He assumes that several interpretations of a poem, explanations of a historical development, or even theories of a class of events in physics may be legitimate "depending on how you look at it." Though he feels a little uneasy in such a kaleidoscopic world, he nonetheless supposes that the lecturer may be about to present three legitimate theories which can be examined for their internal coherence, their scope, their fit with various data, their predictive power, etc.

Whatever the lecturer then proceeds to do (in terms of his own assumptions and intent), these three students will make meaning of the experience in different ways which will involve different assessments of their own choices and responsibilities. (Perry 1999, 1–2)

This unit has been designed to give you the opportunity to "try on" Student C's approach or cognitive orientation (and thus to work as true college-level readers, writers, and thinkers). Because there is no "right answer" to the questions this unit explores, you should find that the readings in this unit will probably push you against your own conceptual boundaries and frontiers. You will no doubt find this challenging, but this challenge is an integral part of the cognitive learning challenge this unit provides!

My goal here is to offer you the opportunity to engage different theories related to poverty, class, and economic inequality that can be examined for "their internal coherence, their scope, their fit with various data, their predictive power, etc."

As you work through this unit, I would like you to focus on discussing the strengths and weaknesses of each theory.

You may organize your essay in whatever way you want, and you are certainly invited to discuss any issues in these readings that you think are important. Feel free to be creative, use personal experience and observation, etc.

Essays should be approximately 1250 words in length. Please quote at least once from each reading in your essay.

My students have found this kind of foregrounding both interesting and very challenging, as I hoped it would be.

## 6
## REVOLUTION

### THE "CENTRAL FACTOR IN THINKING"

Listening is an orientation to the world and a pedagogical practice that is most advantageously paired with reflective writing and reflective thinking. As we know, reflective thinking has a long and distinguished history. John Dewey is perhaps the most influential thinker and educator to discuss reflective thought, and reflection is vitally important to the way he understands and theorizes thinking. For Dewey, reflective thought is, as he famously put it in *How We Think*, the "central factor in thinking" (Dewey 1997, 6):

> To turn the thing over in mind, to reflect, means to hunt for additional evidence, for new data, that will develop the suggestion, and will either, as we say, bear it out or else make obvious its absurdity and irrelevance. Given a genuine difficulty and a reasonable amount of analogous experience to draw upon, the difference, par excellence, between good and bad thinking is found at this point. The easiest way is to accept any suggestion that seems plausible and thereby bring to an end the condition of mental uneasiness. Reflective thinking is always more or less troublesome because it involves overcoming the inertia that includes one to accept suggestions at their face value; it involves willingness to endure a condition or mental unrest and disturbance. . . . As we shall see later, the most important factor in the training of good mental habits consists in acquiring the attitude of suspended conclusion, and in mastering the various methods of searching for new materials to corroborate or to refute the first suggestions that occur. To maintain the state of doubt and to carry on systematic and protracted inquiry—these are the essentials of thinking. (Dewey 1997, 13)

Writing teachers should be in the business of designing assignments that require students to think in ways that are "more or less troublesome" in the sense that Dewey uses here. Moreover, learning theorists would be very supportive of the kind of "mental unrest and disturbance" that Dewey champions here because this kind of "unrest" has the potential to move students toward more sophisticated cognitive orientations

DOI: 10.7330/9780874219449.c006

and a more complex understanding of the nature of knowledge and the construction of meaning and value.

Dewey also suggests in *How We Think* that reflective thought is only required for the most challenging kinds of problems, a class of problem that "perplexes and challenges the mind so that it makes belief at all uncertain" (Dewey 1997, 9). Uncertainty is a key variable here for Dewey, as it is for learning theorists. In his own way, Dewey is discussing ill-structured problems, problems for which there is no obvious or correct solution, as there might be for an algebraic equation or calculating a chemistry problem.

Dewey offers writing teachers a compelling rationale here for bringing reflective thinking (as opposed to simplistic argumentative thinking and its privileging of closure and certainty) to the center of our curriculum.

## REFLECTIVE THINKING IS "OPEN TO SELF-CORRECTION"

Reflective thinking is one of the key focal points in King and Kitchener's developmental scheme, and it is essential for Perry's as well. King and Kitchener note that reflective judgment has become a neglected aspect of the critical thinking process (King and Kitchener 1994, 1–19). The most important and essential point they make about reflective thinking is that it actively resists certainty and closure: "Judgments derived from the reflective thinking process remain open to further scrutiny, evaluation, and reformulation; as such, reflective judgments are open to self-correction" (8). Openness of mind and resistance to certainty and closure are key hallmarks of the pedagogy we are theorizing here. King and Kitchener devote a whole chapter to identifying ways to nurture this kind of openness and reflection during the college years (222–57). At the center of these recommendations is the ill-structured problem. As King and Kitchener suggest (and as we have noted previously), "in the final analysis, the real challenge of college, for students and faculty members, is empowering individuals to know that the world is far more complex than it first appears" (1).

We also see reflective thinking at work in the most advanced stages of Perry's developmental scheme as he reports on what students say about their development in college. It is the essential wellspring that makes possible the kind of ethical and intellectual development that he chronicles in his famous book. Given this important work, why are we still teaching in a manner that actively subverts what we know about how mature thinking and writing is produced?

## HILLOCKS AND YANCEY

Reflective thinking is important for scholars in the field of composition as well. In *Teaching Writing as a Reflective Practice*, George Hillocks situates reflective thinking at the center of teaching writing. At the heart of the pedagogy that Hillocks discusses is an epistemological stance much like the one we are theorizing here. It is focused on inquiry, "the exchange and thoughtful examination of ideas and opinions" (Hillocks 1995, 213), and "requires an epistemological stance quite different from that of current-traditional rhetoric and the textbooks that use it, one which suggests that truth is unambiguous, monolithic, and transportable by means of language" (212).

Hillocks recommends including a richer variety of writing tasks for students, including personal narrative and satire, along with argument (Hillocks 1995, 127–46). Significantly, Hillocks supports the use of personal narrative because it helps build empathy:

> One major concern in schools is with developing potential, providing the bases from which students may grow. A second has been with providing the tools for understanding the culture. If our writing program is to fulfill either of these broad goals, it must include writing for empathic response, both to develop potential and to better understand how such writing operates in the culture.
>
> Beyond that, empathic writing has auxiliary purposes as well. Because students engage with their own stories and like to hear the stories of others, personal narrative can be used in a variety of ways to involve students in high-level discussion of complex ideas and emotions. (Hillocks 1995, 128)

Hillocks values this kind of intellectual work very highly: "Writing that achieves empathic response is arguably the most important kind of writing in our culture" (128). There is much in Hillocks's book that supports the pedagogy we are developing here. Of special note is Hillocks's summary assessment: "If thoughtful inquiry does not lie at the heart of writing, then our students become little more than amanuenses" (214)—that is to say, "manual laborers" who go largely unengaged and unchallenged by the ideas they are writing about. As Hillocks suggests, however, the kind of "thoughtful inquiry" that he advocates must be very carefully theorized and implemented for it to be realized effectively in the classroom. Ultimately, for Hillocks, the teaching of writing involves foundational questions, including "what we hope our students will become through our teaching of writing, both as people and as writers, how our means and methods of teaching influence that, and what must (or may) be taught (the matter of curricula, plural) to reach those goals" (3). A pedagogy focused on listening, empathy, and reflection would certainly be worthy of such noble goals.

Kathleen Blake Yancey has also done important work on reflection and writing. In *Reflection in the Writing Classroom*, Yancey acknowledges that "reflection has played but a small role in the history of composing" (Yancey 1998, 4). This is something we are both interested in changing. Yancey theorizes reflection, building on the important work of Donald Schon (1983, 1987) (*The Reflective Practitioner* and *Educating the Reflective Practitioner*), as both a process of inquiry and a type of writing students do:

> Reflection is both process and product. The process of reflection can be fostered in several ways. Inviting students to reflect in multiple ways is inviting them to triangulate their own truths, to understand and articulate the pluralism of truth. Given what William Perry explains about maturation for the typical college student—that she/he moves from a dualistic stance to a relativistic stance to a reflective stance—such invitations seem particularly appropriate. (Yancey 1998, 19)

Yancey discusses and develops a pedagogy here for three different kinds of reflection:

- **reflection-in-action**: the process of reviewing and projecting and revising, which takes place with a composing event, and the associated texts
- **constructive reflection**: the process of developing a cumulative, multiselved, multi-voiced identity, which takes place between and among composing events, and the associated texts
- **reflection-in-presentation**: the process of articulating the relationships between and among the multiple variable of writing and the writer in a specific context for a specific audience, and the associated text (Yancey 1998, 13–14)

The kind of reflection Yancey champions here is interrogative, dialogic, and collaborative. It is "about learning to ask questions, about the power that asking good questions confers, about the value of doing this collaboratively so that we learn with and from each other. Reflection is, as I've learned, both individual and social" (Yancey 1998, 17). There is also a tentative, cautious quality to this kind of intellectual work for Yancey, and this orientation links her ideas about reflection to the learning theory we reviewed earlier. As Yancey suggests, given the central role that reflection plays in the development of thinking, we have much to gain from moving reflective writing beyond the marginal places it now occupies in our curriculum (i.e., for the reflective portfolio letter, the final reflective portfolio essay, the reflection that sometimes accompanies a more traditional kind of writing task, and the final, cumulative reflective essay at the end of the semester) (see Jung 2011; Yancey 1998, 15). Yancey's most recent book, *Writing across Contexts: Transfer, Composition, and Sites of Writing* (2014), which she co-authored with Liane Robertson and Kara Taczak, positions reflective writing at the center of a writing pedagogy focused on transfer of knowledge. At the moment, however, reflective writing is very much undervalued and underappreciated in the writing classroom. It has been in large measure eclipsed in the writing classroom by simplistic thesis and support argumentative writing.

## THE EXPLORATORY ESSAY

There has been considerable and sustained resistance to argumentative thesis and support writing in the academy now for many years. In fact, a significant oppositional tradition has developed within our scholarship (which, alas, has been generally undervalued, and with which I humbly and respectfully position myself) that seeks to have students focus on more exploratory, open, and dialogic kinds of writing activities. The model for some of these scholars is Montaigne and his example of a writing practice that is fueled primarily by curiosity, openness, and the spirit of intellectual exploration. Generally, these scholars all suggest that a more open-ended, exploratory essay model is better for student learning, offering a more productive and worthwhile kind of writing experience because it privileges a more tentative, cautious, and exploratory orientation toward the world than conventional argumentative writing. I see my own pedagogy here supporting, extending, and attempting to operationalize this important work.

As early as 1971, Keith Fort critiqued the "tyranny" of the thesis/support essay. Fort suggested, in "Form, Authority, and the Critical Essay," that the thesis/support essay perpetuates, among other things, hierarchical power structures in society: "the form we have unconsciously assumed to be the best one (if not the only one) for expressing written ideas on literature both reflects and perpetuates attitudes that generate the structures of our society" (Fort 1971, 629). Furthermore, he suggested that this type of writing activity "*conditions* thought patterns and, particularly, attitude towards authority" (630). It does so because it requires students to think in terms of hierarchy, "mastery," and the belief "in the reality of a transcendent authority" (633): "As will always happen when the mind is patterned to think in terms of hierarchy, it will also have to be competitive. Most basically the critic is competing against his subject to establish his claim of mastery over it. And the form that has internal competition as its motive force will also generate extrinsic competition" (635).

As we have seen from our discussion of learning theory, this kind of thinking produces a number of serious problems for student writers, serving to entrench them in lower order cognitive orientations. This kind of argumentative writing, which privileges the strong thesis statement above almost all else, also reduces writers to "thesis hunters" (633), rather than careful readers and reflective thinkers: "if the only form in which a writer can express himself on literature is one that requires a thesis, then he has to look at literature as a source of theses" (633). This pedagogy requires student writers to think in certain ways—but not others:

> Formal tyranny in essay writing, as in any other expression, is based on the need of those who are in control to make the appearance of the expression confirm a desired idea of which there is doubt. To reach some understanding of what causes the creation of this tyranny, the best approach is to consider the common element in the form that is most generally taken as a rule, for this common element is the one that binds the group together.
>
> In the essay it would seem that this key rule is that there must be a thesis which the essay proves. The first question always asked about a prospective paper is whether the idea is "workable" or can be "handled." As I understand these terms, they mean "do you have a thesis that can be proved?" This formal requirement is a *sine qua non* for a paper. Meeting it does not necessarily mean that a paper will be successful (an A in the classroom or publication), but its absence guarantees failure.
>
> This formal requirement permits an infinite number of individualized expressions, but like any formal limit, it obviously permits freedom only of a kind. And, furthermore, since a relation always exists between form and content, it also imposes broad restrictions on the kind of topics that may be chosen. Only those ideas are acceptable that can be proved. If a writer tries to force the "wrong" kind of idea into the right form failure will result. Teachers and editors look with dismay on "big" or very personal topics. Their abhorrence is reasonable so long as the form is fixed because these topics are not provable. (Fort 1971, 631)

Fort approvingly mentions "conversational, exploratory essays" (632) as a viable alternative to thesis/support essays.

William Zeiger's (1985) essay, "The Exploratory Essay: Enfranchising the Spirit of Inquiry in College Composition" is another important landmark in this oppositional tradition. The title itself suggests a great deal about Zeiger's curricular ideas, and I am especially appreciative of his interest in enfranchising students, something I enthusiastically support as well. Zeiger suggests that our almost exclusive focus on argumentation in the classroom serves to subvert intellectual and emotional exploration and mature meaning-making:

> The ability to construct a logical argument, as in exposition, is of course a critical skill for any educated person. Equally important, however, is the ability to explore—to recognize and weigh alternatives. By concentrating almost exclusively on thesis-support exposition in college composition classes, we are implicitly teaching that the ability to support an assertion is more important than the ability to examine an issue. In doing so, we fall in with the results-oriented popular prejudice and fail in our duties as liberal educators. No doubt we composition teachers extol to our students the need to research a topic carefully and to scrutinize a question from all sides; we even sit in conference over preliminary drafts. But as long as the goal and product of writing is to demonstrate the validity of a thesis, the implicit message is that proving is more important than finding out. (Zeiger 1985, 458)

A powerful and important critique, indeed. Zeiger sees our disciplinary mono-culture of argumentation as dangerous and problematic for a number of reasons:

> It would appear, in sum, that concentration on the expository essay has reached a point of severely diminished returns. It continually demands that the writer prove a thesis, even while slighting the exploration that would provide the substance of the proof; it asks the writer to make bricks without straw. It augments this impediment to free creation by confronting the writer with a critical audience, dispelling the congenial atmosphere in which exploration would thrive. I do not challenge the importance of sound exposition to a college career and a liberal education; but as long as the "bottom line" of an essay is a well-defended thesis, the art of exploration will continue to languish as the poor step-sister of exposition. If we genuinely wish to promote freedom of thought, to balance demonstration with the inquiry which sustains it, then we must establish the art of exploration as an equally acceptable and worthy pursuit. (Zeiger 1985, 459)

In place of argument, Zeiger proposes that we teach "the personal or familiar essay in the manner of Montaigne—an essay in an informal, friendly tone, whose aim is to unfold the intellectual potential of an idea" (460). Zeiger suggests that we adopt an "open form" of essay writing that has as its primary defining characteristic a "quality of accommodating several viewpoints, even contradictory viewpoints, simultaneously. If the expository essay is essentially an argument, the familiar essay is essentially a conversation" (460). The language here of "conversation" brings us back to Bruffee, Salvatori, and Morrow. This kind of writing privileges caution and the value of staying flexible and open to self-correction.

Sheree Meyer has also done important work on this subject. In "Refusing to Play the Confidence Game: The Illusion of Mastery in the Reading/Writing of Texts," Meyer submits to withering critique the standard intellectual orientation of argumentative writing as it typically plays out in our classrooms, which relentlessly requires writers to assume a position of "authority" and mastery. Meyer suggests that this is a very risky "game" to play:

> Some students can play the part; they can assume "authority" in imitation of the models they know. But they may still have a great deal of difficulty overcoming their feelings that they (and therefore their essays) are frauds. Sometimes those feelings are sufficient to create writer's block or dissatisfaction. If we insist that they pose as "acknowledged authorities," then we have contributed not to their learning but to their impostor complex.
>
> Too often, these students are not really confident of their power to write; instead, they are playing a confidence game. One synonym for confident is "cocksure," and indeed, that is my point—to have confidence, the students must participate in an illusion of mastery: an illusion of "being cocksure" of themselves, their control of the language, their mastery of the literary text, and their superiority over their audience. Being "in control," however, exacts a heavy price and, strangely enough, exacerbates rather than relieves anxieties about inadequacy. (Meyer 1993, 47)

Furthermore, the focus of a writer constructing an argument, then, becomes not to listen to or embrace or welcome the other/s, but to annihilate them:

> The act of persuasion is then a verbal assault on that opposition; we have won the argument if the reader moves from his or her opposition to our position—if we annihilate the "other" view" (Meyer 1993, 48).

Deep engagement with the chaos of mature meaning-making also becomes difficult under these conditions (48–9). Like Zeiger, Meyer laments the current state of curriculum in our discipline and seeks to theorize an alternate pedagogy:

> Although challenged from a number of directions, formal argumentation is and will probably continue to be, at least for some time, the dominant mode of academic discourse. As such, it can be seen as empowering— empowering those students who by successfully imitating it convince their readers that they really "know" what they are presumed to know. Whenever students (or we, for that matter) sit down to write, we are all confronting the power of the red pen or the blue pencil. Rather than risk losing their place in academe, students try to play by the rules of the confidence game I have already described. Conformity may appear safer than the alternatives.
>
> What then are the alternatives? What other stances and voices are there? Can we establish an "authority" that is not based on an illusion

of mastery? Can we locate an academic discourse that is not aggressively combative and competitive but that promotes a community that engages in dialogue, not debate? Can we argue differently about literature? These are the questions I ask of myself, my colleagues, and my students. And I am not alone. (Meyer 1993, 52)

Drawing on feminist scholars like Torgovnick, Lamb, and Frey, as well as the work of Jane Gallop, Meyer theorizes an oppositional pedagogy and a writing practice for the classroom that is less monolithic and more fluid than traditional argumentative writing, one that focuses on helping students "attain a degree of flexibility in negotiating the subject/object relations of the reading process and in articulating a multiplicity of 'selves'" (Meyer 1993, 54).

Paul Heilker and Donna Qualley have also contributed significant work to this oppositional tradition. Both of these scholars champion a pedagogy that is less reliant on argumentation and more focused on dialog, openness, and exploratory types of writing assignments. Heilker and Qualley's work warrants careful attention from anyone interested in having students produce mature, intellectually sophisticated work.

Heilker suggests in his notable book, *The Essay: Theory and Pedagogy for an Active Form,* that the thesis/support format, "once learned, works to actually thwart student development" (Heilker 1996, 2) because it embodies an "overly simplistic positivistic epistemology" (4)—one that suggests that truth can be rather easily found and that uncertainty is typically only a temporary condition. Heilker cites James Berlin here to discuss epistemology, but he might have also cited the learning theorists we discussed earlier, all of whom make roughly the same point about this kind of cognitive orientation. Furthermore, Heilker suggests that

> besides being the uncritically and automatically invoked template for producing text, the scaffolding of the thesis/support form that allows students to simply and mechanically organize information reveals a second way this form limits students' development: by closing rather than opening their minds. This closing process begins by requiring students to repeatedly narrow and focus their topics (often to the point of inconsequentiality) in order to find a "workable" thesis, one that is straightforward (often to the point of being obvious, incontestable, or clichéd) and has clear supporting reasons. (Heilker 1996, 3)

Heilker goes on to suggest that this form of writing is inadequate in all sorts of ways—developmentally, epistemologically, and ideologically.

In its place, and drawing on the work of Lukacs, Adorno, Huxley, Holdheim, Good, and Bakhtin, Heilker champions a different kind of essay, which he theorizes and defines, following the example of

Montaigne, as a form of writing and intellectual inquiry that "must be an uncertain exploration of received opinion that searches for truth rather than trying to establish it" (38). Such writing should be characterized by three hallmarks:

- A profound epistemological skepticism. Against the absolute sureness and "airtight closure" (Heilker 1996, 4) of the thesis/support essay, Heilker suggests we embrace and model writing practices in our classrooms that acknowledge (and here he is quoting J. C. Guy Cherica) the "insufficiency" of our own knowledge "and its uncertainty" (17).

- Anti-scholasticism. Heilker is interested in destabilizing the idea that the academy is the only place one can find answers to life's most challenging and important questions and suggests that "truth" can be elusive, context-specific, and various.

- Chrono-logic organization, a form of organization that is much more fluid and organic than argument typically is. This is an organizational strategy that celebrates the mind at work, however associational, asymmetrical, tentative, and nonlinear the results of that thinking and inquiry may be. Again, Montaigne is the model here.

Of course, as Heilker suggests, putting this kind of writing at the center of our curriculum would require "both teachers and students to rethink almost everything they know about writing in academia" (87). This seems to be very much the case, indeed.

Qualley makes similar recommendations in *Turns of Thought: Teaching Composition as Reflexive Inquiry*. As the title of her book suggests, Qualley's pedagogy seeks to promote "reflexive inquiry," a complex intellectual and rhetorical activity that is built around a number of essential components, beginning with an "encounter with the other": "The encounter with the other initiates the reflexive turn to the self and the continual interplay between self and other is what prevents self-consciousness from slipping into narcissism or solipsism" (Qualley 1997, 139). Additional elements of her pedagogy include:

- Developing an "open stance" that is "receptive, deferent, exploratory, tentative" (Qualley 1997, 141).

- Privileging dialog: "Genuine dialog also presupposes that participants are not isolated in their own subjectivism and are open to considerations of other positions" (146).

- Embracing recursiveness: "Such a process helps students to experience revision as a creative and intellectual process. It also nurtures an important, intellectual, and ethical habit of mind in both students *and teachers*" (151).

Qualley also has important things to say about agency and confidence, that bring us again to problematic elements at the heart of "the discourse of mastery":

> A good example of a person with a strong sense of ethical agency—way beyond most of us—is the nun in the film *Dead Man Walking*, who is able to open herself to the other, the convicted killer, without losing herself in the process.
>
> All too frequently, though, our methods in the teaching of composition seem to encourage false or premature agency or an illusion of power. As Sheree Meyer (1993) notes, learning to write in the university can often mean learning to play the "confidence game." When students assume an authority in their written texts before they have had an opportunity to earn it through inquiry, they "participate in an illusion of mastery" that belies an inadequacy they often still feel about themselves as writers. (145)

Qualley's comments here about earned authority through inquiry are vitally important to keep in mind as we consider the simplistic argumentative essay. How much of the authority in these essays is "earned"? How would a student "earn" such authority? Would it be possible for someone who has read only a few short essays about a subject to earn any kind of authority? And what are we teaching students about writing, thinking, and meaning-making with these kinds of argumentative assignments? All important questions, for sure.

Paul Heilker's (2001) more recent essay, "Official Feasts and Carnivals: Student Writing and Public Ritual," extends Fort's discussion about the thesis/support argument and posits an alternative type of writing activity for students, theorized using Bakhtin's ideas about "carnival":

> In teaching writing, we limit students' development by training them to practice only one kind of public ritual: the official feast of thesis-and-support writing. This kind of ritual, Mikhail Bakhtin notes, serves only to reinforce extant discursive, epistemological, and ideological boundaries, to buttress and sanction the existing ideas, hierarchies, prohibitions, and truths that proscribe the possible limits of students' thought, actions, and identities (Rabelais 9). Students also need to learn to practice the opposing and complementary public ritual of the carnival and thus come to transgress and transcend these forces which would place such hard limits on their senses of who they are, what they can do, and who they might become. By training students to also write in carnivalesque genres like the exploratory essay or Winston Weathers's Grammar B, for example, we train them to engage in a ritual which, according to Bakhtin, exists to offer temporary liberation from the established, enforced, and accepted conventions of the world and, thus, to consecrate inventive freedom. By teaching students to engage in the public ritual of carnivalesque writing, we can provide them with powerful practices with which to think, act, and

write differently—and, thus, to reinvent both who they are and the worlds in which they live. (Heilker 2001, 77–78)

Heilker suggests here that "the thesis/support form celebrates a positivistic epistemology and corresponding rhetoric in which truth is eternal and indisputable" (Heilker 2001, 79). As James Berlin has noted, in this epistemological orientation, "all truths are regarded as certain, readily available to the correct method of investigation" (Berlin 1987, 9). As we know from our review of learning theory, this is deeply problematic for student development. In its place, Heilker proposes that we embrace the models provided by Montaigne and Bakhtin:

> In contemporary terms, the Montaignean essay, in stark contrast to the official feast of academic discourse, serves as one form of carnivalesque writing. The Montaignean essay counters official ideology, ritual, and dogmatism by embodying a spirit of discovery at work in an uncertain universe that leaves old, inadequate orders behind in its quest for new ideas, new insights, and new visions of the truth. It operates in opposition to the scholastic delineation of experience into discrete disciplines and their respective discourses, offering instead a transgressive and more inclusive discourse that temporarily brings together contrasting and incongruous points of view in an attempt to more fully and deeply address whole problems of human existence. In this, it enacts a conscious and conscientious act of resistance, one characterized by the free and familiar contact and discourse among people usually divided by a variety of cultural barriers. It encourages students to endlessly open and complicate their topics, to examine how and why they came to think and feel as they do, to follow an idea wherever it may lead, to entertain multiple (even contradictory) simultaneous theses, to enact the perpetual mobility that characterizes a freed mind. (Heilker 2001, 80)

There is much to be said for this kind of "resistance." This is the kind of intellectual work that should be at the center of our writing instruction, grade 6–13.


## FEMINIST SCHOLARSHIP AND THE "ADVERSARIAL METHOD"

Feminist scholars have also urged compositionists to rethink our reliance on argumentation and thesis and support so that our assignments require more dialogic and collaborative intellectual work. Feminist theory has long been interested in moving our discipline away from what Catherine Lamb has called "monologic argument" (Lamb 1991, 13). Lamb suggests, in fact, that "we have uncritically assumed that there is no other way to write" (13). This seems to be clearly and certainly the case. Argumentative academic writing is devoted almost exclusively to what Olivia Frey has characterized as the "adversarial method" (Frey 1990, 512). Deborah Tannen has written a whole book on this question (*The Argument Culture*), and she has suggested that, in the final analysis, "our spirits are corroded by living in an atmosphere of unrelenting contention" (Tannen 1999, 3). We have had many calls over the years from feminist scholars and others for classroom writing activities that, following Lamb, move us away from the almost gladiatorial writing practices of argument and thesis/support toward writing activities that promote "cooperation, collaboration, shared leadership, and integration of the cognitive and the affective" (Lamb 1991, 11; Clinchy 2000; Gannett 1992; Kirsch et al. 2003). I would like to add my name to that list.

## ROGERIAN ARGUMENTATION

We should pause here briefly to consider rhetorical tradition itself and the appealing example of Rogerian argumentation, a style of argumentation and negotiation founded perhaps most essentially on listening. Rogers identified and framed the key issues facing us in terms of rhetoric and argument much the way I am framing them here. As he notes in *On Becoming a Person*, "I would like to propose, as an hypothesis for consideration, that the major barrier of mutual interpersonal communication is our very natural tendency to judge, to evaluate, to approve or disapprove, the statement of the other person, of the other group" (Rogers 1961, 330).

This is a disposition enabled and encouraged, in some unfortunate ways, by simplistic argumentative writing. The solution to this problem, for Rogers, is increased priority given to listening and empathy:

> But is there a way of solving this problem, of avoiding this barrier? I feel we are making exciting progress toward this goal and I would like to present it as simply as I can. Real communication occurs, and this evaluative tendency [to judge others] is avoided, when we listen with understanding. . . . We know from our research that such empathic understanding—understanding *with* a person, not *about* him—is such an effective approach that it can bring about major changes in personality. (331–32)

Rogerian argumentation is also built around furthering legitimate dialog and finding common ground. In response to the kind of culture of contentiousness that alarmed Deborah Tannen many years later, Rogers laid the foundation here for a more humanistic, dialogic, and less adversarial argumentative rhetoric. As Doug Brent has noted in *Theorizing Composition: A Critical Sourcebook of Theory and Scholarship in Contemporary Composition Studies*, "Rogerian rhetoric has had difficulty achieving unqualified acceptance. Yet it has had an uncanny persistence. For many scholars, the turn toward dialogism, collaborative learning and social construction of knowledge makes Rogerian rhetoric more rather than less interesting, despite problems with its earliest formulations" (Brent 1998, 264).

There is much that Rogers says about human communication here and elsewhere in his work that can provide important guidance to us as we develop pedagogy and curriculum for our students.

## PETER ELBOW AND THE BELIEVING GAME

Peter Elbow's work also supports a pedagogical focus on listening, empathy, and reflection. Elbow has spent his career resisting many of the accepted and dominant traditions and pedagogical practices in our discipline in an effort to create a space where students could write freely and enthusiastically, liberated from "the gateway power that teachers have in institutional classrooms to determine a student's experience of writing and to judge whether writing is good or bad" (Elbow 2008, 520). In his comments on receiving the Exemplar Award from CCC (in 2007), Elbow returns again to one of his primary concerns as a teacher and scholar—championing the value of "the believing game" and listening:

> I knew that it would seem anti-intellectual to suggest a class where no one has any training or authority or sanction to judge writing. This was exactly the charge that Joe Harris later came to make: "the students in [my teacherless] workshops . . . do not seem to be held answerable to each other as intellectuals" (31). That's why I wrote the appendix essay and started off this way:
>
> > To academics especially, the idea of listening to everyone else's reading no matter what it is, refraining from arguing, and in fact trying to *believe* it, seems heretical and self-indulgent. Many people would dismiss the charge: "Intellectual schmintellectual! Who cares?" The trouble is I care. I think of myself as an intellectual! (Elbow 2008, 147)
> >
> > In that appendix on the believing game, I was trying to show how deeply intellectual it is to harness both intellect and will in the job of believing multiple and conflicting views. I was arguing (as I still am) that the notion of "intellectual" work is far too permeated by a hunger for better answers and therefore toward premature judging and arguing. I tried to show that conventional assumptions about "good thinking" tend to preclude a kind of smartness and perceptivity that depend on maximum responsiveness and the willful withholding of judgment. (Elbow 2008, 521)

That's beautifully put, as we might expect from a scholar who has made it his life's work to find new ways to make us listen, to "voice," to the music of vernacular language (Elbow 2012), to others as a matter of principle, and to students. "Listening and silence are hallmarks of the believing game. All input, no output" (Elbow 1973, 189). One listens most effectively and productively, Elbow suggests, while also "fighting the itch for closure" and certainty (Elbow 1973, 176–81). There is much in Elbow's work that supports the pedagogy we are theorizing here.

## WHITHER COMPOSITION?

Given this long and distinguished tradition within our scholarship, we can now consider a simple question: What's not to love about the kind of writing described here by this rather long list of distinguished scholars and teachers? And why aren't we asking students to do more of it?

And two last questions if I may: Doesn't the research and scholarship we have carefully reviewed overwhelmingly indicate that it is time to make a change? And doesn't this scholarship and research give us a clear sense of what direction that change should take? I think it does.

## UNIQUE FEATURES OF THIS PEDAGOGY

While I draw on a large body of scholarship from both within and outside our discipline, there are some unique features to the pedagogy I am proposing here that I would like to briefly highlight. First of all, this approach to teaching writing has been carefully theorized to incorporate learning theory into our teaching practice. While scholars in our discipline have long been interested in learning theory, none has developed a theory and practice of teaching writing linked so closely to learning theory or developed such a full range of pragmatic applications that seeks to incorporate what we know about learning theory into our daily classroom activities. This is an important, unique, and foundational element of the pedagogy we are discussing here. In addition, this approach to teaching writing has been designed to be responsive to scholarship from a variety of important subject areas for our discipline, including scholarship related to critical thinking, transfer of learning, and the nature of writing expertise. I am unaware of any pedagogy whose foundational practices can be tied so transparently and intentionally to such a broad range of important scholarship and research. This linkage to such a wide range of foundational scholarship should provide teachers of writing at all levels of instruction with confidence that this pedagogy has been carefully theorized and that it can offer students at all ranges of instruction important opportunities for growth and development as writers. This pedagogy also offers teachers of writing strong philosophical validation for moving away from a focus on argument and toward a curriculum that embraces listening, empathy, and reflection as its most valued classroom practices. I know of no other pedagogy that does this.

Furthermore, this curriculum moves the ill-structured problem to the center of the intellectual work students do in our classrooms, an approach that provides instructors at all levels of instruction with a very pragmatic focal point for a whole range of classroom activities that can serve to center the work we do in the classroom on a common, simply stated, and theory-supported purpose. I know of no other writing pedagogy that makes this link to ill-structured problems so overtly and centrally. I am also suggesting here that assignment design, long an unheralded and undervalued component of our teaching practice, must be regarded as a complex and vitally important art form and linked in overt ways to learning theory and scholarship related to critical thinking, transfer of learning, and the nature of writing expertise. Readings must be very carefully selected, sequenced, and scaffolded. I know of no other writing pedagogy that makes assignment design so centrally important. So although there are some common features here informed by other research and scholarship, the pedagogy we are discussing updates and contemporizes that work in substantial, productive, and positive ways.

## ALIGNMENT

This approach to teaching composition also aligns well with a number of important recent statements about writing and "college readiness." For example, this pedagogy supports many of the objectives articulated in the "Framework for Success in Postsecondary Writing," a document developed collaboratively by the Council of Writing Program Administrators, the National Council of Teachers of English, and the National Writing Project. Of particular note for our purposes here are the "habits of mind" that are the foundational elements of this approach to college readiness:

> The concept of "college readiness" is increasingly important in discussions about students' preparation for postsecondary education.
> This Framework describes the rhetorical and twenty-first-century skills as well as habits of mind and experiences that are critical for college success. Based in current research in writing and writing pedagogy, the Framework was written and reviewed by two- and four-year college and high school writing faculty nationwide and is endorsed by the Council of Writing Program Administrators, the National Council of Teachers of English, and the National Writing Project.

Habits of mind refers to ways of approaching learning that are both intellectual and practical and that will support students' success in a variety of fields and disciplines. The Framework identifies eight habits of mind essential for success in college writing:

- Curiosity—the desire to know more about the world.
- Openness—the willingness to consider new ways of being and thinking in the world.
- Engagement—a sense of investment and involvement in learning.
- Creativity—the ability to use novel approaches for generating, investigating, and representing ideas.
- Persistence—the ability to sustain interest in and attention to short- and long-term projects.
- Responsibility—the ability to take ownership of one's actions and understand the consequences of those actions for oneself and others.
- Flexibility—the ability to adapt to situations, expectations, or demands.
- Metacognition—the ability to reflect on one's own thinking as well as on the individual and cultural processes used to structure knowledge. (Council 2011)

The pedagogy we are theorizing here seeks to nurture and privilege each of these habits of mind. We will discuss this document and these dispositional characteristics in more detail in the final section of this book. This new pedagogy is built around the belief that these habits of mind are essential to helping students develop more sophisticated cognitive orientations about the world and essential to helping them become stronger, more mature readers, writers, and thinkers.

The kind of reflective writing practice that I am advocating here also aligns well with a number of the Common Core State Standards (2010, 35–47 [reading and writing]; 48–50 [speaking and listening]), especially those related to reading. A focus on listening, empathy, and reflection in the writing classroom would, for example, help students meet the ambitious reading goals set forth in these standards:

Key Ideas and Details

1. Read closely to determine what the text says explicitly and to make logical inferences from it; cite specific textual evidence when writing or speaking to support conclusions drawn from the text.

2. Determine central ideas or themes of a text and analyze their development; summarize the key supporting details and ideas.

3. Analyze how and why individuals, events, and ideas develop and interact over the course of a text.

### Craft and Structure

4. Interpret words and phrases as they are used in a text, including determining technical, connotative, and figurative meanings, and analyze how specific word choices shape meaning or tone.

5. Analyze the structure of texts, including how specific sentences, paragraphs, and larger portions of the text (e.g., a section, chapter, scene, or stanza) relate to each other and the whole.

6. Assess how point of view or purpose shapes the content and style of a text.

### Integration of Knowledge and Ideas

7. Integrate and evaluate content presented in diverse formats and media, including visually and quantitatively, as well as in words.

8. Delineate and evaluate the argument and specific claims in a text, including the validity of the reasoning as well as the relevance and sufficiency of the evidence.

9. Analyze how two or more texts address similar themes or topics in order to build knowledge or to compare the approaches the authors take.

### Range of reading and Level of text Complexity

10. Read and comprehend complex literary and informational texts independently and proficiently. (CCSS, 35)

The focus on listening in the Core Standards is also another obvious area of alignment, although I am advocating here for a broader and more philosophically-informed understanding of listening. The Common Core Standards puts argumentative writing at the center of our national curriculum, however, and this is a priority I do not support and would like to see modified.

This approach also aligns very well with the outcomes articulated in AACU's important report, *College Learning for the New Global Century*, especially the focus on developing skills in "inquiry and analysis" (Association of American Colleges and Universities 2007, 3) and assessing "students' ability to apply learning to complex problems" (26). As we noted previously, this report echoes Robert Kegan's claim about the cognitive challenges adults face in modern life, calling for a curriculum that invites students to engage "challenging questions": "In a world of daunting complexity, all students need practice in integrating and applying their learning to challenging questions and real-world problems" (Kegan 1994, 13).

This report also calls on educators to become more "intentional" about the kinds of learning students need:

The council further calls on educators to help students become "intentional learners" who focus, across ascending levels of study and diverse academic programs, on achieving the essential learning outcomes. But to help students do this, educational communities will also have to become far more intentional themselves—both about the kinds of learning students need, and about effective educational practices that help students learn to integrate and apply their learning. (Association 1007, 4)

Our focus here on learning theory, critical thinking scholarship, and work done on transfer of knowledge and the nature of writing expertise seeks to do precisely this, anchoring the work we do in writing classes firmly and intentionally in foundational research and scholarship.

## DISCERNMENT, JUDGMENT, AND CAUTION

Finally, the approach to thinking and writing that we are theorizing here is similar in many important ways to the one advanced by Sam Wineburg for thinking and writing about history in his book, *Historical Thinking and Other Unnatural Acts*. Wineburg suggests that the teaching of history should be used "as a tool for changing how we think, for promoting a literacy not of names and dates of discernment, judgment, and caution" (Wineburg 2001, ix). A pedagogy for the writing classroom focusing on listening, empathy, and reflection could be said to be built around the same principles—discernment, judgment, and caution. Wineburg asks, "What is it, exactly, that historians do when they 'read historically'? What concrete acts of cognition lead to sophisticated historical interpretations?" (xii). One of his answers is that history can "teach us what we *cannot* see," can "acquaint us with the congenital blurriness of our vision" (11). Mature historical cognition, he suggests, "is an act that engages the heart" and begins to embrace "a humility before the narrowness of our contemporary experience and an openness before the expanse of the history of the species" (22). He explains:

> Coming to know others, whether they live on the other side of the tracks or the other side of the millennium, requires the education of our sensibilities. This is what history, when taught well, gives us practice in doing. Paradoxically, what allows us to come to know others is our distrust in our capacity to know them, a skepticism about the extraordinary sense-making abilities that allows us to construct the world around us.
>
> A skepticism toward the products of the mind can sometimes slide into cynicism and solipsism. But this need not be the case. The awareness that the contradictions we see in others may tell us more about ourselves is the seed of intellectual clarity. It is an understanding that counters narcissism. For the narcissist sees the world—both the past and the present—in his

own image. Mature historical knowing teaches us to do the opposite: to go beyond our own image, to go beyond our lived life, and to go beyond the fleeting moment in human history into which we have been born. History educates ("leads outward" in the Latin) in the deepest sense. Of the subjects in the secular curriculum, it is the best at teaching those virtues once reserved for theology—humility in the face of our limited ability to know, and awe in the face of the expanse of human history. (Wineburg 2001, 23–24)

Note here Wineburg's emphasis on openness and humility. (This is not typically something that argumentative writing does much to nurture.) The model of historical thinking that Wineburg advances, foregrounds caution and respect for uncertainty and indeterminacy as being among its primary values. Advanced historical thinking as it is theorized here understands history as "context-bound and context-sensitive" (Wineburg 2001, 42).

Furthermore, Wineburg suggests that effective learning activities in the history classroom must be very carefully constructed with these goals in mind. He demonstrates one such activity with a case study assignment, "Reading Abraham Lincoln," a fascinating project focused on exploring Lincoln's ideas about slavery and African Americans (Wineburg 2001, 89–112). Texts for this project were carefully chosen not from textbooks, but from primary documents (a speech by Stephen Douglas, a letter to Mary Speed, etc.), and they provide a very rich and complex picture of Lincoln. Assignments for writing classes must be as carefully designed and crafted, with cognitive outcomes clearly in mind. In many important ways, the curriculum we are discussing for writing classrooms closely parallels the curriculum Wineburg outlines in his book for history teachers.

### YES WE CAN

Why do smart, perceptive, well-read writing teachers sometimes feel compelled to teach reading and writing in ways that are sometimes reductive, not always conducive to real learning, and not always congruent with scholarship and research? How might we move beyond simplistic argumentation to develop a deeper, richer, more effective teaching practice that is built around current research and scholarship and that will work in a variety of classrooms, grades 6–13? As a discipline, we know a lot about writing and reading and their importance for thinking and learning. So why are we teaching writing in a manner that often subverts so much of what we know is good for students and good for their development as writers and thinkers?

For those of us who teach FYC and prepare others to do so, our sense of purpose and direction continues to evolve as we listen to the various voices participating in our scholarly and disciplinary conversation. Even when we work out in our own minds what our purpose and pedagogy will be (at least for the moment, as this process is often one that is ongoing and responsive to new ideas and scholarship, as it should be), we are confronted with many factors that can complicate or even prevent our ever fully implementing this purpose: high-stakes testing and accountability to others outside of our discipline; common core curricula; standardized textbooks; teaching staffs comprised of over-worked teachers who are responsible for too many students; graduate students (in some cases with little training) and part-time teachers with little job security; too many papers to grade and too little time or energy to think creatively or purposefully about curriculum and pedagogy; and the often invisible power of routine, entropy, and old patterns and beliefs.

I am calling for a new writing curriculum built around listening, empathy, and reflection. This is a pedagogy that would support all forms of serious intellectual work and would help nurture essential cognitive and dispositional orientations that are the wellsprings of mature meaning-making. Such a pedagogy would also offer us the chance to teach knowledge that transfers to other disciplines and to contexts outside the classroom. This is something that a curriculum focused on argument and thesis/support simply cannot claim.

Given what we have surveyed in terms of scholarship and research from a variety of fields including composition, learning theory, critical thinking, neuroscience, transfer of knowledge, and work related to teaching thinking in the classroom, it is clearly time to develop curriculum nationwide that is more responsive to this important work. It is time to liberate our classrooms from the stranglehold of simplistic argumentation. The time for revolution is now.

There may well be important civic benefits for our democracy that issue from this pedagogy as well: citizens in potentially great numbers who understand and appreciate the transformative power of listening, who are willing and interested in engaging others with empathy, and whose first response to a complex problem is to read, research, and reflect. The benefits to the nation and for our democracy could be substantial.

# PART II

*Motivation*

# 7

# "A LIFELONG AVERSION TO WRITING"

## What If Writing Courses Emphasized Motivation?

Now that we have examined learning theory, scholarship in the field of critical thinking, neuroscience, and work related to transfer of knowledge and the nature of writing expertise—and considered adjusting our curriculum to be congruent with this important work—we can turn our attention to the second major component in the pedagogy we are theorizing here: motivation. Each of the three components in this pedagogy—listening, motivation, and habits of mind—is developmentally scaffolded and linked, and is an interrelated part of the approach to composing that we are building.

We can have the best pedagogy and curriculum in the world, but if students are not engaged and motivated, all of this does us very little good. "Intrinsic motivation" is a key variable here, and there are many ways that writing teachers can help unleash and nurture the transformative power of intrinsic motivation. There may not be anything more important that we do.

Our focus on motivation here, to borrow an eloquent formulation by Carol Dweck, is "part of a tradition in psychology that shows the power of people's beliefs. These may be beliefs we're unaware of, but they strongly affect what we want and whether we succeed in getting it. This tradition also shows that changing people's beliefs—even the simplest beliefs—can have profound effects" (Dweck 2007, ix).

This tradition in psychology includes Aaron Beck's development of cognitive behavior therapy designed to address negative "automatic" thinking; Albert Ellis's work helping individuals to identify and replace self-defeating thoughts and beliefs; Albert Bandura's work on agency and self-efficacy; Ellen Langer's work on mindfulness and "automatic behavior"; Martin Seligman's work on optimism and positive psychology;

DOI: 10.7330/9780874219449.c007

Robert Sternberg's work on creativity; Angela Lee Duckworth's work on "grit"; and Carol Dweck's work on "mindsets." Our goal in this major section of the book is to examine the beliefs that students bring with them to the writing classroom and explore how changing negative, self-limiting, self-deconstructing beliefs about reading and writing can produce profound effects in our classrooms. Intrinsic motivation is a luminous, powerful, inexhaustibly vital force. Writing teachers need to understand how intrinsic motivation works and how we can nurture this type of motivation and its incredible power to transform lives and improve performance in the writing classroom.

## WRITING PERMITTED IN DESIGNATED AREAS ONLY

With all due respect to the many excellent scholars working in the field of composition, I would like to suggest that the single most important sentence in the last twenty-five years of composition scholarship may very well occur in Linda Brodkey's essay "Writing Permitted in Designated Areas Only":

> While it appears to take longer in some cases than in others, composition instruction appears to have succeeded best at establishing a life-long aversion to writing in most people, who have learned to associate a desire to write with a set of punishing exercises called writing in school: printing, penmanship, spelling, punctuation, and vocabulary in nearly all cases; grammar lessons, thesis sentences, paragraphs, themes, book reports, and library research papers in college preparatory or advanced placement courses. (Brodkey 1995, 220)

These are dire and troubling words, indeed. Is it true that we encounter significant levels of aversion to reading and writing in our typical high school classes, in our basic writing classrooms, in our first-year composition courses? Let us each answer this question with as much candor and courage as we can. I would certainly have to answer in the affirmative. I have taught composition at an open admissions institution now for twenty-five years, and I have certainly encountered my fair share of aversion to writing, especially in my basic writing classes. I have also worked with a number of area high school English teachers over the last several years, and I have heard much from them about student aversion to writing as well. Is it possible that the most lasting and significant learning outcome many students take away from composition classes is a lifelong aversion to writing? Alas, I think it may be.

Another way to begin understanding the scope and significance of this problem is to ask a corollary question: How many students do we routinely encounter in high school and college writing classes who are curious about ideas, who enjoy reading and have done a lot of it, and who are enthusiastically committed to becoming better writers? Not nearly as many as there should be, it seems to me, given how much time students spend in English classes, K–12.

Furthermore, I believe that at least part of our current national college readiness crisis stems directly from this aversion problem. In *The Condition of College and Career Readiness* the American College Testing Association (ACT) reports that only 66 percent of all ACT-tested high school graduates met the English College Readiness Benchmark for writing in 2010, which tests usage, mechanics, and rhetorical skills (American 2010, 8). An even smaller number (52 percent) met this benchmark for reading (8). In broad terms, these numbers indicate that roughly half of all high school graduates who took the ACT are not ready to be successful college-level readers, writers, or thinkers. This data is drawn from tests taken by 1.57 million students, approximately 47 percent of all 2010 high school graduates in the nation. The National Center for Education Statistics reports, moreover, that 29.8% of students attending public 4-year colleges in 2011–12 took at least one developmental course. 19.1% of students attending private nonprofit 4-year institutions took at least one developmental course. And 40.4% of students attending public 2-year institutions took at least one developmental course (United States Department of Education 2013).

There is justifiable concern about this poor performance. It is expensive and, in the long run, dangerous in terms of the nation's economic vitality, global competitiveness, and national security—for all the obvious reasons. In 1998, for example, Breneman and Haarlow estimated that "remedial education costs the nation's public colleges and universities about $1 billion annually" (Breneman and Haarlow 1998, 2; see also Saxon and Boylan 2001). The Strong American Schools organization notes in its 2008 report with the chilling title, *Diploma to Nowhere*, that the number of "remedial" students in American colleges now exceeds 1 million (1,305,480), incurring an estimated cost to taxpayers of over two billion dollars (Strong American Schools 2008, 3). I do not want to put too fine a point on this, other than to note that there is a great deal at stake here.

I believe that our national remediation problem is directly related to our aversion problem. After all, two of the three most important gateway college readiness skills are taught primarily by English teachers—reading and writing (the other gateway skill, of course, is math). My suggestion here is a simple one: we must attend carefully and systematically to issues related to motivation because students who are motivated typically do not underachieve. Recent research has provided a compelling theoretical rationale for this focus on motivation. This work suggests that intrinsic motivation is a prerequisite for any kind of real learning and achievement. It is essential that writing teachers begin to engage this research carefully and begin developing curriculum designed specifically to promote and nurture intrinsic motivation.

## "INTRINSIC" VERSUS "EXTRINSIC" MOTIVATION

The first step we need to take as we begin engaging our lifelong aversion problem is to think carefully about student motivation and how we attempt to nurture and promote student engagement in writing classes. There are many different ways that we might theorize even the general purpose of education that will make important differences in how we develop writing assignments, classroom activities, and curriculum for our students. For me, no one gets it better than Yeats: "Education is not the filling of a bucket, but the lighting of a fire." The presence or absence of this "fire" affects everything students experience in our classrooms, usually in profound ways. As we know, students who are engaged and motivated learn almost effortlessly. Those who are not engaged almost always struggle, resist, and often fail. Unmotivated students often become disruptive and troublesome influences in our classrooms.

What Yeats is talking about here is "intrinsic" motivation, the kind of passion for a subject that leads to deep and significant achievement and learning. As Alfie Kohn notes, "psychologists typically distinguish between 'intrinsic' and 'extrinsic' motivation, depending upon whether one sees a task as valuable in its own right or merely a means to an end. . . . Adults who consistently do excellent work, and students whose learning is most impressive, are usually those who love what they do, not those who see what they do as a way to escape a punishment" (Kohn 2000, 22).

As a profession we need to do a much better job creating activities, learning environments, and writing projects for students that target this kind of intrinsic motivation. In fact, this needs to become one of our primary goals as writing teachers, across institutional boundaries and at all grade levels. If we can inspire sincere student interest in reading, writing, and thinking, much else will take care of itself, without us having to lecture, harangue, prod, threaten, test, quiz, or plead. We all try to do this to some extent, of course. I am proposing that we make it one of the primary guiding principles of our profession, in an attempt to reverse the production of life-long aversion to writing in students. To do this will require creativity, patience, and perhaps even courage.

## RECENT RESEARCH ON MOTIVATION

There has been a great deal of groundbreaking work done on motivation during the last twenty-five years, and all of it points to the importance of intrinsic motivation. This research has very significant ramifications for teachers of writing. However, as Daniel Pink notes in his book *Drive: The Surprising Truth about What Motivates Us*, there is currently a "mismatch between what science knows" about motivation and the kind of attention organizations, educators, and parents devote to it (Pink 2009, 145). Anderman and Anderman make exactly the same point in their recent book, *Classroom Motivation*: "Despite ongoing development of motivation theories and continued progress in empirical studies within the research literature, many important implications of this scholarly work do not get translated into the everyday practice of education" (Anderman and Anderman 2009, v).

Our focus in this section of the book will be on rebalancing this asymmetrical relationship. We will examine what research tells us about intrinsic motivation, and then we will explore ways that we might translate this research into everyday classroom practice.

Edward Deci is perhaps the most important scholar in this field of study, and his work (much of which he co-authored with Richard M. Ryan) has become foundational among scholars, researchers, and educators interested in motivation. What he has to say about motivation, for example, in his book, *Why We Do What We Do* (which he wrote for a popular audience with the help of *New York Times* science writer Richard Flaste), is something that all teachers (as well as principals, superintendents, legislators, advocates for national and statewide testing programs, and citizens concerned about education) should be familiar with:

> All the work [Richard M.] Ryan and I have done indicates that self-motivation, rather than external motivation, is at the heart of creativity, responsibility, healthy behavior, and lasting change. . . . Because neither compliance nor defiance exemplifies autonomy and authenticity, we have continuously had to confront an extremely important—seemingly paradoxical—question: How can people in one-up positions [i.e., in positions of authority], such as health care providers or teachers, motivate others, such as their patients or students, who are in one-down positions, if the most powerful motivation, leading to the most responsible behavior, must come from within—if it must be internal to the self of the people in the one-down positions? . . . In fact, the answer

to this important question can be provided only when the question is reformulated. The proper question is not, "how can people motivate others?" but rather, *"how can people create the conditions within which others will motivate themselves?"* (Deci and Flaste 1996, 9–10; see also Deci and Ryan 1985, 2005).

There are few questions more essential for teachers of writing than this one: How can composition instructors create classroom conditions within which students will motivate themselves?

Unfortunately, as Deci notes, attendance at school often tracks concurrently with a catastrophic loss of curiosity and motivation for learning:

> For young children, learning is a primary occupation; it is what they do naturally and with considerable intensity when they are not preoccupied with satisfying their hunger or dealing with their parents' demands. But one of the most troubling problems we face in this culture is that as children grow older they suffer a profound loss. In schools, for example, they seem to display so little of the natural curiosity and excitement about learning that was patently evident in those very same children when they were three or four years old. What has happened? (Deci and Flaste 1996, 19)

Deci poses a vital question for writing teachers at all levels of instruction and across institutional boundaries: "Why is it that so many of today's students are unmotivated, when it could not be more clear that they were born with a natural desire to learn?" (19). The problem Deci and Flaste are describing is the problem we seeking to address here.

As Ryan and Powelson suggest, it is imperative that we not "conceive of the central goal of 12 years of mandatory schooling as merely a cognitive out-come" (Ryan and Powelson 1991, 62). Instead, one of our primary goals, they suggest, should be to create learners who are "willing and even enthusiastic about achieving something in school, curious and excited by learning to the point of seeking out opportunities to follow their interests beyond the boundaries of school" (62). This motivation needs to come from our students' own natural curiosity, interests, and passions. It should be characterized, as Deci, Koestner, and Ryan note, by "genuine interest, enjoyment and excitement" (Deci, Koestner, and Ryan 1999, 189).

Boiled down to its most essential, this body of work suggests that educators must devote careful attention to motivational factors in the classroom—in terms of course design, general course outcomes, assignment design, and even a host of smaller, less obvious aspects of classroom environment and classroom management strategies.

## MOTIVATION AND COMPOSITION SCHOLARSHIP

Situating my recommendations about motivation within the long history of composition scholarship is not difficult, since there has not been a great deal of attention paid to intrinsic motivation in our literature. Part of the reason for this is that much of this research has been conducted outside of our discipline, and, as we know, it sometimes takes many years for work conducted in other disciplines to make its way into our scholarly conversations. This appears to be changing, however. A recent special issue of *English Journal*, for example, was devoted entirely to motivation (Lindblom 2010). There has also been some significant discussion of intrinsic motivation in the scholarship related to reading instruction (in Atwell 1998, 2007 and in Smith and Wilhelm 2002). Again, however, many writing teachers are not familiar with research related to reading development. A number of recent books—Paul Tough's (2012) *How Children Succeed: Grit, Curiosity, and the Hidden Power of Character*, Amanda Ripley's (2013) *The Smartest Kids in the World: And How They Got That Way*, and *The Handbook of Competence and Motivation* edited by Andrew J. Elliot and Carol Dweck (2007)—suggest that issues related to motivation are beginning to move into the mainstream educational conversation.

Alfie Kohn has also been doing important work on this subject for many years, but he is a bit of an absolutist in terms of classroom applications of intrinsic motivation, and this appears to have contributed to keeping intrinsic motivation on the periphery of our scholarly conversation. His theoretical discussions of intrinsic motivation have obviously been groundbreaking. But his practical classroom suggestions can sometimes strike readers as impractical. Unfortunately, this may be part of the reason why intrinsic motivation is not more widely discussed and implemented in classrooms. Kohn suggests, for example, that we "reduce the number of possible grades to two: A and Incomplete. The theory here is that any work that does not merit an A isn't finished yet" (Kohn 1993, 208). As personally appealing as I find this idea, it is not easy to operationalize in the classroom. Like Kohn, I believe that any student work that has not earned an A or a B is simply unfinished—and I tell my students this. Nonetheless, like most teachers, I still find myself at the end of the semester reporting final grades other than A and Incomplete.

Kohn also speaks against most kinds of "praise" (Kohn 1993, 96–116), and much of what he says about this subject is important. Obviously, certain kinds of praise can damage intrinsic motivation, especially if such praise is perceived as empty, unearned, or used to manipulate or control. But praise doesn't always have to be damaging as Kohn acknowledges (106–110; see also Dweck 2007, 71–74, 169–72). Deci, Koestner, and Ryan, for example, have shown in an important study published a few years after Kohn's famous book, *Punished by Rewards*, that "verbal rewards" (i.e., positive feedback) do not have much of an effect on children but do have a consistently "significant positive impact" on the intrinsic motivation of college students: "verbal rewards—or what is usually labeled positive feedback in the motivation literature—had a significant positive impact on intrinsic motivation, although the effect on free-choice behavior was found for college students but not children" (Deci, Koestner, and Ryan 1999, 653). Part of the reason for this, as we will see, is "age effects" and the cognitive sophistication of older students that enables them to distinguish between different kinds of praise.

The subject of motivation is clearly a very complex area of human psychology, as Deci, Koestner, and Ryan (1999) demonstrate in their exhaustive meta-analytic review of 128 research studies examining the effects of extrinsic reward on intrinsic motivation. What I attempt to chart here is a pragmatic "middle way" for teachers of writing—offering our profession a practical, replicable way to begin applying the wisdom of Kohn, Deci, and Ryan in the classroom. We can begin doing this by focusing on three major areas: designing curriculum that offers students *variety*, *choice*, and *disguised repetitions*. To show how these strategies can be used in a classroom, I will be sharing examples from my own teaching practice, using my basic writing course again, where issues of motivation come into play every day. I would like to see our profession situate intrinsic motivation at the very heart of what we do in the writing classroom, grades 6–13.

## WHAT DO STUDENTS SAY ABOUT WRITING CLASSES?

One way to begin exploring this subject is to ask students themselves what they have enjoyed, valued, and learned in their writing classes. I have been doing this recently, and the results have been fascinating. Here is the simple survey I have been using:

1. Taking into account all of your experiences in writing classes throughout your years in school, what kinds of assignments and activities have inspired you to enjoy reading and writing?

2. What kinds of assignments and activities have led you to dislike reading and writing?

3. If you could design curriculum to promote enjoyment of reading and writing in, say, a junior high school or senior high school writing class, what kinds of activities and assignments would you include and why?

Here is one typical response:

1. Throughout my experiences in English classes I have typically only had very traditional assignments that have included reading either a book, play, or some other reading and then writing a paper on it. I feel these are beneficial to an extent but they tend to become somewhat repetitive rather quickly. One activity that I particularly liked was one involving a movie. We watched *Blood Diamond* in class. We did this after reading a book dealing with child soldiers. We were then asked to pick an aspect of the movie (i.e. the symbolism of diamonds, what they represent) and write a paper on it. Although this assignment did involve a paper, it was more enjoyable to me because of watching a film that so closely paralleled the book we were reading. It made it much more interesting.

2. Like I said above, reading and then writing a paper is beneficial to an extent, but doing the same thing over and over again doesn't, in my opinion, instill a love of reading and writing. I think assignments that tend to involve creativity and different mediums are far more interesting.

3. Creative assignments. Reading more recent literature as it may be easier to relate to. Activities involving more mediums. Perhaps things like, film, music, and theatre.

There is important wisdom here that confirms what the research on intrinsic motivation is telling us about student engagement and learning.

My work as one of the editors of *What Is "College-Level" Writing?* Volume 2: *Assignments, Readings, and Sample Student Writing* (Sullivan, Tinberg, and Blau 2010) also greatly deepened my appreciation for intrinsic motivation. We included three student-authored essays in this book, inviting these college students to talk about their writing histories and to discuss landmark experiences in their precollege writing careers. To my great surprise, all three of our student contributors singled out creative assignments as crucial to nurturing their interest in reading and writing. These creative assignments appear to have one thing in common—they introduce variety, choice, and disguised repetition into the curriculum. That is, they are assignments that involve reading, writing, and thinking, but they do not present themselves to students as typical writing assignments.

Casey Maliszewski, one of our student contributors, was home-schooled from kindergarten through twelfth grade. She attended a community college after getting her GED, and served from 2007–2008 as the international president of Phi Theta Kappa, the international honor society for junior, community, and technical colleges. She recently received her Bachelor of Arts degree from Mount Holyoke College (majoring in sociology) and is pursuing a law degree at Columbia Law School. Creative assignments were crucial to her development as a writer:

> My parents' creative approach to English was no formal writing—none. My writing assignments consisted of fiction stories, poems, fables, and journals, just enough to get a handle on basic grammar. I remember marveling when my friends told me of their latest book report due. Asking my mother why I never had to do any book reports, she responded with a shriveled face as if she had just tasted bad milk. "Book reports made me hate reading when I was kid. I do not want to do the same thing to you." I suppose my parents' approach worked because I always was and still am an obsessive reader. One story assignment comes to mind during my earlier years of high school work. My assignment was to write a fable about why robins are red breasted. First, I had to do research on the computer on what a fable was and what components it consisted of (a brief story that features animals, inanimate objects, and forces of nature to illustrate a moral lesson). Then, I had to find a fable already written to get an example. Last, I had to let my imagination do the rest. Such an assignment might seem odd, but by this time I was used to these creative assignments from my parents. (Sullivan, Tinberg, and Blau 2010, 257–58)

Casey notes in her essay that completing these creative assignments throughout her high school years kindled in her "a great interest in writing." Casey is now an active and joyful learner, and despite never having written a formal essay until she was preparing for her GED, she has had a very successful college career.

Lindsay Larsen, one of our other student contributors, reports a similar experience:

> One of the best assignments I had in high school was to create a newspaper about *Romeo and Juliet,* and my friend and I wrote articles about the tragic events in the play, including police reports about the deaths of Romeo, Juliet, Mercutio, and other characters, and an investigative article on apothecaries. In middle school, I had a teacher who had us write creative works for every book or poem we were reading—we created a poem version of Poe's "The Pit and the Pendulum," or wrote a creative piece on the Holocaust after reading about Anne Frank. Creative assignments helped open my imagination and helped me grow as a thinker. With creative writing assignments, you are not restricted to a certain form and your ideas are not stifled. The real world is filled with different problems and issues, and dealing with them in creative ways will help you immensely in life. Creative assignments allow for more freedom and less boredom for students. It is important to master all forms of writing, and this in turn will improve a student's essays. (Sullivan, Tinberg, and Blau 2010, 282–83)

There is important wisdom here.

## A "CAPTIVE AUDIENCE"

Some of the students we meet in writing classes are, indeed, enthusiastic and motivated learners. It is also probably fair to say, however, that a large number of students that we meet in writing classes (especially 6–13 and in basic writing classes) are not. They do not necessarily bring a compelling interest in reading, writing, or thinking with them into our classrooms, and they often simply try to "get through" and "survive" writing classes.

Think about it for a second: there are millions of students in English classes across the country at this very moment—in primary and secondary schools, in basic writing classes, and also in first-year composition courses—who do not particularly want to be there. In some very real ways, they are a "captive audience"—captive, of course, accurately suggesting a condition of being unhappily and "forcibly confined or restrained" and "unable to escape." It is our job to help these students want to be in our classes—day after day, year after year. We cannot continue to present as self-evident the value of reading and writing. We need to work every day to help students discover, experience, and feel the joys of reading and the magic of written communication. It has become very clear that traditional motivational chestnuts like "This class will really help you improve your SAT scores" are not working.

## HOW "AVERSION" IS CREATED AND NURTURED

There are many factors that help promote aversion to writing in our school systems and classrooms. Some of this aversion appears simply to be the result of our profession not having systematically engaged the issue of intrinsic motivation before. Certainly, some of this aversion is also created by high-stakes local, national, and state-mandated standardized testing programs. Such programs negatively affect motivation in all sorts of ways. One obvious factor, of course, is the proportion of class time available to spend on any activities other than preparing for high-stakes tests, taking such tests, and reviewing the results. The relief and joy that the students at Tyler Heights Elementary School express in Linda Perlstein's book, *Tested*, for example, when their state-mandated testing cycle ends and the school is free to move on to different kinds of learning activities suggests what is at stake here in terms of motivation and student success. The change is so significant, in fact, that one young student remarks, "It feels like a different school" (Perlstein 2007, 246). A qualitatively different kind of engagement and student learning also begins to take place.

Some of this aversion is also probably our own fault. We have relied perhaps too much on traditional kinds of assignments, traditional classroom strategies, and readings drawn from what Lynn Bloom calls the "essentially conservative" essay canon (Bloom 1999, 417) that results in a few "classic" essays and readings getting recycled over and over again. Most high school reading lists focus on a very narrow list of traditional titles that dominate reading assignments year after year. Furthermore, as Smith and Wilhelm note, teachers canonize (and have students write about) certain kinds of texts—especially those that allow readers to provide nuanced interpretations (Smith and Wilhelm 2002, 195)—at the expense of others. Smith and Wilhelm's interviews with male students in middle school and high school provide compelling evidence for broadening the variety of readings we assign, teach, and invite students to write about. One of the students Smith and Wilhelm interview, in fact, addresses this issue—and speaks to our aversion problem—with devastating effect: "I will read books that other people tell me I should read—except for my English teachers" (143).

Aversion is also created in structural and systematic ways by national and statewide curriculum requirements and by less than helpful or sympathetic superintendents, principals, deans, department chairs, and parents. There is much working against us here.

## BALANCE

We obviously need to continue to design curriculum that provides traditional kinds of challenges for students as readers, writers, and thinkers. Given that understanding, however, the typical 6–13, basic writing, and first-year composition class clearly needs to achieve a richer, more diverse blend of reading and writing activities.

Proportionately, it seems to me that we should probably devote approximately twenty percent of our class time to this important endeavor, with the remainder dedicated to traditional kinds of assignments and activities. This is the approximate percentage of time that I devote to this kind of work in my classes, and the results have been encouraging. (I provide specific examples from my own teaching practice below.) Practically speaking, I do not think we necessarily need to see immediate positive results from this work with all students in every class. I think we can think longitudinally and across the entire span of students' academic experience in our classes. Somewhere along the line, and hopefully before they come to college, we want that "fire" to be lit. And we will no doubt need to be patient. It may take years and many positive experiences in our classrooms for some students to finally enjoy reading, writing, and thinking.

This kind of curriculum development can be viewed as a long-term, low-risk, high-yield investment strategy, one that has the potential to pay extraordinary dividends over the course of a student's academic career. It can also generate great value for students after they leave school, potentially producing adults in greater numbers who will become thoughtful, passionate, lifelong learners. There is also no more important gift that we can hope to give to our nation and to our democracy than this—citizens who like to read, write, and think.

Before moving forward with a discussion of practical classroom strategies, I would like to state for the record that I do not believe that all students are resistant writers and learners. During my career as a teacher, I have certainly had the pleasure of working with many enthusiastic, fully engaged students. But I must also say, in terms of full disclosure, that I have also worked with many students who have not been particularly engaged or enthusiastic about being in an English class. Many would rather have been almost anywhere else. I also do not wish to diminish or dismiss the literacies that students bring with them or to suggest that what I define here as reading, writing, and thinking is the only type of reading, writing, and thinking worth doing.

## PRACTICAL CLASSROOM APPLICATIONS

There are probably thousands of different ways to nurture intrinsic motivation in the writing classroom, and this in itself should make this enterprise fascinating and enjoyable for teachers and students as well. I will be sharing assignments from one of the classes that I teach, English 93, a course we have already discussed in some detail. For purposes of illustrating a general pedagogical strategy, I believe this course is a good choice to discuss here because it likely resembles writing courses taught at many other colleges and in many high schools as well. This class is a good example because it is also a site where I routinely encounter strong aversion to writing. Obviously, students cannot be considered "ready for college" if they do not enjoy reading, writing, or thinking. So the stakes are high here for all sorts of reasons, including our ongoing national conversation related to articulation, college readiness, and alignment across institutional boundaries. Although the focus here is on English 93, I have developed activities like the ones we will be discussing for all of my courses, including upper-level writing courses and survey literature courses.

The core of my English 93 class is built around three major essays (which we have already discussed). These assignments are traditional and challenging and focus on listening, empathy, and reflection. As we work on these units as a class, I do things many writing teachers typically do: I assign journal writing for each of these readings; I discuss the readings in class with my students; I have students develop rough drafts of their essays in response to these readings; and I meet with each student individually to talk about and assess the progress of their drafts. I also require students to meet with a tutor at our writing center. So this is serious, focused work.

These three major writing projects, along with other traditional kinds of activities that I have designed for this class take up roughly eighty percent of my class time (this includes introducing students to important research and theory related to reading, writing, and thinking as well as work related to motivation, critical thinking, habits of mind, the value of a "growth mindset," among others).

## VARIETY, CHOICE, AND DISGUISED REPETITIONS

I devote the remainder of my available time to activities designed to promote and nurture intrinsic motivation. My focus here is on adding variety, choice, and disguised repetitions to my curriculum. By design, this turns out to be about twenty percent of my total class time. Some of the days I use for these activities I consider "gimmees." I have found, for example, that students are usually incapable of doing much work on days when major essays are due, so I can use these days however I wish without feeling like I might be wasting class time. For the remainder, I use what I think of as "good work days"—valuable teaching days when students are likely to be mentally fresh and willing to work hard. I could, of course, be using this class time to do more traditional kinds of work or having students engage in more repetitions of traditional work, but I have come to believe that the time I spend in class on activities designed to nurture intrinsic motivation is a more worthwhile use of our time. These activities, regardless of when they are scheduled, really do make a significant positive difference in the way students think about my class and about "English." They also nurture a positive long-term attitude toward reading and writing. For the remainder of this chapter, I would like to share with readers how I attempt to realize this in my classroom.

## VARIETY: WRITING ABOUT ART ON CAMPUS

In calling for introducing more variety into our curriculum, we are following the work of composition scholars like Curtis and Herrington and their important research on writing development in the college years. In their essay, which we have already discussed, Curtis and Herrington call for broadening the types of writing students are required to do (Curtis and Herrington 2003, 86–88). (As Lunsford and Lunsford have shown, there does not appear to be much variety in the English curriculum. Most of the writing assigned in FYC, for example, is either argument or close analysis [Lunsford and Lunsford 2008, 793].) We are also following the advice of Alfredo Lujan, who recommends that students "write and write often in multigenres: stories, personal essays, critical essays, parodies, poems, freewrites, letters to teachers, journals, jingles, reader responses, lists" (Lujan 2010, 56). We are also following Alfie Kohn, who likewise supports bringing more variety into our classrooms (Kohn 1993, 220). We are also responding here to the opinions of Casey Malszewski and Lindsay Larsen, the two student contributors to *What Is "College-Level" Writing?* Volume 2 (Sullivan, Tinberg, and Blau 2010) that we discussed above, both of whom recommend bringing more creativity into our curriculum. Variety is one very important way we can nurture intrinsic motivation. Variety can serve to deepen students' understanding and appreciation of writing, and can make the classroom experience more diverse and interesting. It also allows different kinds of learners to encounter different kinds of challenges, provides pacing and rhythm over the course of the semester, and disguises repetitions.

One example of how I introduce variety into my English 93 class is writing about art on campus. Here I am following the work of Elliot Eisner, who champions in *The Arts and the Creation of Mind* curricular diversity as well as the value of incorporating art and aesthetics into our curriculum. As he suggests, "Meaning is not limited to what words can express" (Eisner 2004, 280). We are blessed to have a campus extraordinarily rich in art work (we have student and professional art on many walls and public places on campus and we have an art gallery). The assignment I describe here is designed to diversify our class's writing activities and to have students engage art and aesthetics. This assignment also helps students work on their concentration and observational skills. Good writers, I tell them, are good observers, and they are able to sustain focus and concentration. This activity also provides me with an excellent opportunity to talk about audience and to highlight the difference between reader-based and writer-based prose (Flower 1979). This assignment requires students to imagine an audience that is unfamiliar with their work of art and then write for it. This helps my basic writing students begin to make the crucial cognitive transition from writing for themselves (writer-based) to writing for others (reader-based), a key transition point for developing writers. Finally, I also like to do some things with my classes during the semester that gets my students active and up and moving in order to show them that writers do more than just sit in front of computers all day and write.

For this assignment, we tour the campus looking at art. I ask students to select a single work that they like and then return to it and study it carefully. Students then write about the work they select. Here is the assignment:

### Writing about Art on Campus

Today, we will tour the campus looking at the art on display. Your job will be to find a piece of art that you really like. Once you have found a work you like, I would like you to write a response to the piece you've selected. I will be collecting these at our next class meeting, and you will be presenting the work you chose to the class in a short speech. Word count: 500 word minimum!

Here's how our day will go:

- We will spend 30 minutes touring campus and taking notes.
- I would like you to select a work that you want to write about and then return to it to sit in front of it. Please spend some time looking at it carefully. I'd like you to take notes and begin a preliminary draft of your response (at least 15 minutes).
- Take a picture of the work you've chosen so you can show it to the class.
- We will all return to class during the final 10 minutes of class to finish up this activity and begin writing our responses.

Here's what I would like you to do in each paragraph:

Paragraph 1: Please describe the piece of art that you have selected as carefully and fully as you can. Please assume that the audience you are writing for has not seen the work you have selected. Readers will only be able to "see" your work of art from your written description, so make it full and strong!

- What is it? (A painting? A sculpture? Pottery?) What is it made of? (Paint? Wood? Steel? Something else?)
- What colors or textures or patterns does it feature that you find interesting or appealing?

Paragraph 2: Think carefully about the piece you've selected. What does it make you feel? What does it make you think? Does it recall or remind you of anything?

- Why do you like this piece of art? Why did you select it?

This kind of assignment adds a very welcome element of variety to the semester, and most students find the assignment fascinating and enjoyable, regardless of how much exposure they have had to art before. Many students develop a proprietary sense of ownership toward the work they have chosen, and for this reason they usually look forward to writing and speaking about it. All of this helps nurture intrinsic motivation for writing, and students are still required to "read" their piece of art carefully, think about why the piece moves them, and then write an effective description and response. This is one of many ways that I seek to add variety to this class over the course of the semester. We have much to gain from making variety a hallmark of our curriculum development.

## CHOICE: READING FOR PLEASURE

Choice is something that everyone interested in motivation and teaching agrees is important. It is one of Kohn's three major curricular recommendations for teachers, along with richer, more meaningful content and more opportunities for students to collaborate (Kohn 1993, 213–26). It is foundational to Atwell's approach to teaching reading (Atwell 1998, 37–39; 2007, 26–35). It is supported by many other reading scholars as well, including DeBenedictus; Gallagher; Krashen; Manning and Manning; Miller; and Worthy, Turner, and Moorman. Deci and Flaste also consider it essential in the classroom because it helps promote intrinsic motivation and autonomy (Deci and Flaste 1996, 34–36, 144–49). My own journey toward providing students with choice has been a long one. I highlight one assignment here that resulted from this important journey.

By way of background, I have always wanted my English 93 students to love reading, but I was never willing to devote any class time to this important learning outcome. I also believed until recently that this was something students should really be able to get to on their own. For many years, I would simply tell students that they should love reading, and I thought that they would. Like most teachers, I felt as if I already had enough material to cover, and I would always think, "I just can't spare the time."

I have recently changed my mind about this, though, and as a result I have developed an assignment that targets this learning outcome specifically—getting students to enjoy reading. My thinking now is this: "If I really believe this is an important outcome for my courses—if I really want students to read for pleasure on their own—I ought to have an assignment that specifically targets that outcome." So learning how to "read for pleasure" and seeing reading as enjoyable are the two major learning outcomes I am after here. I also want students to begin to see the library for the miraculous and amazing place it is. So in response to this thinking, I developed the following book review activity, with the goal of designing a book report assignment that even Casey's Mom could love:

### Essay #3: Book Review!

For this assignment, I am asking you to select a book from the library about a subject that interests you. It can be fiction, poetry, biography, a graphic novel, a book about art or food or national parks—anything that you are interested in. The only requirement is that you select something that you will enjoy reading! Once you have made your selection and read your book, I would like you to write a review of the book that will include the following:

1. An interesting and creative introduction that will get readers interested in reading your review.
2. Author, title, publication date, and subject.
3. Why you selected this book.
4. What you found interesting in this book.
5. What you enjoyed in this book.
6. What you learned from this book.
7. Please include at least two quotes from your book and discuss why you found these quotations important or interesting.
8. Your overall assessment of the book.

The guidelines are as follows:

1. The book cannot be one you are reading for another class.
2. The book cannot be one that you've read before.
3. I would like this book to be one you've always wanted to read or about a subject you've always wanted to know more about.
4. You may also purchase a book at a bookstore or borrow it from your home library or a friend.

Your focus here should be on enjoyment! Have some fun! You can organize your review however you want—but I want you to think creatively and remember that you are writing for an audience, as we will be posting these reviews on our class website. Reviews should be approximately 750 words in length.

Each student will also be presenting a 2-minute speech on the book they have chosen to read.

To prepare for this assignment, about a week before we begin this activity I survey my students about their reading practices and what subjects interest them. I then personalize my feedback to them as we look around the library as I help them find a book they might enjoy. Here are some comments my students made recently about the subjects they wanted to read about:

- Society, psychological issues, urban life, political issues, other cultures, their beliefs and way of life.
- I would like to read about a true story, nothing fiction. I would like to read about something exciting or a bio on someone.
- I want to read more, but not sure what I want to read about.
- I like to read about the military.
- I do not like books, books make me tired and bored. I hate books so I do not want to read any book.

Some students choose urban fiction, some choose books about sports, some choose popular novels, and some surprise me with what they pick. I let students choose anything they want. If I can see a spark of interest and enthusiasm, then I know they have the right book.

This activity is designed to address our national aversion to reading problem, a problem linked in many important ways to our aversion to writing problem. As Worthy, Turner, and Moorman suggest, research related to student reading is not encouraging:

> While most children begin their school careers with positive attitudes toward reading, many show a steady decline in reading attitudes and voluntary reading as they progress through school (Allington, 1975; McKenna, Ellsworth, & Kerr, 1995; Shapiro & White, 1991). Negative attitudes become especially prevalent beginning in middle and high school years (Anderson, Tollefson, & Gilbert, 1985; Cline & Kretke, 1980). In fact, according to a report from the California Department of Education (cited in Morrow, 1991), 70% of the over 200,000 sixth graders surveyed almost never read for pleasure. Other researchers paint similarly bleak pictures of students' leisure reading. (Worthy, Turner, and Moorman 1998, 296)

It is imperative that we design and implement curriculum to reverse this unfortunate trend. We are also attempting with assignments like this to plant seeds that may flower later in students' lives or careers, even if they do not bear the immediate fruit of turning students instantly into voracious readers. *Choice* is essential to this process. As Nancie Atwell notes,

> In the classrooms at CTL [the school Atwell founded, the Center for Teaching and Learning, in Edgecomb, Maine] choice is a given: kids choose what they read because children who choose books are more likely to grow up to become adults who read books. Students who read only a steady diet of assigned titles don't get to answer, for themselves, the single most important question about book reading: why does anyone want to? As William Dean Howells put it, "The book which you read from a sense of duty, or because for any reason you must, does not commonly make friends with you."
> . . . For students of every ability and background, it's the simple, miraculous act of reading a good book that turns them into readers, because even for the least experienced, most reluctant reader, it the *one good book* that changes everything. The job of adults who care about reading is to move heaven and earth to put that book into a child's hands. (Atwell 2007, 27–28)

Smith and Wilhelm offer similar advice about literacy in the lives of young men (Smith and Wilhelm 2002, 108–10). This book review assignment is one way we can attempt to do precisely that—to move heaven and earth to put that *one good book* that changes everything into a student's hands. Let us return again to the important national report, *To Read or Not to Read: A Question of National Consequence*, and remember what is at stake here:

> *To Read or Not to Read* confirms—without any serious qualification—the central importance of reading for a prosperous, free society. The data here demonstrate that reading is an irreplaceable activity in developing productive and active adults as well as healthy communities. Whatever the benefits of newer electronic media, they provide no measurable substitute for the intellectual and personal development initiated and sustained by frequent reading. (Gioia 2007, 6)

Following this activity, I do a satisfaction survey to see what students like about this assignment and what they learned from it. Most really enjoy it. Here is a representative sampling of this feedback:

- I enjoyed reading what I wanted.
- I learned books are different than movies.
- I enjoyed the assignment because it was a nice break from all the hardcore college books. It was fun.
- I learned that everyone has a different preference in what they like to read for fun. Each was unique in its own way.
- Yes, I liked my book.

- Yes, I liked it because we got to pick whatever we wanted to read. It was nice to have a little freedom.
- Yes, I enjoyed the opportunity to read what I chose.
- I learned that there are lots of books in the library that I would like to read.

In terms of course design and the overall rhythm and trajectory of this class, I place this assignment immediately after the most challenging assignment of the semester, as a kind of palate cleanser and enjoyable interlude before we begin the intense final weeks of the semester. As one of the comments above suggests, students are very aware of pacing and rhythm issues in classes ("I enjoyed the assignment because it was a nice break from all the hardcore college books. It was fun."). I find that this break allows students to concentrate more fully and with more engagement on the final writing projects to come.

## DISGUISING REPETITIONS: THE BONNIE AWARDS

I believe the testimony from our student contributors to Volume 2 of *What Is "College-Level" Writing?* tells us a great deal about the value of disguising repetitions. They have shown us how powerfully these kinds of creative assignments can improve student engagement, motivation, and learning. I think there is a great deal we have to gain from thinking creatively and designing activities that disguise repetitions in our classrooms—that is, developing assignments that require students to read, write, and think, but that do so in ways that are creative and nontraditional. I would like to see us make this a central part of curriculum development at all levels of writing instruction.

One of the ways that I disguise repetitions in my English 93 class is a playful awards ceremony I have developed called the Bonnie Awards (named after my daughter). I have found this activity does a great deal to nurture intrinsic motivation.

Before I describe this activity, let us first review what we know about "rewards," a subject that Kohn has written about extensively. It is important for teachers interested in nurturing intrinsic motivation to have a clear understanding of what the current research says about rewards, as this is a subject that routinely comes into play in all sorts of ways in our classrooms and schools (the honor roll, the National Honor Society, Phi Theta Kappa, the dean's list, the president's list, Phi Beta Kappa). As the title of his best-known book suggests, Kohn has claimed famously that students are "punished by rewards" because "rewards undermine interest" (Kohn 1993, 140). Again, I believe that

Kohn makes a very important point here. Reward systems that seek to "bribe" students into controlling or improving behavior and performance will be effective only in the short term—and they will often actually damage long-term motivation and excitement about learning. This kind of incentivization can never be as powerful or as transformative as intrinsic motivation in terms of a student's long-term success. But as with the issue of "praise," more recent research related to rewards has complicated our understanding of how students respond to rewards. Research has shown, for example, that certain kinds of rewards can be worthwhile and can nurture intrinsic motivation. There are a number of variables that come into play here, as Deci, Koestner, and Ryan suggest, including the age of the student and how a student perceives the intention of a reward:

> For more than 25 years, we have argued that predictions about the effects of rewards necessitate a differentiated analysis of how the rewards are likely to be interpreted by the recipients based on a consideration of the type of rewards (Deci, 1971, 1975), the type of contingency [i.e., what kind of performance or behavior is required to earn the reward] (Ryan et al., 1983), the type of participants (Deci et al., 1975), and the type of interpersonal climate within which the rewards are administered (Deci, Nexlek, et al., 1981; Ryan et al., 1983). (Deci, Koestner, and Ryan 1999, 658)

Rewards can function in different ways, and this is particularly dependent on how students perceive the intention of these rewards—their "functional significance" (Deci, Koestner, and Ryan 1999, 628). Rewards that are perceived to control or influence behavior and self-determination will have a negative effect on intrinsic motivation. Rewards that are "positively informational"—that is, rewards that are used as "indicators of competence" (628)—can be positive motivators: "where rewards are positively informational, they are predicted to provide satisfaction of the need for competence and thus to enhance motivation" (628; see also Ryan, Mims, and Koestner 1983).

The Bonnie Awards were designed with these kinds of variables in mind, and this activity has been designed in a way that is consistent with what research tells us about nurturing intrinsic motivation. After students submit their work for one of my major assignments (usually my second major assignment, around midterm), essays that have earned a B+ or better are presented to the class as our Bonnie Award nominees. I copy these essays and distribute them to students along with a Bonnie Award ballot. Everyone in class is asked to submit votes in five categories:

1. Best Overall Performance by a Writer in an English 93 Class

2. Best Engagement of the Big Ideas in the Readings

3. Best Use of Readings

4. Best Introduction

5. Most Fun to Read

I continue to be impressed each semester by how well this activity works. Intrinsic motivation for reading, writing, and thinking surges once students realize that someone other than me will read their work and that their work on this essay will have some meaning beyond learning how to write. Students also are usually eager to read the work of their peers. I am always surprised how much I am able to gain simply by framing a rather standard peer writing activity in this way.

In terms of the variables Deci, Koestner, and Ryan discuss related to rewards, this assignment has been designed to maximize impact on intrinsic motivation:

- The type of rewards: These awards are symbolic and playful, and students clearly recognize this (and enjoy it).
- The type of contingency: Students receive a letter grade for their essay independent of the Bonnie Awards. These awards are, in some important ways, simply extensions of grades they have already earned. Winners are selected by their classmates, not by me.
- The type of participants: These are college students, and as Deci, Koestner, and Ryan note about "age effects," "college students have greater cognitive capacity for separating the informational and controlling aspects of rewards" (Deci, Koestner, and Ryan 1999, 656). My students clearly understand that this activity has been designed to motivate them to do their best writing, to reward excellent work, and to help them learn from other writers in the class.
- The interpersonal climate: Again, the climate is playful, friendly, and supportive, and students understand and appreciate this.

This activity works in many positive ways. It provides me with an opportunity to publicly recognize excellent work in my class. It also provides students with an opportunity to read strong writing produced by their classmates. And it has proved to be an especially powerful learning activity for my less accomplished writers because they get to see how other students—some sitting right next to them—have responded to the same assignment they struggled with. For many students, these essays often speak more eloquently and powerfully about good writing than anything I can say in class about it. This activity has proved to be a very powerful learning and teaching tool.

After students have read each of the essays and submitted their ballots, we discuss the essays together as a class. I ask students to identify the qualities that they liked about the essays they chose as winners, and we develop a rubric for "good writing" that comes out of this student work. Here is one such rubric that we developed from one of these discussions:

### Qualities You Liked about the Bonnie Award Essays

1. Depth. Personal engagement.
2. Engaged readings effectively.
3. Used personal experience well (related to the readings; used experience to explore and discuss ideas in readings).
4. Used quotes from the readings. Then explained the quotes. Then discussed the quote and the meaning.
5. Good intro! Got my attention!
6. Flow! Stayed on topic. Good transitions. I got involved with reading it!
7. Juicy details! ("el encondido"/"Merengue and Bachata/palm trees, sunny beaches, colorful cement houses").
8. Engaged me as a reader.
9. The writing is alive.
10. Good paragraphs and good grammar.
11. Rhythm.
12. Interesting to read.
13. The writer appears to care that the writing is interesting!

Once we have developed a rubric in class, we continue to use it throughout the semester and for many students it becomes a handy touchstone and pocket-guide for what they know about good writing. Because this rubric is generated by students themselves, it carries more weight and authority than most documents I might be able to provide to them about good writing.

I complete this project with an Academy Awards–style ceremony that I conduct to announce the winners in each category. I present Bonnie Awards that I make myself to the winners. I've had students tell me with a smile long after a particular semester has ended that they still keep their Bonnie Awards proudly displayed in their homes. This activity orients student writers in a very positive way toward their work and toward each other. It is also simply a creative way to disguise repetitions—a way that invites students to read student writing and then discuss the components of good writing in ways that engage their attention and interest.

## CONCLUSION

Speaking about American high schools and the discouraging news coming from ACT about college readiness, Jack Jennings, president of the Center on Education Policy in Washington, DC, recently touched on precisely this issue of intrinsic motivation: "We haven't figured out how to improve them [high schools] on a broad scope and if our kids aren't dropping out physically, they are dropping out mentally" (Banchero 2010). That's very well said. The key phrase here is "dropping out mentally." Unless students are engaged, interested, and intrinsically motivated, the best curriculum in the world will not make much difference in terms of student learning and achievement. Furthermore, if our goal is to create active and engaged life-long learners and to build a strong democracy full of thoughtful, curious, intellectually vibrant and well-read adults, a great deal is at stake here in terms of what goes on in writing classes. After all, this is the primary place where Americans learn to read, write, and think.

Since I have begun targeting intrinsic motivation in this way, I have noticed improved student engagement and performance. The pacing of my classes is different, and many students appear to be able to make it to the end of a basic writing class, for example, and still stay engaged. Students are also very perceptive and recognize the efforts I am making on their behalf in this regard. They have communicated to me in all sorts of ways how much they appreciate the nontraditional, "creative" curricular elements I have built into my classes, even as they recognize the value and importance of the more traditional work we do together.

There is probably less urgency to concern ourselves with intrinsic motivation in upper-level and advanced placement classes, as the students who have made it to these curricular levels have already demonstrated some degree of motivation and can be assumed to be ready to focus on serious business (although I personally think it is important to target intrinsic motivation at all curricular levels; I do so in all my courses). But for students in basic writing classes in college, for students in high school English classes, and for all those students in 6–13 English classes, I think it is very clear that there is much we need to do in terms of nurturing intrinsic motivation.

As writing teachers, we have in our care the most potent of all human creations—written language. We need to provide opportunities for students to experience for themselves the joy of reading and the power of language to move, transform, and inspire. It is a privilege to be given this task. Let us begin finding ways to light this "fire"—so that reading and writing become an essential and beloved part of our students' lives.

# PART III

## Habits of Mind

# 8

# DISPOSITIONAL CHARACTERISTICS

Having discussed the value of listening and motivation, we can now turn our attention to the final major component in this new pedagogy: habits of mind. Again, each of these three major components—listening, motivation, and habits of mind—is developmentally scaffolded and linked, and each is an interrelated part of the approach to composing that we are theorizing here.

It is essential to the development and design of any pedagogy to look beyond our own classrooms and our own discipline to consider transfer of knowledge and the kind of learning that will be of value to students in broader contexts and situations. Research related to critical thinking and the development of writing expertise suggests that intellectual and dispositional "habits of mind" may be more valuable to students, especially in the long run, than knowledge about traditional subjects at the center of most writing instruction, including the thesis statement, MLA format, and even essays themselves. Readers may be surprised to learn, for example, that Tim, the student Anne Beaufort tracks through his college career and into his professional life in *College Writing and Beyond*, never uses thesis statements, MLA format, or even essays as an engineer. (He uses bullet points instead.) These habits of mind, as we know, include dispositional characteristics like curiosity, openness, engagement, creativity, persistence, responsibility, flexibility, and metacognition.

I would like to see us bring these important habits of mind to the center of our teaching practice. A classroom focused on listening and empathy, for example, is designed to help build curiosity, openness, and engagement. A focus on reflection is designed to help build flexibility, metacognitive skills, and responsibility ("Judgments derived from the reflective thinking process remain open to further scrutiny, evaluation, and reformulation; as such, reflective judgments are open to self-correction" [King and Kitchener 1994, 8]). Attention to motivational factors in the classroom actively seeks to help nurture persistence,

DOI: 10.7330/9780874219449.c008

engagement, and creativity. This is another way that the pedagogy we are theorizing has been designed to be responsive to—and congruent with—landmark scholarship and research.

As a profession we need to foreground these essential habits of mind in every writing class we teach. In addition to building these habits of mind into the pedagogy we use in the classroom, we can also use these habits of mind to help students respond proactively to challenges and difficulties throughout the semester. These habits of mind communicate to students some of the most important things we have to say to them about reading, writing, and thinking—and about the academic enterprise in general, in all classrooms and courses, regardless of discipline or grade level. We can also help students understand that an impressive and growing body of scholarship and research suggests that these dispositional characteristics transfer to other contexts and will be of great value to them across their entire life span. Here we will be intentionally building the kind of "sideways learning" environment championed by Ellen Langer, one that privileges mindfulness in a number of important ways: (1) openness to novelty; (2) alertness to distinction; (3) sensitivity to different contexts; (4) implicit, if not explicit, awareness of multiple perspectives; and (5) orientation in the present (Langer 1997, 22–23).

## COSTA AND KALLICK

Perhaps the best place to begin our discussion of this subject is with Costa and Kallick's foundational work on "habits of mind" (2008, 2009, 2013). As they note in their preface to *Learning and Leading with Habits of Mind*, "We want students to appreciate the value of and to develop the propensity for skillful problem solving using a repertoire of mindful strategies applied in a variety of settings. So we came to call these dispositions Habits of Mind, indicating that the behaviors require a discipline of the mind that is practiced so it becomes a habitual way of working toward more thoughtful, intelligent action" (2008, xvii). Note here the language of "mindfulness" being used to discuss critical thinking and mature problem solving. Costa and Kallick's work has been ongoing since 1982, producing a body of scholarship that has been widely embraced among educators, cognitive psychologists, learning theorists, and teachers. As they note,

> Vast research on effective thinking, successful people, and intelligent behavior by Ames (1997), Carnegie and Stynes (2006), Ennis (1991), Feuerstein, Rand, Hoffman, and Miller (1980), Freeley (as reported in Strugatch, 2004), Glatthorn and Baron (1991), Goleman (1995), Perkins

(1991), Sternberg (1984), and Waugh (2005) suggests that effective thinkers and peak performers have identifiable characteristics. These characteristics have been identified in successful people in all walks of life: lawyers, mechanics, teachers, entrepreneurs, salespeople, physicians, athletes, entertainers, leaders, parents, scientists, artists, teachers, and mathematicians. (Costa and Kallick 2008, 16)

Costa and Kallick have identified sixteen characteristics or "habits of mind" that they regard as essential for students. They are:

- Persisting
- Managing Impulsivity
- Listening With Understanding and Empathy
- Thinking Flexibly
- Thinking About Thinking (Metacognition)
- Striving For Accuracy
- Questioning and Posing Problems
- Applying Past Knowledge to New Situations
- Thinking and Communicating with Clarity and Precision
- Gathering Data through All Senses
- Creating, Imagining, Innovating
- Responding with Wonderment and Awe
- Taking Responsible Risks
- Finding Humor
- Thinking Interdependently
- Remaining Open to Continuous Learning (Costa and Kallick 2008, xx–38)

Costa and Kallick suggest that these habits of mind are broad, enduring intellectual and dispositional skills that can be nurtured in classrooms and then used across a student's lifespan (Costa and Kallick 2008, xvii), equipping them for adult challenges and uncertainties. This work supports the pedagogy we are theorizing in a number of ways. Many of these habits of mind are built around or designed to encourage listening, empathy, and reflection. These include (in addition to "listening with understanding and empathy") "thinking flexibly," "thinking interdependently," and "remaining open to continuous learning." Other habits of mind including "persisting," "managing impulsivity," and "thinking about thinking (metacognition)" also support the discourse of mindfulness we are attempting to promote.

It should be noted that Costa and Kallick situate their work on habits of mind in opposition to traditional, reductive approaches to accountability, testing, and teaching and learning: "Educational outcomes in traditional settings focus on how many answers a student knows. When we teach the Habits of Mind, we are interested also in how students behave when they don't know an answer. . . . We are interested in enhancing the ways students *produce* knowledge rather than how they merely *reproduce* it" (Costa and Kallick 2008, 16). This is a vitally important distinction. Significantly, and perhaps not surprisingly, they note that a focus on habits of mind in the classroom would require "a shift toward a broader conception of educational outcomes and how they are cultivated, assessed, and communicated" (xviii).

## "THINKING DISPOSITIONS"

Other thinkers have made similar claims about critical thinking and these kinds of habits of mind and intelligent behaviors. Tishman, Perkins, and Jay, for example, in *The Thinking Classroom: Learning and Teaching in a Culture of Thinking*, suggest that "thinking dispositions" are at the heart of what we call "good thinking." These "dispositions," they note, help us put good thinking into practice, help make us aware of our own thinking patterns, give us a better understanding of what good thinking is, and help us cultivate habits that lead to good thinking (Tishman, Perkins, and Jay 1994, 42–43):

> Thinking dispositions are abiding tendencies toward distinct patterns of thinking behaviors. Just as we can talk about a person's tendency to be friendly or to work hard, we can talk about someone's tendency to be curious or systematic or persistent in their thinking. Good thinkers are disposed to explore, to question, to probe new areas, to seek clarity, to think critically and carefully, to consider different perspective, to organize their thinking, and so on. (39–40)

As writing teachers, we should be keenly interested in these conclusions and others like them. Tishman, Perkins, and Jay identify five dispositions that they regard as essential for mature intellectual work and the production of good thinking:

1. The disposition to be curious and questioning
2. The disposition to think broadly and adventurously
3. The disposition to reason clearly and carefully
4. The disposition to organize one's thinking
5. The disposition to give thinking time (Tishman, Perkins, and Jay 1994, 41–42)

Note that these "dispositions" are similar to those we discussed in the literature related to critical thinking and transfer of knowledge earlier.

Scholars in this field have also identified a list of "affective dispositions of critical thinking" that are similar to Costa and Kallick's habits of mind. These include:

- open-mindedness regarding divergent world views
- flexibility in considering alternatives and opinions
- understanding of the opinions of other people
- honesty in facing one's own biases, prejudices, stereotypes, egocentric or sociocentric tendencies
- prudence in suspending, making or altering judgments
- willingness to reconsider and revise views where honest reflection suggests that change is warranted (Facione 1990, 25)

We have some very good reasons, then, to develop curriculum designed to nurture and develop these important habits of mind.

Significant recent work on transfer of knowledge also suggests that dispositional characteristics are essential to the "broad transfer" of knowledge (Bereiter 1995, 24–25), as we have seen. Both Langer as well as Salomon and Globerson privilege a quality that they call "mindfulness," a habit of mind that can be characterized as an "attentive, nonautomatic, and volitional" disposition to learning and thinking (Marini and Genereaux 1995, 8). Bereiter, in his important essay, "A Dispositional View of Transfer," suggests that this kind of focus in the classroom is very likely to yield positive results:

> Although the intelligent behavior of the dairy truck loader cannot be expected to transfer to, let us say, behaving intelligently as a restaurant waiter, it may be that there are certain dispositions of mindfulness and willingness to learn that will assist one in learning to act intelligently in any situation. If schooling could inculcate those transferable dispositions, it would justify the higher hopes that have been invested in it, hopes that have seemed to be demolished by the research on transfer and on the situatedness of cognitive skills. (Bereiter 1995, 30)

Bereiter also suggests that transfer of knowledge is perhaps most productively theorized in terms of broad ways of engaging the world and thinking about knowledge and problem solving. In discussing a 5th-grade science classroom activity that focused on gravity, for example, Bereiter notes that the lesson is designed to do more than simply help students understand gravity and that the direction "down" is relative and not an absolute:

> Will the gravitational principle transfer to other situations? Even more strongly than before, it can be argued that transfer of the principle will depend on how well the principle is understood, and that instead of

being concerned about transfer the teacher ought to be concerned about understanding. If the students understand gravity only as "what holds us on the earth," the concept will not be much good for explaining anything else, whereas if they actually grasp the notion that it is an attractive force between any two bodies in the universe, it has broad potential for making sense of the world (Bereiter 1992). But what does transfer of disposition mean in the science learning case? The students described in the vignette were not simply receiving a lesson about gravity. They were engaged in a group effort at sense-making that the teacher guided in a scientific direction. They were led to question common sense assumptions and everyday meanings of terms like *down*. They were led to strive for explanations that provided coherent accounts of all the facts, which philosophers of science take to be the hallmark of scientific thinking (Thagard 1989). So it is this disposition to think scientifically that we might hope would transfer to other situations. In other words, we do not want students to think scientifically only in science class, but to do so in their daily lives, when there are puzzling facts to be accounted for. Will they think scientifically when there is no teacher to guide them, and when the surrounding milieu may encourage uncritical belief or superficial explanation? (Bereiter 1995, 23)

The questions Bereiter asks here are essential ones for anyone interested in helping students become better readers, writers, and thinkers. Obviously, curriculum in writing classes should be carefully designed to nurture these kinds of dispositional qualities. These habits of mind would, following Bereiter, help students think carefully not only in school, but also in their daily lives, at work, at home, and with their families and in their communities. Such dispositions would also empower students to think carefully when there is no teacher to guide them, and when the surrounding milieu may, indeed, encourage uncritical belief, automatic kinds of thinking, or superficial explanations. This is one way as a discipline that we can help students move beyond routine, automatic, and largely unexamined ways of looking at the world and engaging complex problems. It would also provide us with effective ways to nurture what Sam Wineburg calls "the invaluable mental power which we call judgment" (Wineburg 2001, 5).

There has been some very important work related to this kind of "automatic" thinking in the fields of social and cognitive psychology. John Bargh, for example, in his landmark essay "The Automaticity of Everyday Life," has demonstrated that much of our thinking is done uncritically, automatically, and (alas) "nonconsciously" (see also Bargh and Chartrand 1999). Daniel Kahneman, in his book, *Thinking, Fast and Slow*, suggests much the same thing. Kahneman suggests that we each have two processing systems, one that is intuitive, fast, nonrational, and often unreliable, and another that is much more deliberate, reflective, and "effortful" (Kahneman 2011, 408)—that is to say, much slower but also more likely to produce consistently better results. Kahneman defines human cognition in ways that are dauntingly complex, but for our purposes here it seems clear that a pedagogy that privileges listening, empathy, and reflection would help students to "slow down" (417), resist cognitive biases, stereotypes, and automatic kinds of thinking, and ultimately produce better thinking. Ellen Langer makes a similar point in her book *Mindfulness*.

Finally, a recent essay by David Perkins and Gavriel Salomon, influential scholars in the field of transfer of knowledge, updates and supports many of the claims we have been discussing concerning the importance of dispositional characteristics and habits of mind. Perkins and Salomon theorize transfer of knowledge as a complex cognitive activity and suggest that transfer "benefits from motivational and dispositional drivers" (Perkins and Salomon 2012, 248). Perkins and Salomon note that dispositional and motivational aspects related to transfer of knowledge are drawing increased attention from scholars in the field of educational psychology, and their work suggests that a growing interest is developing about the importance of these qualities for both student learning and the development of educational pedagogy. They suggest, in fact, that this research will require us to shift our "mind-set about the nature of knowledge and learning" (248). They summarize their current thinking about transfer of knowledge this way:

> So, are we ready to teach for transfer? Perhaps not completely. There is still both the matter of the three bridges of detect, elect, and connect and relatedly the role of motivations and dispositions in transfer. Teaching for transfer ideally not only prepares the learner to figure out how what's been learned connects to new situations but also to detect the opportunities and elect to pursue them. Unfortunately, detect and elect pose major challenges of their own, even more so "in the wild," away from focusing and motivating laboratory or classroom contexts.
>
> As to detect, recall how the clutter of events in another context, comfort with the messages one is hearing even though they have flaws, or functional fixedness and mental set can mask potential transfers. Patterns of instruction that encourage reflective mindful processing (high-road processing as we called it before) *not just in the classroom but beyond* can be expected to increase rates of detection. Indeed, all the authors champion in one way or another the cause of motivated reflective mindful processing. Their visions of good learning seem likely to cultivate broad dispositional characteristics such as mindfulness (Langer 1989), need for cognition (Cacioppo & Petty 1982), need for validity more than quick cognitive closure (Kruglanski & Webster 1996), and

incremental versus entity stances toward intellectual challenge (Dweck 1975, 2000).

As to elect, recall how strong rival habitual responses and urgent counter-motives, or also total indifference to a theme, can preempt potential transfers. Intellectual understanding alone is not likely to save the day when such interference is involved. To add to previous examples, consider Zimbardo's (2006) students who abused their fellow students despite humane principles they must have held, or the observations of Darley and Latane (1968) about the indifference of bystanders who fail to apply simple principles of helping a person in need. Called for are patterns of instruction that change the emotional and motivational landscape through such means as re-imagining scenarios, cultivating empathy, and role-playing, as for instance in some school programs addressing sexual behavior and school violence (e.g. Reyna, et al., 2005). More broadly, Bereiter (1995) urges cultivating general dispositions that motivate transfer, mentioning moral dispositions such as respect for human life and thinking dispositions such as a scientific approach to natural phenomena. (Perkins and Salomon 2012, 253–54)

Note that many of the key points that Perkins and Salomon stress in this summative account of transfer research include qualities we have identified as important for the pedagogy we are theorizing here. These include reflection, motivation, dispositional characteristics, and empathy. Of utmost importance for our purposes here is the suggestion that "patterns of instruction that encourage reflective mindful processing (high-road processing as we called it before) *not just in the classroom but beyond* can be expected to increase rates of detection." The pedagogy we are theorizing—one that privileges listening, empathy, and reflection—establishes this goal as one of its primary learning outcomes.

### "A FRAMEWORK FOR COLLEGE SUCCESS"

Closer to home, the WPA/NCTE/NWP document, "A Framework for College Success" represents our profession's best current thinking on the subject of college readiness and teaching composition. The framers of this document were obviously aware of this important work related to transfer of knowledge, critical thinking, the nature of writing expertise, and habits of mind. As we have seen, this document identifies eight "habits of mind" as essential for success in college:

- Curiosity—the desire to know more about the world.
- Openness—the willingness to consider new ways of being and thinking in the world.
- Engagement—a sense of investment and involvement in learning.

- Creativity—the ability to use novel approaches for generating, investigating, and representing ideas.
- Persistence—the ability to sustain interest in and attention to short- and long-term projects.
- Responsibility—the ability to take ownership of one's actions and understand the consequences of those actions for oneself and others.
- Flexibility—the ability to adapt to situations, expectations, or demands.
- Metacognition—the ability to reflect on one's own thinking as well as on the individual and cultural processes used to structure knowledge.

Although this document also acknowledges the importance of rhetorical knowledge, critical thinking, writing processes, knowledge of conventions, and the ability to compose in multiple environments, the most interesting, unexpected, and perhaps even revolutionary aspect of this document is this focus on "habits of mind." These qualities may well be more vital to college success than SAT scores or recommended high school course sequences or even rhetorical knowledge and knowledge of writing conventions, which are mentioned later in the document (and are, of course, also important). This list communicates to students some of the most significant things we have to say to them about writing, about success in school, and about the ways one may choose to understand and live in the world.

## Curiosity and Openness

For example, there are few qualities more essential to success in college as a writer than curiosity and openness. These habits of mind make learning possible. Students come to a liberal arts college, after all, not only to earn credentials and train for a career but also to open themselves up to a grand enterprise of exploration and discovery (Astin 1993; Astin 1997; Hirst 1973). We might also say that, ideally, students come to a liberal arts college to become more truly awake and alive. ("'Then are you a teacher?' the student persisted. 'No, I am not a teacher.' 'Then what are you?' asked the student, exasperated. 'I am awake,' the Buddha replied.") Curiosity and openness make this kind of powerfully transformative learning possible. They are the primary drivers that enable us to productively engage the "chaos" of real meaning making, to borrow a phrase from Ann Bertoff. They are also the wellsprings of intrinsic motivation, where passion and engagement begin. They are essential to any kind of success in college and vital for writers at all grade levels.

## Creativity

Creativity is another extraordinarily important human capacity that has been routinely overlooked and undervalued in recent discussions of academic rigor, curricular alignment, and the teaching of writing. There is considerable theoretical support for moving creativity to the center of our discussions of college readiness, school reform, and the teaching of writing. Here we are following Csikszentmihalyi's important work:

> To achieve the kind of world we consider human, some people had to dare to break the thrall of tradition. Next, they had to find ways of recording those new ideas or procedures that improved on what went before. Finally, they had to find ways of transmitting the new knowledge to the generations to come. Those who were involved in this process we call creative. What we call culture, or those parts of our selves that we internalized from the social environment, is their creation. (Csikszentmihalyi 1996, 317)

Creativity is very highly valued in the business community, in the sciences, and in the global marketplace, and it is often valued above other, more traditional types of academic skills (Friedman and Mandelbaum 2011, 133–52; Peterson and Seligman 2004, 109–23; Sternberg and Lubart 1995). Langer has suggested, in fact, that "'creativity' and 'mindfulness' may be two ways of looking at many of the same qualities of mind" (Langer 1989, 129). Despite this, pedagogy and curriculum in writing classes often end up focusing only on a narrow range of analytical thinking skills, typically defined as "critical thinking," and a very narrow range of writing activities, as we have seen, mostly focused on argumentative writing.

Robert Sternberg, one of the preeminent scholars on the subject of intelligence, has recently suggested that any understanding of intelligence must also include our capacity for creativity (Sternberg 2007; see also Sternberg 1999). Ken Robinson, a scholar in the field of education and creativity, makes this point even more bluntly: "Creativity is the greatest gift of human intelligence. The more complex the world becomes, the more creative we need to be to meet its challenges" (Csikszentmihalyi 1996; Kaufman and Sternberg 2006; Kaufman and Sternberg 2010; Robinson 2011, xiii; see also Gardner 1993; Gardner 2006, 3–24; Ravitch 2010; Sacks 1999; Sahlberg 2011).

We know that creativity will be increasingly important in the competitive global marketplace. Clearly, creativity should be intentionally and systematically nurtured throughout a student's academic career and especially in writing classes.

To that end, I'd like to propose that we replace the phrase "critical thinking" in our literature with the phrase "creative and critical thinking." All good thinking is also creative in some way—in math, in the sciences, in business, and in writing classes. It's vitally important that we acknowledge this essential human capacity in our scholarship and official statements and that we actively seek ways to nurture it in our classrooms.

## Accountability

Engagement, responsibility, and persistence" are also essential for success in the writing classroom, of course, and in most other areas of life as well. We have heard so many pronouncements in recent years about "holding teachers more accountable for student performance" that many citizens outside the nonacademic community appear to believe that this is all anyone needs to know about teaching and learning. (As William James noted, "There's nothing so absurd that if you repeat it often enough, people will believe it.") What's missing from this conversation are equally impassioned calls to *hold students and parents accountable for student performance as well.* After all, shouldn't students be encouraged to take responsibility for their own learning? Isn't this much better than constantly theorizing and positioning students as if they are only passive spectators, helpless before the grand sweep of their own learning and their own lives?

When we look at the high schools that we know—with their learning centers, writing centers, counseling centers, advisement programs, basic writing and basic math curriculum, computer labs, peer tutors, and reference librarian staffs—don't we see institutions doing everything they possibly can to help students succeed? For the student who needs it and has the desire to find it, help is almost always available. This is an issue complicated in complex ways by race and class, of course (Haskins and Sawhill 2009; Massey 2007; Rothstein 2004; Sullivan 2005; Tough 2012). Global economics might also be said to play a role here as well, especially in terms of the changing American workplace and the catastrophic loss of blue-collar jobs (mostly in manufacturing) that pay a living wage. This has had a devastating effect on families and communities, and thus on student learning across America, especially in poor communities (Duncan and Murnane 2011; Wilson 1996). Nonetheless, we ultimately empower and enable students when we require them to take responsibility for their own learning, for their own choices, and for their own successes and failures. Here we are following the work of Albert Bandura (1997) on agency and self-efficacy.

## Humility

*Noble has humble as its root.*

—Lao Tzu

One disposition we might consider adding to the habits of mind list is humility. Humility opens us up to difference, to ideas, and to others in powerfully positive ways. It also provides students with an extremely valuable general disposition toward the world, intellectual work, and the production of meaning and value in their lives.

For inspiration and direction we might follow Sam Wineburg's work on teaching history, which we have already discussed. Mature historical thinking, Wineburg suggests, "is an act that engages the heart" and begins to embrace "a humility before the narrowness of our contemporary experience and an openness before the expanse of the history of the species" (Wineburg 2001, 22):

> Coming to know others, whether they live on the other side of the tracks or the other side of the millennium, requires the education of our sensibilities. This is what history, when taught well, gives us practice in doing. Paradoxically, what allows us to come to know others is our distrust in our capacity to know them, a skepticism about the extraordinary sense-making abilities that allows us to construct the world around us.
>
> A skepticism toward the products of the mind can sometimes slide into cynicism and solipsism. But this need not be the case. The awareness that the contradictions we see in others may tell us more about ourselves is the seed of intellectual clarity. It is an understanding that counters narcissism. For the narcissist sees the world—both the past and the present—in his own image. Mature historical knowing teaches us to do the opposite: to go beyond our own image, to go beyond our lived life, and to go beyond the fleeting moment in human history into which we have been born. History educates ("leads outward" in the Latin) in the deepest sense. Of the subjects in the secular curriculum, it is the best at teaching those virtues once reserved for theology—humility in the face of our limited ability to know, and awe in the face of the expanse of human history. (Wineburg 2001, 23–24)

The model of historical thinking that Wineburg advances here foregrounds caution and respect for uncertainty and indeterminacy as among its primary values. There is much that student writers can gain from embracing such an outlook as a primary value and orientation in the writing classroom. A pedagogy focused on listening, empathy, and reflection and built around ill-structured problems actively seeks to encourage this kind of "humility in the face of our limited ability to know, and awe in the face of the expanse of human history."

## "Grit"

A fascinating body of research is also developing around issues related to character and student achievement, and this work also supports a focus on habits of mind and dispositional characteristics. This is work that all writing teachers should be familiar with. Angela Lee Duckworth's work on "grit"—a personal quality that includes self-discipline, perseverance, and passion—for example, strongly supports a pedagogical focus on dispositional characteristics in the writing classroom. An important early research study by Duckworth and Martin Seligman (2005) found that character traits like passion and perseverance were more important to academic success than IQ or "smarts" (as the title of this famous study suggests: "Self-Discipline Outdoes IQ Predicting Academic Performance in Adolescents"). Duckworth and her colleagues have come to define grit as self-discipline and perseverance, but it also includes passion as well: "We define grit as perseverance and passion for long-term goals. Grit entails working strenuously toward challenges, maintaining effort and interest over years despite failure, adversity, and plateaus in progress" (Duckworth, Peterson, Matthews, and Kelly 2007, 1087–88).

As Peter Doskoch notes in an essay about Duckworth's research, grit is not simply a matter of just working hard. There appears to be an important element of joyfulness in this quality as well: "That quality Duckworth finds so intriguing has little to do with clenched teeth. Rather, it's a force of motivation so luminous that, as mathematician Andrew Wiles found, it constantly renews itself" (Doskoch 2005, 8).

As Duckworth and Eskreis-Winkler note, the implications of this research on our understanding of human achievement and development are just beginning to be recognized and understood:

Our research suggests that prodigious talent is no guarantee of grit. In fact, in most samples, grit and talent are either orthogonal or slightly negatively correlated. To the extent that talented people are, on average, less gritty, individuals who are both extremely talented and extremely gritty should be particularly rare. Indeed, objective measures of achievement are typically log-normal in distribution; the most accomplished scientists, novelists, artists and entrepreneurs are dramatically more successful than what would be expected were achievement distributed in a normal bell curve. A hypothesis we aim to test in future research is that talented individuals, for whom learning and advancement come easily, have fewer opportunities (or, more aptly, necessities) to develop a resilient approach to failure and setbacks.

In our cross-sectional analyses, grit increases monotonically throughout adulthood. One possibility is that people have a growing appreciation of the efficacy of effort as they age. Alternatively, consistent with the literature on identity formation, it may be that the value of specializing versus exploring diverse pursuits shifts as we age. Early in life, it may make more sense to privilege exploration over specialization. Until we develop a solid understanding of our own inherent interests and abilities, it may make sense to hold off on committing to lifelong goals. Later in development, it may be increasingly adaptive to stay with a particular vocational (or avocational) pursuit, especially since division of labor in our modern economy tends to reward specialization. (Duckworth and Eskreis-Winkler 2013)

This important body of research strongly supports a focus on habits of mind in the classroom.

Peterson and Seligman's book, *Character Strengths and Virtues*, offers additional support for this kind of curricular focus on character traits. As Peterson and Seligman note in their introduction,

> The classification of strengths presented in this book is intended to reclaim the study of character and virtue as legitimate topics of psychological inquiry and informed societal discourse. By providing ways of talking about character strengths and measuring them across the life span, this classification will start to make possible a science of human strengths that goes beyond armchair philosophy and political rhetoric. We believe that good character can be cultivated, but to do so, we need conceptual and empirical tools to craft and evaluate interventions. (Peterson and Seligman 2004, 3)

Paul Tough's (2012) book, *How Children Succeed: Grit, Curiosity, and the Hidden Power of Character,* provides additional support for a curricular focus on dispositional characteristics. Roy F. Baumeister and John Tierney's *Willpower: Rediscovering the Greatest Human Strength*, which focuses on the power of self-regulation, does as well. The work of researchers like Walter Mischel, popular writers like Geoff Colvin, and others we might mention here lend support to this approach as well. As Ron Ritchhart notes in his book, *Intellectual Character*, "Rather than working to change who students are as thinkers and learners, schools for the most part work merely to fill them up with knowledge" (Ritchhart 2002, 7).

The work we do to nurture these kinds of dispositional characteristics may, in the long run, prove to be more important than anything we might teach students in writing classes about thesis statements, essay structure, and MLA format.

## CLASSROOM APPLICATIONS

Scholarship and research provide us, then, with compelling reasons to embrace these habits of mind and to actively nurture them in our classrooms. This can be accomplished in many ways. In one classroom strategy that Tishman, Perkins, and Jay highlight, for example, a science teacher developed an interactive classroom activity that allowed students to recreate Darwin's fascinating intellectual journey as he struggled to make sense of what he found on the Galapagos Islands during his historic voyage aboard *The Beagle*. This arduous intellectual work, of course, eventually produced Darwin's theory of evolution. After participating in a series of activities that put students on the Galapagos Islands with Darwin confronting what appeared to be insoluble mysteries, and after recreating some of Darwin's thinking processes as a class, the teacher then asked students to identify the key elements of Darwin's "good thinking." Here is the list they came up with:

- Don't give up
- Ask lots of questions
- Generate multiple ideas and explanations
- Be critical
- Don't stop too soon (Tishman, Perkins, and Jay 1994, 47)

This list is an excellent example of a pedagogical entry point to begin talking about "good thinking" with a class. These are habits of mind that are likely to transfer to almost any situation or context because these dispositions are not context-, discipline-, or field-dependent. These are habits of mind that all good thinkers and writers need to produce strong work, regardless of field, occupation, or discipline. In terms of the pedagogy we are discussing here, a classroom focused on ill-structured problems, for example, actively seeks to develop these characteristics because the intellectual work is challenging, easy answers are not available, and the assignment has been designed with the expectation that in order to be successful students will need to not give up, ask lots of questions, generate multiple ideas and explanations, be critical, and not stop too soon. A focus on motivation helps build passion, perseverance, and grit so that this important work can be accomplished.

## CHARACTER

Overall, we have much to gain from encouraging students in our writing classes to think about the nature of writing expertise in ways that focus not on standardized test scores or particular curricular achievements and skill sets but on dispositional qualities, character traits, and habits of mind. If we can help students develop habits of mind like curiosity, openness, engagement, creativity, persistence, responsibility, flexibility, humility, grit, and metacognition, then very good things will happen.

Our profession has a great deal to gain from moving these habits of mind to the center of our curriculum. There is a growing consensus, as we have seen, that these dispositional characteristics are vitally important in all sorts of ways for students. One way we can effectively nurture such dispositions is by adopting a pedagogy that privileges listening, empathy, and reflection as its central values and attending carefully to nurturing intrinsic motivation. Such a pedagogy would help develop these essential habits of mind, and would also provide our profession with a strong, research-based theoretical model for seeking ways in our classrooms to help nurture these essential dispositional characteristics at every grade level and across institutional boundaries.

# 9

## AN OPEN LETTER TO FIRST-YEAR HIGH SCHOOL STUDENTS

### THE "EXPECTATIONS GAP"

As we know, and as any number of important recent reports make clear, college readiness has become the single most urgently discussed concern in our profession. The Common Core Standards were developed and adopted nationwide in response to this problem. As our discipline has engaged this work, we have come to understand how poorly we have managed curricular alignment between our high schools and colleges and how much confusion still remains about what college readiness means.

Being ready for college means a lot of different things—all of them complex, all of them interrelated, and all of them essential. In fact, to describe someone as being "ready for college" is to describe a person who has often painstakingly, and almost always intentionally, developed an extensive variety of distinct proficiencies, habits of mind, and personal values related to the world and to the academic enterprise. Regardless of how good a high school may be, without systematic engagement and particular kinds of long-term preparation by high school students, college readiness will continue to be elusive and worrisome national problem.

To help promote better understanding of college readiness, I have composed the following open letter addressed to first-year high school students. I have included here everything that I think might be useful to high school students thinking about college. I have tried to narrow down what I know about succeeding in college into a few pages of practical advice. Although I have addressed this letter to first-year high school students specifically, the advice here is designed to be useful to any student who plans or hopes to attend college. I use this letter in my basic writing and reading classes, and students have found it very useful (and often very surprising: there's so much expected of them!). I have also developed a handy checklist for students (which follows the open letter)

DOI: 10.7330/9780874219449.c009

so that students can get a sense of where they stand and what they need to work on.

### AN OPEN LETTER TO FIRST-YEAR HIGH SCHOOL STUDENTS

Dear First-Year High School Students,

Greetings!

I am one of the editors of *What Is "College-Level" Writing?* and *What Is "College-Level" Writing?* Volume 2: *Assignments, Readings, and Student Writing Samples*—two scholarly books that explore the difference between high school writing and college-level writing. Because of my work on these books, I've spent a great deal of time during the last ten years thinking about what students need to successfully navigate the transition from high school to college.

Many studies and reports in recent years have suggested that there's an important "expectations gap" between the skills students are *typically bringing* to college and what college teachers like myself think students *should be bringing with them* to college. This letter is an attempt to state those expectations clearly, at least from my perspective.

I offer you my advice and encouragement here as you embark on your high school career because I think there's a lot that you can do on your own to get ready for college.

A good place to start is with some advice from Stephen Covey's book *The Seven Habits of Highly Effective People*: "Begin with the end in mind." I am advising you to set clear and specific long-term goals for yourself, and then to work incrementally over a period of time to meet them. I would like to provide you here with a number of specific goals that you can work toward over the next four years.

Let's begin with perhaps the most fundamental of all college readiness skills—reading.

### Reading

Reading comprehension, as measured by standardized tests like the SAT and ACT, is certainly an essential college-level skill. Students in college are required to read an enormous amount of material across a formidable range of disciplines, and college students must be able to understand and engage this material thoughtfully. Reading is a foundational skill that makes success possible in virtually all areas of your college education.

Strong reading comprehension skills, though, do not in themselves guarantee that you are ready for college. The best college students I've worked with over the years have had a number of other reading-related strengths in addition to strong comprehension skills, and I would like to briefly outline them for you here. Remember, you still have time to work on these!

- *Students who are ready for college like to read.* If you don't like to read, you are going to find college very difficult.
- *Students who are ready for college have read some* good *books as well as some* important *books while they were in high school.* I want you to know that I read for fun and enjoyment, and I want to encourage you to read for this reason as well. I also want you to know that I'm not suggesting that you need to follow any particular or prescriptive reading list to get ready for college, like the one E. D. Hirsch includes, for example, in his book, *Cultural Literacy.* But a high school student who wants to be ready for college should have at least some sense of our shared intellectual and cultural history, as well as at least some exposure to work outside the Western cultural tradition. A high school student who is ready for college should be able to recognize and respond in some thoughtful way to, say, a reference in a lecture to *King Lear.* Ideally, a student ready for college would have some visceral sense of what *King Lear* feels like as a dramatic experience and as a point of reference in our common heritage. The same can be said about the Book of Job, Toni Morrison's *The Bluest Eye,* Cervantes's *Don Quixote,* Willa Cather's *My Antonia,* Gabriel Garcia Marquez's *One Hundred Years of Solitude,* and Richard Rodriguez's *Hunger of Memory,* among others.
- *Students who are ready for college read for pleasure.* Reading is not something that a student who is ready for college always associates with "work," "discomfort," "inconvenience," or "pain." Students who are ready for college enjoy reading.

Being able to enjoy reading is often the result of a long engagement with books and the written word that cannot be replaced by "cramming" or taking special college preparatory classes. The students who I have found to be most ready for college have loved books and loved to read. If you don't, you will probably be confused and frustrated while at college. This is because reading is perhaps the most paradigmatic activity of a liberal arts education. Reading is where learning begins at college. You have four years to learn to love to read.

**Writing**

Strong writing skills are, of course, essential to college success, and as a long-time composition instructor, I know that there are many things that high school students can do to become strong writers.

First of all, you should expect any piece of serious writing to require considerable effort. Students who are ready for college routinely plan to produce multiple drafts of essays; expect to read and reread assigned texts; expect to think and rethink key ideas they are exploring in their essays; and routinely ask friends, family members, tutors, and teachers for feedback about their work. High school students who are ready for college know that good writing does not get produced without considerable effort, and they are willing to make that effort. Most of the time they do such work enthusiastically.

Students who are ready for college come here interested in learning how to become better writers. Many of the most problematic students I've encountered in my teaching career come to college unable or unwilling to believe that they have anything left to learn as writers. (I've been writing seriously now for about thirty years, and I'm still actively looking for ways to become a better writer.) Students should come to college with the understanding that they have a great deal to gain from listening to their professors as they discuss and evaluate their written work. In fact, students who are ready for college understand that this is where much of the most important learning in college takes place.

A whole range of behavioral and attitudinal qualities are also essential to anyone who hopes to be a successful college-level writer. English professor Kathleen McCormick articulated these quite memorably during an online exchange that we conducted a few years ago among contributors to *What Is "College-Level" Writing?* (Kathy was commenting on an essay by Kim Nelson, one of our student contributors to this volume; Kim's essay described the process of completing a college-level essay on J.R.R. Tolkien):

> Let's begin by just listing many of the skills with which Kim entered college. I think they should be divided into two types: behavior skills and writing skills. Behavioral skills are not exclusive to college-level writing, but without them, it is hard to achieve anything, and they are skills that few of us articulate as explicitly as Kim does, so I think they deserve to be underscored:

- Work through "panic" and refuse to procrastinate.
- Pace yourself to work on assignments for an extended period of time.
- Find others to help you (mother; teachers; friends at dinner; tutors at the writing center).
- Recognize that critique by a professor, while initially disheartening, is helpful.
- Initiate repeated visits to the professor.
- Value intellectual work and collaboration and validation more than the grade.
- Brainstorm in note form.
- "Bang out" an outline and critique it.
- Chose quotations.
- Develop a thesis.
- Transfer writing skills learned in high school to the college situation.
- Maintain sensitivity to language use.
- Reread texts you plan to write about; underline.
- Do library research.
- Listen to multiple levels of textual analysis.
- Rewrite and revise your thesis and writing.

## Thinking

I would advise you to seek out classes and learning experiences that legitimately challenge you. Research now shows that the brain responds in very powerful and positive ways to cognitive challenges. Don't limit yourself only to subjects or activities that are familiar or easy or comfortable.

Students who are ready for college bring with them a curiosity about ideas and an interest in encountering new ways of looking at the world. In fact, one of the reasons they come to college in the first place is to expand their minds, to encounter new ideas and perspectives, and to grow. High school students who are ready for college have genuine curiosity about the world and the people in it. Do you?

## Listening

Listening is a vastly undervalued and underappreciated skill in our culture. Strong listening skills (and the patience and empathy that make listening possible) will be enormously valuable to you in all areas of your life, in college and beyond. Listening skills will certainly help you move toward a more open and positive engagement with the world and with others.

Strong listening skills also make possible healthy, positive, respectful human relationships. Much of college success depends on establishing strong working relationships with professors, college staff, and fellow students, and such relationships are built, of course, with strong listening skills. Students who are unable to listen are typically unable to learn, for all the obvious reasons.

Good listeners bring to any interaction with others a number of important qualities, including patience, empathy, personal generosity, emotional intelligence, and respect for others. Good listeners are also able to suspend an interest in themselves and focus instead in respectful ways on what others think and feel. Students who are ready for college have done some of the important personal work that makes this possible. Listening is a skill, like many others, that improves with practice, and one can become a better listener simply by endeavoring to be one.

## "Grit"

"Grit" is another quality that is vitally important for college readiness. Researchers who use this term suggest that it includes self-discipline, perseverance, and passion. As psychologists Angela Duckworth and Martin Seligman note in their recent essay "Self-Discipline Outdoes IQ in Predicting Academic Performance of Adolescents," grit appears to be at least as important to academic success as IQ or "smarts." In fact, all high school students should hear what they have to say about self-discipline:

> Underachievement among American youth is often blamed on inadequate teachers, boring textbooks, and large class sizes. We suggest another reason for students falling short of their intellectual potential: their failure to exercise self-discipline. . . . We believe that many of America's children have trouble making choices that require them to sacrifice short-term pleasure for long-term gain, and that programs that build self-discipline may be the royal road to building academic achievement. (Duckworth and Seligman 2005,944)

Furthermore, as Peter Doskoch notes in an essay about Duckworth's research, "grit" is not simply a matter of working hard.

There appears to be an important element of joyfulness in this quality as well:

> That quality Duckworth finds so intriguing has little to do with clenched teeth. Rather, it's a force of motivation so luminous that, as mathematician Andrew Wiles found, it constantly renews itself. (Doskoch 2005, 8)

Any student is capable of bringing a quality of joyfulness to their work at college, and the same can be said for the qualities of self-discipline, perseverance, and passion. Without these qualities, students can only be considered ready to be bored, lost, angry, or confused at college.

## Attitude toward College

Drinking, socializing, and taking reckless advantage of "freedom" on campus lead many students to squander their time at college. I've seen many young men and women in my teaching career trapped in a protracted adolescence that often lasts well into their late teens, early 20s, and beyond. As teachers, we want students to have a youthful spirit (however old they may be), but we also want them to bring maturity to the college enterprise.

Some students, usually as a result of difficult life experience, arrive at college with such maturity. But many do not. It has been my experience that mature students are often able to engage the college experience in very productive ways. Those who do not bring such maturity, however, typically cannot. Such students often find themselves distracted, confused, and without any real direction.

You also need to understand that the chance to attend college is an opportunity of incalculable value. Because many students take this opportunity for granted, I recommend that community service be a required part of every high school student's preparation for college. Community service is an excellent way for you to begin building a balanced and mature perspective about life. Such a perspective will be invaluable to you when you attend college.

Sincerely,
Patrick Sullivan

### Determining College Readiness

To give you a very practical document to work from, I have developed the following college readiness checklist. Only students who score a perfect 100 percent (or check every item) can be considered ready for college. Good luck! Remember: you have four years to work on these!

## College Readiness Checklist

❑  1. I like to read.

❑  2. I have read a number of *good* books as well as some *important* books. Here is a list of some of them:

_____

_____

_____

_____

_____

_____

_____

_____

_____

❑  3. I am open-minded and curious about ideas, and I am interested in encountering new ways of looking at the world.

❑  4. I read for pleasure.

❑  5. I understand that any piece of serious writing will require considerable effort.

❑  6. I am interested in becoming a better writer. I understand that there are always ways to improve my writing, no matter how good I may think I am.

❑  7. I understand that some of the most important learning I do takes place when I discuss my written work with my teachers.

❑  8. I work through "panic" when I get a writing assignment, and I refuse to procrastinate.

❑  9. I am able to pace myself to work on assignments for extended periods of time.

❑  10. I routinely ask others to give me feedback about my written work in draft stage (this includes parents, teachers, friends, and writing center tutors).

❑ 11. I initiate repeated visits to teachers to discuss my work.

❑ 12. I value intellectual work, collaboration, and validation more than grades.

❑ 13. I use brainstorming strategies when I begin a writing assignment.

❑ 14. I produce a working outline for writing assignments and critique it.

❑ 15. I chose quotations effectively, and I can discuss them thoughtfully.

❑ 16. I can develop a point of view and maintain a consistent focus when I am writing an essay.

❑ 17. I always maintain sensitivity to language use.

❑ 18. I always reread texts I plan to write about, and I interact physically with these texts by underlining and highlighting key passages.

❑ 19. I am able to conduct library research on my own, and I don't settle for the first items that may come to hand.

❑ 20. I always revise my work a number of times before I hand it in.

❑ 21. I am eager to move outward from myself toward a more open and broad-minded engagement with the world and others.

❑ 22. I understand that listening is an important life skill and an essential college skill.

❑ 23. I enjoy listening to others, and I bring to all my encounters with others the qualities of patience, empathy, personal generosity, and respect.

❑ 24. I bring self-discipline, perseverance, and passion to whatever I do.

❑ 25. I understand what "grit" is, and I understand why it is essential for success in any long-term endeavor like college.

❑ 26. I understand that the chance to attend college is an opportunity of incalculable value.

❑ 27. I understand that many students squander this opportunity by drinking, socializing, and taking full advantage of the freedom they have at college. I will not be one of these students.

❑ 28. I understand the value of being involved in my community.

❑ 29. I have demonstrated my commitment to my community and to community service in the following ways (100 hours minimum):

_____

_____

_____

_____

_____

❑ 30. I have done community service not because it looks good on my college application, but because this is how I choose to live my life. I choose to be involved with my community, and I choose to spend some of my time "giving back" to my community.

# CONCLUSION

The dogmas of the quiet past are inadequate to the stormy present.
The occasion is piled high with difficulty, and we must rise with the
   occasion.
As our case is new, so we must think anew and act anew.
We must disenthrall ourselves, and then we shall save our country.

—Abraham Lincoln,
Annual Message to Congress. December 1, 1862

I was hurrying
through my own soul,
opening its dark doors—
I was leaning out;
I was listening.

—Mary Oliver, from "Mockingbirds"

Now that we have drawn to the conclusion of our journey together, I
would like to invite readers to return to the questions we began with.
We have examined a broad range of scholarship and research, and we
are perhaps in a better position now to engage these essential questions
about our teaching practice and our pedagogy. Following Lorraine
Code, and keeping in mind the understanding that knowing is always
a matter of degree, let's see what kind of answers we are now comfortable providing for those essential questions. Here is how I would answer
them, given what we have read, discussed, and shared together.

## 1. WHAT MIGHT WE BE ABLE TO SAY THAT WE KNOW FOR SURE ABOUT LEARNING HOW TO READ AND WRITE?

There is considerable debate about this, and there are only a few things
we appear to know for sure. First, we know that motivation plays a fundamental role in any kind of learning, and in some very real ways it
can be said to make learning possible. Motivated students learn joyfully
and almost effortlessly. Unmotivated students, as we also know through

DOI: 10.7330/9780874219449.c010

painful field experience in the classroom, often do not learn at all and can become disruptive influences in the classroom.

Second, we know that certain kinds of dispositional characteristics and habits of mind are essential to the development of mature cognitive orientations, and are prerequisites for mature critical thinking. There is much that we can do to help nurture these habits of mind in our classrooms. Research from a variety of disciplines makes this course of action very compelling.

Third, following David Jolliffe (and a variety of gloomy recent national reports on student reading ability), we know that writing teachers need to teach reading. Strong reading skills are essential to good writing and thinking. We must also seek to nurture a lifelong passion for reading in our students, 6–13. There are few things that we do that will be more important than this. We know, for example, that reading, especially at a young age, is crucial to a student's intellectual development, preparation for college, and long-term prospects. As Richard Rothstein has noted, "the number of books in students' homes, for example, consistently predicts [achievement] scores within almost every country" (Rothstein 2004, 20). This is an issue related to race and class (and perhaps to parenting styles as well, as Annette Lareau and others have suggested). As Rothstein notes,

> If children see parents read to solve their own problems or for entertainment, children are more likely to want to read themselves. . . .Parents who read to children but don't read for themselves send a different message. . . . Furthermore, parents who are more literate are more likely to ask questions that are creative, interpretive, or connective, like "What do you think will happen next?" "Why do you think this happened?" "Does that remind you of what we did yesterday?" . . . Stark social class differences arise not only in how parents read but in how they converse. Explaining events in the broader world to children, in dinner talk, for example, may have as much of an influence on test scores as early reading itself. (Rothstein 2004, 21)

We must keep in mind, as we noted above, that reading skills have been eroding nationally for some time. As NCTE notes in a recent policy brief on adolescent literacy, "it is easy to summon the language of crisis in discussing adolescent literacy" (National Council of Teachers of English 2007, 1). The brief goes on to state:

> Less than half of the 2005 ACT-tested high school graduates demonstrated readiness for college-level reading, and the 2005 National Assessment of Educational Progress (NAEP) reading scores for 12th graders showed a decrease from 80 percent at the *proficient* level in 1992 to 73 percent in 2005.

Recent NAEP results also reveal a persistent achievement gap between the reading and writing scores of whites and students of color in 8th and 12th grades. Furthermore, both whites and students of color scored lower in reading in 2005 as compared with 1992, and both male and female students also scored lower in 2005. (1)

Reading is perhaps the most vitally important gateway skill for college readiness and participation in a democracy, and striving to help students see reading as an enjoyable, lifelong activity is something that we all must embrace regardless of institution or instructional level. Report after report makes this very clear.

Beyond this, alas, it seems the rest may be up for grabs. The very existence of FYC, for example, has been challenged and called into question (Petraglia 1995; Smit 2004; Wardle 2009; see also Hansen 2012). As Smit notes in *The End of Composition*, "No one can doubt that the field has become increasingly divided into narrow areas of concern with little indication that scholars and researchers in one area read, respect, or deal substantively with the work of those in other areas" (Smit 2004, 7). This is not hyperbole, unfortunately. There is still a great deal that is unsettled and unsure in our discipline.

It seems clear, however, that we can improve teaching and learning if we focus on motivation, nurture habits of mind like curiosity and openness, and seek ways to make reading an enjoyable and lifelong activity for students. There also appears to be a great deal of evidence to support a pedagogy that would bring listening, empathy, reflection, and mindfulness to the center of our teaching practice.

## 2. HOW ARE STUDENTS IN THE UNITED STATES DOING RIGHT NOW IN TERMS OF READING, WRITING AND COLLEGE READINESS?

Here, I'm afraid we may have to turn to Auden and "In Memory of W. B. Yeats":

> He disappeared in the dead of winter:
> The brooks were frozen, the airports almost deserted,
> And snow disfigured the public statues;
> The mercury sank in the mouth of the dying day.
> What instruments we have agree
> The day of his death was a dark cold day.

What instruments we have agree that students in the United States are underachieving as readers, writers, and thinkers, perhaps in ways that might be described as catastrophic. We have reviewed a wide variety of research data that suggests that vast numbers of students in the United States read and write poorly, and when compared with students from other countries our students can only be described, at best, as mediocre (Sahlberg 2011; United 2014; Wagner 2008). The data on reading is particularly disheartening. *The Condition of Education 2011*, for example, shows that in 2009, 26 percent of 12-grade students read at "below basic" level, 36 percent read at a "basic" level, and 33 percent read at a "proficient" level (Figure 10–2) (United States Department of Education 2011, 43). Only 5 percent of 12-graders read at an "advanced" level. This is data that we probably already have a strong sense about just from classroom experience, as we routinely encounter students who hate to read, who don't read at all, or who resist reading anything longer than a few pages. It is much rarer than it should be that we encounter students in our classrooms who are dedicated and passionate readers.

In terms of writing, perhaps the single most disheartening and troubling bit of data is the National Commission on Writing's remark that 12th-grade students currently produce writing that is "relatively immature and unsophisticated" (National 2003, 17). I have attempted to explain why this is the case.

I think we can say with some confidence that we have significant challenges before us regarding reading, writing, and college readiness.

## 3. WHAT DO WE KNOW ABOUT THE CURRENT STATE OF TEACHING READING AND WRITING IN THE UNITED STATES?

There is considerable disagreement in our discipline about how writing teachers should be spending their time in writing classes. There also appears to be considerable disagreement about what constitutes effective teaching in writing classes. There appear to be factions everywhere—some teachers focusing on grammar and punctuation, some on rhetorical strategies, some on argumentation, some on the five-paragraph essay, some on the personal essay, some on close reading or analysis, some on research, some on process, some on comparing and contrasting, some on definition or description, some on various combinations of these different approaches (Lunsford and Lunsford 2008, 793). As Smit notes:

> In 2001, Gary Tate, Amy Rupiper, and Kurt Schick edited a collection entitled *A Guide to Composition Pedagogies*. The Collection included twelve chapters, each devoted to a different pedagogy used in the teaching of writing: "Process Pedagogy," "Expressive Pedagogy," "Rhetorical Pedagogy," "Collaborative Pedagogy," "Cultural Studies and Composition," "Critical

Pedagogy," "Feminist Pedagogy," "Community-Service Pedagogy," "The Pedagogy of Writing Across the Curriculum," "Writing Center Pedagogy," "Basic Writing Pedagogy," and "Technology and the Teaching of Writing." These chapter titles give us a fair indication of the many different ways writing is taught in our colleges and universities.

Now what I find interesting about these twelve different ways of conceptualizing writing and writing instruction is that they have very little in common; they do not agree on the kinds of writing that should be taught or the methods to be used in writing instruction. Even more interesting, they do not agree on what courses in writing should ultimately accomplish. (Smit 2004, 137)

Much of this writing appears to function in what Elizabeth Wardle has famously described as "mutt genres":

The types of writing asked for in the assignments [in our discipline] can generally be grouped into the following genres:

- Autobiography/personal narrative
- Profile of a person
- Argument/position paper
- Interview
- Travel narrative
- Evaluation/review
- Observation
- Reflection
- Rhetorical analysis

Most of the assignments are described by one of the doctoral students who analyzed assignment sheets with me as "mutt genres." The mutt genres teachers assigned mimic genres that mediate activities in other activity systems, but within the FYC system their purposes and audiences are vague or even contradictory. They are quite different from and serve very different purposes in FYC than they do in other disciplinary activity systems. (Wardle 2009, 773–74)

There does not at the moment appear to be a national consensus related to best practices in the classroom, despite the work of organizations like the WPA, which has sought to establish common ground. The "WPA Outcomes Statement for First-Year Composition," for example, lists a number of important outcomes related to "critical thinking, reading, and writing," for example, and these include using writing and reading "for inquiry, learning, thinking, and communicating"; understanding a writing assignment "as a series of tasks, including finding, evaluating, analyzing, and synthesizing appropriate primary and secondary sources"; integrating a student's own ideas with those of others; and understanding "the relationships among language, knowledge, and power" (Council of Writing Program Administrators 2000). These are excellent outcomes, of course, but they may be too generic, especially in terms of how teachers might practically operationalize such goals in their classrooms on Monday morning when they meet their classes. How best to do this? I think it is fair to say that there is considerable difference of opinion in our discipline on this question at the moment. And certainly in individual classrooms across the United States these differences may well be more pronounced, were we able to accurately measure them.

### 4. IS THERE ANY SCHOLARSHIP *OUTSIDE OF OUR DISCIPLINE* THAT WE MIGHT NEED TO CONSIDER AND BE FAMILIAR WITH AS TEACHERS OF WRITING?

It looks like there is a great deal of this, much of which, it turns out, is directly applicable to what we are trying to accomplish in the writing classroom. We have reviewed research in this book related to learning theory, critical thinking, transfer of knowledge, neuroscience, motivation, cognitive psychology, and characterological dispositions. I will let readers decide for themselves the value and importance of this work. For me, it is beyond dispute—it is essential and foundational work that all writing teachers should be familiar with. Taken in aggregate, it emphatically suggests shaping our curriculum and pedagogy in very specific ways (and not in others). I have attempted to shape the pedagogy we are theorizing here in ways that is responsive to this important work.

### 5. CONSIDERED CUMULATIVELY, WHAT DOES ALL THE RESEARCH AND SCHOLARSHIP WE HAVE REVIEWED HERE (INCLUDING COMPOSITION SCHOLARSHIP) TELL US ABOUT WHAT WE SHOULD BE DOING IN THE ENGLISH CLASSROOM AND HOW WE MIGHT BE ABLE TO TEACH WRITING MOST EFFECTIVELY?

This is a question that each reader and teacher will have to answer for herself, of course. I think that the review of research that we have conducted here strongly supports the development of the pedagogy that brings listening, empathy, and reflection to the center of our teaching practice. Although the problems we seek to address together are complex and multi-faceted, it seems clear that research and scholarship strongly supports the following:

- Reduce our overreliance on argumentative writing, especially simplistic argumentative writing.
- Make listening, empathy, and reflection the primary skills we value in our classrooms.
- Develop curriculum with learning theory clearly in mind, especially the landmark work of Perry, Kegan, King and Kitchener, and Baxter Magolda.
- Bring "ill-structured problems" to the center of our pedagogy.
- Teach reading.
- Theorize reading and writing as dual and essential elements of the same activity—thinking.
- Teach reading and writing together. Most writing that students do in writing classrooms should be linked to reading, and should require, following Hillocks, a rigorous "process of inquiry" (Hillocks 2010, 26).
- Construct and design learning activities and writing assignments very carefully and purposefully, targeting key areas identified by learning theory, cognitive psychology, and critical thinking scholarship.
- Move reflective, dialogic, exploratory writing to the center of our pedagogy and curriculum.
- Make transfer of knowledge an essential consideration in any pedagogical or curricular choice or decision. Knowledge of the scholarship on this subject should be considered essential for anyone discussing curriculum for our discipline.
- Develop curriculum that acknowledges the powerful links between writing expertise and genre.
- Make improving student motivation a primary concern for teachers of writing. This should be an essential part of what it means to teach writing.
- Promote variety in the writing curriculum. Students should have to "write and write often in multigenres: stories, personal essays, critical essays, parodies, poems, freewrites, letters to teachers, journals, jingles, reader responses, lists" (Lujan 2010, 56).
- Find ways to bring choice into the classroom.
- Design activities that disguise repetitions of writing tasks.
- Develop policies and practices that require students to take responsibility for their own learning and their own development as readers, writers, and thinkers.
- Adopt an active learning pedagogy: "Teach less, learn more." Reduce "teacher talk" (Hillocks 2002, 7–9) in the classroom so that teachers "teach less" and students "learn more" (Sahlberg 2011, 62–69). Active learning is widely acknowledged as an important component of good teaching, and conventional wisdom suggests it is widely practiced in our profession. Evidence provided by Hillocks and others, though, appears to suggest otherwise. In *The Testing Trap*, for example (see Hillocks 2002, 5–33), Hillocks still finds a great deal of

"teacher talk" and reductive epistemologies driving much classroom practice.

- Intentionally and systematically nurture creativity and creative thinking, 6–13. Creativity is an extraordinarily important human capacity that has been routinely overlooked and undervalued in recent discussions of academic rigor, curricular alignment, and articulation. As Ken Robinson notes, "Creativity is the greatest gift of human intelligence. The more complex the world becomes, the more creative we need to be to meet its challenges" (Robinson 2011, xiii).

- Attend carefully to critical thinking scholarship and the "habits of mind" identified in the WPA/NCTE/NWP document, "Framework for Success in Postsecondary Writing." Dispositional characteristics like curiosity, open-mindedness, flexibility, as well as a "willingness to reconsider and revise views where honest reflection suggests that change is warranted" (Facione 1990, 25) are essential to good writing and good thinking. Furthermore, these are habits of mind that are likely to transfer to almost any situation or context because these dispositions are not context-, discipline-, or field-dependent. These are habits of mind that all good thinkers and writers need to produce strong work, regardless of field, occupation, or discipline.

- Embrace recent work from neuroscience, especially "the revolutionary discovery that the human brain can change itself" (Doidge 2007, xvii). Active learning, a focus on questions, and a curriculum that nurtures curiosity should be key elements for all writing curriculum (see Healy 1999, 73).

- Attend carefully to international models that produce engaged students and quality learning.

This final item is particularly important. We can learn a great deal by attending carefully to international educational models that produce engaged students and quality learning. There is much we might learn from such models about how to effectively balance the need for accountability and standardization with high quality teaching and innovation (a balance that we have yet to achieve, alas). Pasi Sahlberg's recent book on Finland's highly successful educational system, *Finnish Lessons*, might be a good place to start. I was particularly impressed with the Finnish focus on risk-taking and embracing uncertainty: "School-based and teacher-owned curricula facilitate finding novel approaches to teaching and learning, and encourage risk-taking and uncertainty in leadership, teaching, and learning" (Sahlberg 2011, 103). This is something that is probably essential for building a robust and dynamic teaching practice. Unfortunately, the U.S. appears to be moving in the opposite direction.

One of Sahlberg's main points is that our high-stakes testing policies thwart effective teaching, learning, and pedagogical innovation:

One of the key messages of this book is that unlike many other contemporary systems of education, the Finnish system has not been infected by the market-based competition and high-stakes testing policies. The main reason is that the education community in Finland has remained unconvinced that competition and choice with more standardized testing than students evidently require would be good for schools. The ultimate success of a high-stakes testing policy is whether it positively affects students learning, not whether it increases student scores on a particular test (Amrein & Berliner, 2002). If student learning remains unaffected, or if testing leads to biased teaching, the validity of such high-stakes tests must be questioned. Finnish education authorities and especially teachers have not been convinced that frequent external census-based testing and stronger accountability would be beneficial to students and their learning. (Sahlberg 2011, 39).

There is growing consensus among United States educators that market-based competition and high-stakes testing policies—which are part of a global trend in education—have, indeed, had a negative impact on student learning and have led to more narrow and "biased" teaching practices (Koretz 2008; Perlstein 2007; Ravitch 2010; Sacks 1999). As Rothstein, Jacobsen, and Wilder have suggested, "Standardized tests that assess only low-level skills and that can be scored electronically cost very little to administer—although their hidden costs are enormous in the lost opportunities to develop young people's broader knowledge, traits, and skills" (Rothstein, Jacobsen, and Wilder 2008, 7). As they note, for example, "making reading drills a chore can destroy children's potential to love literature or to understand and interpret history" (13). Dismantling this system is going to take vision, great leadership, perseverance, and determination, among many other things. In its place, perhaps we can begin thinking about Rothstein, Jacobsen, and Wilder's more thoughtfully balanced curriculum that includes not only "basic academic knowledge and skills" but also "appreciation of the arts and literature," "citizenship and community responsibility," "physical health," and "emotional health" (14).

In closing, I would like to wish my readers and colleagues in this enterprise courage, hope, and patience as we move forward together transforming our curriculum and our teaching practice. A utopian endeavor, for sure. But here we have the comfort of Peter Elbow's inspirational words and example to guide us:

It makes me mad when people criticize me as utopian. Surely there is something misguided when the term "utopian" is used to criticize and is taken to mean "unrealistic" and "unsophisticated." We need the utopian or visionary impulse to keep from being blinded by what seems normal—to help us see that what is natural is constructed, not inevitable. When I get stuck I can often help myself by asking, "How should things be?" This helps me pry myself loose from the web of assumptions we live in. (Elbow 1996, 83)

Indeed, how should things be?

I am calling for a new writing curriculum built around listening, empathy, reflection, motivation, and habits of mind. This is a pedagogy that would help nurture essential cognitive and dispositional orientations that are the wellsprings of mature meaning-making and serious intellectual work. This pedagogy also offers us the opportunity to teach knowledge that transfers to other types of writing situations and disciplines and to contexts outside the classroom. Given the scholarship and research that we have surveyed together here—from a variety of fields including composition scholarship and theory, learning theory, neuroscience, critical thinking scholarship, research related to transfer of knowledge, and work related to the teaching of thinking in the classroom—it is clearly time to develop curriculum nationwide that is more congruent with this important body of work.

The time for revolution is now.

# APPENDIX 1

*Reading Guide for "Sonny's Blues" by James Baldwin*

"Sonny's Blues" is a short work of fiction by the celebrated American writer James Baldwin (1924–1987). "Sonny's Blues" is a short story, and it shares many features with novels (but, of course, it is much shorter in length). This story focuses on the relationship between two brothers—the narrator of the story, who is a teacher and is not given a name in the story by Baldwin (you can refer to him as "the narrator"), and his younger brother, Sonny, who loves music and eventually becomes a jazz musician.

To help you get deeper into the story, I invite you to consider the following questions:

### 1. "You never hear anything I say."

During much of the story the older brother struggles to understand the choices his younger brother, Sonny, makes: "I simply couldn't see why on earth he'd want to spend his time hanging around nightclubs, clowning around bandstands, while people pushed each other around a dance floor. It seemed—beneath him, somehow."

". . . beneath him, somehow." What should we make of that phrase? Is this harsh and unfair? Or is this just something an older brother thinks about when he's trying to look out for his younger brother?

Sonny also feels that that his older brother doesn't really listen to him:

> "Sonny," I said, "I know how you feel, but if you don't finish school now, you're going to be sorry later that you didn't." I grabbed him by the shoulders. "And you only got another year. It ain't so bad. And I'll come back and I swear I'll help you do whatever you want to do. Just try to put up with it till I come back. Will you please do that? For me?"
> He didn't answer and he wouldn't look at me.
> "Sonny. You hear me?"
> He pulled away. "I hear you. But you never hear anything I say."

The brothers certainly have their differences, don't they? What causes these differences? Are they typical of the kind of differences that you

DOI: 10.7330/9780874219449.c011

find in sibling relationships that you've observed in your own life and in the lives of others? Why can't the narrator simply be supportive of Sonny and his interest in becoming a jazz musician?

## 2. Philosophies about Life

The brothers have very different outlooks on life, don't they? The older brother is rather conservative, and he believes that people can't always do what they want to do in life. For the older brother, life necessarily involves some level of sacrifice and compromise. The younger brother has a very different attitude about life. He is not willing to compromise or abandon his dream:

> He turned back to me and half leaned, half sat, on the kitchen table. "Everything takes time," he [Sonny] said, "and—well, yes, sure, I can make a living at it [playing music]. But what I don't seem to be able to make you understand is that it's the only thing I want to do—"
>
> "Well, Sonny," I said gently, "you know people can't always do exactly what they want to do—"
>
> "No, I don't know that," said Sonny, surprising me. "I think people ought to do what they want to do, what else are they alive for?"

An intriguing exchange, to say the least! What do we make of it? Can they both be right? Is Sonny just being irresponsible and childish? Does he need to grow up? Or is the older brother being too intrusive? It's not his life, after all. Which of these attitudes about life and career most closely matches your own? Is there any evidence here that the author favors one attitude or approach to living over the other? What path do most people choose?

## 3. Suffering Begets Wisdom

What leads the older brother to finally write to Sonny in jail and reach out to try to reconnect with him is a horrific trauma in his own life. His daughter dies a sudden and violent death, and that experience opens the older brother up to understanding Sonny's life and suffering in a radically new way:

> I read about Sonny's trouble in the spring. Little Gracie died in the fall. She was a beautiful little girl. But she only lived a little over two years. She died of polio and she suffered. She had a slight fever for a couple of days, but it didn't seem like anything and we just kept her in bed. And we would certainly have called the doctor, but the fever dropped, she seemed to be all right. So we thought it had just been a cold. Then, one day, she was

up, playing, Isabel was in the kitchen fixing lunch for the two boys when they'd come in from school, and she heard Grace fall down in the living room. When you have a lot of children you don't always start running when one of them falls, unless they start screaming or something. And, this time, Gracie was quiet. Yet, Isabel says that when she heard that *thump* and then that silence, something happened to her to make her afraid. And she ran to the living room and there was little Grace on the floor, all twisted up, and the reason she hadn't screamed was that she couldn't get her breath. And when she did scream, it was the worst sound, Isabel says, that she'd ever heard in all her life, and she still hears it sometimes in her dreams. Isabel will sometimes wake me up with a low, moaning, strangled sound and I have to be quick to awaken her and hold her to me and where Isabel is weeping against me seems a mortal wound.

    I think I may have written Sonny the very day that little Grace was buried. I was sitting in the living room in the dark, by myself, and I suddenly thought of Sonny. My trouble made his real.

Does this make sense psychologically? What does that phrase mean, "My trouble made his real"? The ancient Greek tragic dramatists like Sophocles and Aeschylus are famous for suggesting that "suffering begets wisdom." Are they right? Is that's what's going on here? Does suffering beget wisdom? If so, how does that work and why does it work that way? Are there any implications in this for our own lives and relationships?

### 4. "The Darkness"

Baldwin uses the phrase "the darkness" at many key points throughout this story. What is he up to here? In the fourth sentence of the story, for example, Baldwin introduces this phrase, which he will return to again and again throughout the story:

I stared at it [a newspaper story about his brother] in the swinging lights of the subway car, and in the faces and bodies of the people, and in my own face, trapped in the darkness which roared outside.

What is he suggesting here? What should we make of that powerful and memorable phrase: "the darkness which roared outside"? What is "the darkness"? And why is it "roaring"? Can darkness "roar"?

    In the fifth paragraph, Baldwin uses the image of darkness again:

I was sure that the first time Sonny had ever had horse, he couldn't have been much older than these boys are now. These boys, now, were living as we'd been living then, they were growing up with a rush and their heads bumped abruptly against the low ceiling of their actual possibilities. They were filled with rage. All they really knew were two darknesses, the darkness of their lives, which was now closing in on them, and the darkness of the movies, which had blinded them to that other darkness, and in which they now, vindictively, dreamed, at once more together than they were at any other time, and more alone.

What are these "two darknesses"?

Another memorable paragraph in the story describes the narrator and Sonny driving in a taxi through Harlem and looking out the window at their old neighborhood, and Baldwin again employs the image of "the darkness":

> So we drove along, between the green of the park and the stony, lifeless elegance of hotels and apartment buildings, toward the vivid, killing streets of our childhood. . . . houses exactly like the houses of our past yet dominated the landscape, boys exactly like the boys we once had been found themselves smothering in these houses, came down to the streets for light and air and found themselves encircled by disaster. Some escaped the trap, most didn't. Those who got out always left something of themselves behind, as some animals amputate a leg and leave it in the trap.

There is some powerful language here: "smothering," "encircled by disaster," "escaped the trap." What should we make of that concluding image: "as some animals amputate a leg and leave it in the trap"? This is certainly an arresting phrase, but what does it mean? What is Baldwin suggesting here?

Baldwin mentions darkness again later in the story, in the section that describes a large family gathering, with everyone lounging around after a big Sunday meal:

> This was the last time I ever saw my mother alive. Just the same, this picture gets all mixed up in my mind with pictures I had of her when she was younger. The way I always see her is the way she used to be on a Sunday afternoon, say, when the old folks were talking after the big Sunday dinner. I always see her wearing pale blue. She'd be sitting on the sofa. And my father would be sitting in the easy chair, not far from her. And the living room would be full of church folks and relatives. There they sit, in chairs all around the living room, and the night is creeping up outside, but nobody knows it yet. You can see the darkness growing against the windowpanes and you hear the street noises every now and again, or maybe the jangling beat of a tambourine from one of the churches close by, but it's real quiet in the room. For a moment nobody's talking, but every face looks darkening, like the sky outside. And my mother rocks a little from the waist, and my father's eyes are closed. Everyone is looking at something a child can't see. For a minute they've forgotten the children. Maybe a kid is lying on the rug, half asleep. Maybe somebody's got a kid in his lap and is absent-mindedly stroking the kid's head. Maybe there's a kid, quiet and big-eyed, curled up in a big chair in the corner. The silence,

the darkness coming, and the darkness in the faces frightens the child obscurely. He hopes that the hand which strokes his forehead will never stop—will never die. He hopes that there will never come a time when the old folks won't be sitting around the living room, talking about where they've come from, and what they've seen, and what's happened to them and their kinfolk.

But something deep and watchful in the child knows that this is bound to end, is already ending. In a moment someone will get up and turn on the light. Then the old folks will remember the children and they won't talk any more that day. And when light fills the room, the child is filled with darkness. He knows that every time this happens he's moved just a little closer to that darkness outside. The darkness outside is what the old folks have been talking about. It's what they've come from. It's what they endure. The child knows that they won't talk any more because if he knows too much about what's happened to them, he'll know too much too soon, about what's going to happen to *him.*

How can a light fill a room and also fill a child with "darkness"? What is Baldwin trying to tell us here? What does all this talk of darkness accomplish and communicate to us?

### 5. "There's a lot that you don't know. But you are going to find out."

In a very memorable section of this story, the narrator's mother tells him the story about his father and his brother—about the trouble they had and the tragedy that came into their lives. This is something the narrator never knew about his father until this moment:

"I ain't telling you all this," she said, "to make you scared or bitter or to make you hate nobody. I'm telling you this because you got a brother. And the world ain't changed."

I guess I didn't want to believe this. I guess she saw this in my face. She turned away from me, toward the window again, searching those streets.

"But I praise my Redeemer," she said at last, "that He called your Daddy home before me. I ain't saying it to throw no flowers at myself, but, I declare, it keeps me from feeling too cast down to know I helped your father get safely through this world. Your father always acted like he was the roughest, strongest man on earth. And everybody took him to be like that. But if he hadn't had *me* there—to see his tears!"

She was crying again. Still, I couldn't move. I said, "Lord, Lord, Mama, I didn't know it was like that."

"Oh, honey," she said, "there's a lot that you don't know. But you are going to find it out." She stood up from the window and came over to me. "You got to hold on to your brother," she said, "and don't let him fall, no matter what it looks like is happening to him and no matter how evil you gets with him. You going to be evil with him many a time. . . . You may not be able to stop nothing from happening. But you got to let him know you's *there*."

This is a powerful and very memorable conversation, and the narrator's mother appears to be passing down wisdom to her oldest son. What is this wisdom? What does the mother mean when she says, "I ain't telling you all this," she said, "to make you scared or bitter or to make you hate nobody. I'm telling you this because you got a brother. And the world ain't changed"?

What does she mean when she says "the world ain't changed"?

Also, what does she mean when she says that she is not telling him this story to make him "scared" or "bitter" or "hate nobody"? Instead, she is telling him this "because you got a brother." What is the mother trying to communicate here to her son?

And what does she mean when she says, "there's a lot that you don't know. But you are going to find out"? What doesn't the narrator know? What is he going to find out?

## 6. Listening

Finally, Baldwin appears to want to say something to readers of this story about "listening" because he uses the word "listening" at a number of crucial moments in the story. Sonny accuses his brother at one important point in their relationship, as we've already noted, of not listening to him: "I hear you. But you never hear anything I say."

The story concludes with the narrator listening to Sonny play music, and he ends up hearing some remarkable things. In this final and very powerful concluding section of the story, Baldwin makes a number of references to "listening" and "hearing":

> Then Creole stepped forward to remind them that what they were playing was the blues. He hit something in all of them, he hit something in me, myself, and the music tightened and deepened, apprehension began to beat the air. Creole began to tell us what the blues were all about. They were not about anything very new. He and his boys up there were keeping it new, at the risk of ruin, destruction, madness, and death, in order to find new ways to make us listen. For, while the tale of how we suffer, and how we are delighted, and how we may triumph is never new, it always must be heard. There isn't any other tale to tell, it's the only light we've got in all this darkness.
>
> And this tale, according to that face, that body, those strong hands on those strings, has another aspect in every country, and a new depth in every generation. Listen, Creole seemed to be saying, listen. Now these are Sonny's

blues. He made the little black man on the drums know it, and the bright, brown man on the horn. Creole wasn't trying any longer to get Sonny in the water. He was wishing him Godspeed. Then he stepped back, very slowly, filling the air with the immense suggestion that Sonny speak for himself.

Then they all gathered around Sonny and Sonny played. Every now and again one of them seemed to say, amen. Sonny's fingers filled the air with life, his life. But that life contained so many others. And Sonny went all the way back, he really began with the spare, flat statement of the opening phrase of the song. Then he began to make it his. It was very beautiful because it wasn't hurried and it was no longer a lament. I seemed to hear with what burning he had made it his, with what burning we had yet to make it ours, how we could cease lamenting. Freedom lurked around us and I understood, at last, that he could help us to be free if we would listen, that he would never be free until we did. Yet, there was no battle in his face now, I heard what he had gone through, and would continue to go through until he came to rest in earth. He had made it his: that long line, of which we knew only Mama and Daddy. And he was giving it back, as everything must be given back, so that, passing through death, it can live forever. I saw my mother's face again, and felt, for the first time, how the stones of the road she had walked on must have bruised her feet. I saw the moonlit road where my father's brother died. And it brought something else back to me, and carried me past it, I saw my little girl again and felt Isabel's tears again, and I felt my own tears begin to rise. And I was yet aware that this was only a moment, that the world waited outside, as hungry as a tiger, and that trouble stretched above us, longer than the sky.

Then it was over. Creole and Sonny let out their breath, both soaking wet, and grinning. There was a lot of applause and some of it was real. In the dark, the girl came by and I asked her to take drinks to the bandstand. There was a long pause, while they talked up there in the indigo light and after awhile I saw the girl put a Scotch and milk on top of the piano for Sonny. He didn't seem to notice it, but just before they started playing again, he sipped from it and looked toward me, and nodded. Then he put it back on top of the piano. For me, then, as they began to play again, it glowed and shook above my brother's head like the very cup of trembling.

How is it possible that the narrator "hears" all these things in this song? What's going on here? What is Sonny communicating, and what is the narrator hearing? What do you make of this list of things the narrator hears and sees:

> . . . I heard what he [Sonny] had gone through, and would continue to go through until he came to rest in earth. He had made it his: that long line, of which we knew only Mama and Daddy. And he was giving it back, as everything must be given back, so that, passing through death, it can live forever. I saw my mother's face again, and felt, for the first time, how the stones of the road she had walked on must have bruised her feet. I saw the moonlit road where my father's brother died. And it brought something else back to me, and carried me past it, I saw my little girl again and

felt Isabel's tears again, and I felt my own tears begin to rise. And I was yet aware that this was only a moment, that the world waited outside, as hungry as a tiger, and that trouble stretched above us, longer than the sky.

What is Baldwin suggesting here in this concluding passage? What is he trying to tell his readers?

What do you make of this as a conclusion to this story? What's going on here, exactly?

What happens when people don't listen to each other in this story? What happens when they do?

# APPENDIX 2
## *Reading Guide for "Patterns of Culture" Assignment*

**RUTH BENEDICT, FROM** *PATTERNS OF CULTURE*
**(CHAPTER ONE: THE SCIENCE OF CUSTOM)**

### 1. "Pristine Eyes"

Benedict discusses culture in terms of "looking at the world" with "pristine eyes":

> No man ever looks at the world with pristine eyes. He sees it edited by a definite set of customs and institutions and ways of thinking. Even in his philosophical probings he cannot go behind these stereotypes; his very concepts of the true and the false will still have reference to his particular traditional customs. (2)

There seems to be a great deal at stake here for Benedict. The "very concepts of true and false" related to "particular traditional customs"? What could she possibly be suggesting here?

A good place to start thinking about this excerpt is with that adjective, "pristine." What does "pristine" mean? Well, "pristine" means:

pris·tine adj
    1. so clean and neat as to look as good as new
    2. pure; uncorrupted
    3. fresh, clean, and unspoiled

So we can translate the phrase "pristine eyes" into something like "No man or woman looks at the world in a way that is pure and unspoiled." But "unspoiled" by what? "Pure" in what way?

### 2. "There is no social problem it is more incumbent upon us to understand than this of the role of custom."

Benedict then goes on to make the claim that these customs begin to shape our experience and our behavior from the moment of birth:

> The life history of the individual is first and foremost an accommodation to the patterns and standards traditionally handed down in his community. From the moment of his birth the customs into which he is born shape his experience and behaviour. By the time he can talk, he is the little

DOI: 10.7330/9780874219449.c012

creature of his culture, and by the time he is grown and able to take part in its activities, its habits are his habits, its beliefs his beliefs, its impossibilities his impossibilities. . . . There is no social problem it is more incumbent upon us to understand than this of the role of custom. Until we are intelligent as to its laws and varieties, the main complicating facts of human life must remain unintelligible. (2–3)

What is Benedict getting at here? What do those phrases mean: "its habits are his habits, its beliefs his beliefs, its impossibilities his impossibilities"?

"Its impossibilities his impossibilities"? What does this mean? Aren't we free to be whoever we want to be and do whatever we want to do, regardless of where we're brought up and what our culture is?

There also seems to be something crucial at stake here as well for Benedict. One of the most eminent anthropologists who has ever lived is telling us something she obviously regards as vitally important: "There is no social problem it is more incumbent upon us to understand than this of the role of custom. Until we are intelligent as to its laws and varieties, the main complicating facts of human life must remain unintelligible."

There is considerable urgency in this statement. What does that phrase mean: "Until we are intelligent as to its [i.e. culture's] laws and varieties, the main complicating facts of human life must remain unintelligible"? What are the dangers here that Benedict seems intent on warning us about? What do we know about human history that might allow us to understand and appreciate what Benedict is saying here?

### 3. "Chosen people and dangerous aliens"

Benedict then goes on to discuss a kind of thinking and behavior that she says goes back to ancient cultures:

It is the same whether it is a question of our ethics or of our family organization. It is the inevitability of each familiar motivation that we defend, attempting always to identify our own local ways of behaving with Behaviour, or our own socialized habits with Human Nature.

Now modern man has made this thesis one of the living issues in his thought and in his practical behaviour, but the sources of it go far back into what appears to be, from its universal distribution among primitive peoples, one of the earliest of human distinctions, the difference in kind between "my own" closed group and the outsider. All primitive tribes agree in recognizing this category of the outsiders, those who are not only outside the provisions of the moral codes which holds within the limits of one's own people, but who are summarily denied a place anywhere in the human scheme. A great number of the tribal names in common use, Zuni,

Dene, Kiowa, and the rest, are names by which primitive peoples know themselves, and are only their native terms for "the human beings," that is, themselves. Outside of the closed group there are no human beings. And this is in spite of the fact that from an objective point of view each tribe is surrounded by peoples sharing in its arts and material inventions, in elaborate practices that have grown up by a mutual give-and-take of behaviour from one people to another. (6–7).

What does that phrase mean: "attempting always to identify our own local ways of behaving with Behaviour, or our own socialized habits with Human Nature"? Why has Benedict used capital letters for "Behaviour" and "Human Nature" here?

And what is she suggesting about "outsiders"? Do people really treat "outsiders" this way? There is a phrase here that is pretty chilling, isn't it: "Outside of the closed group there are no human beings"?

Is this true? Do people think this way? And what are we to make of that concluding point that she follows that sentence with: "Outside of the closed group there are no human beings. And this is in spite of the fact that from an objective point of view each tribe is surrounded by peoples sharing in its arts and material inventions, in elaborate practices that have grown up by a mutual give-and take of behaviour from one people to another."

What is she saying here? Is there any evidence to support this claim of Benedict's from what we know about human history?

*****

## II. KATHRYN EDIN AND MARIA KEFALAS'S *PROMISES I CAN KEEP*

### 1. Race and Class

In terms of research design, Edin and Kefalas looked at the "problems of family formation through the eyes of 162 low-income single mothers living in eight economically marginal neighborhoods across Philadelphia and its poorest industrial suburb, Camden, New Jersey" (5).

They chose the site for their research for an important reason, and I think it is crucial to look carefully at this rationale before we begin talking about what they found:

America's fifth-largest city entered the twenty-first century with almost a quarter of its citizens, and nearly a third of its children, living in poverty. This is precisely why it was a perfect site for our research. Because of the high rates of poverty there, we found poor whites, blacks, and Latinos living in roughly similar circumstances. Though racial minorities often live in high-poverty neighborhoods, cities where whites live in the same circumstances are rare. The white urban poor usually live in mixed-income neighborhoods, and thus have considerable advantages over the minority poor—better schools, better parks and recreational facilities, better jobs, safer streets, and so on. But in Philadelphia, the high poverty rate in several former white ethnic strongholds—those once-proud industrial villages—create a rare opportunity for students of race and inequality to study whites, Latinos, and African Americans whose social contexts were quite similar. This unique feature of our study may explain why we found the experiences and worldviews of these groups to be so similar, and why class, not race, is what drives much of our account. (13–14)

That last sentence seems very important: "This unique feature of our study may explain why we found the experiences and worldviews of these groups to be so similar, and why class, not race, is what drives much of our account." If we understand "class" to mean "a group of people within a society who share the same social and economic status" and "the structure of divisions in a society determined by the social or economic grouping of its members," what are the authors suggesting here about race and class as factors in this study?


## 2. "Hunger" for Love

Edin and Kefalas go on to acknowledge that the young men and women in this community sometimes have children to get away from their parents, "escape a troubled home life" (33), further a romantic relationship, or because "they have little to lose if they fail to time their births as precisely as the middle class does" (48).

But they also discovered that "children are no mere escape from strained family relationships" (34). Love appears to play a very important role here as well:

> Young women also hunger for the love and intimacy they can provide. Aliya, a twenty-seven-year-old African American mother, who got pregnant at seventeen with her one child, passionately exclaims, "Some people may say it was for the wrong reasons, but it was like too much around me going on. . . . I guess that was my way out of all these situations. {But} I wanted a child that was *mine*. It was [for] love." For those like Aliya, pregnancy offers the promise of relational intimacy at a time few other emotional resources are available. (34)

How are we to explain this "hunger"? And is this "hunger" any different than the kind of hunger for love and intimacy we might find in the hearts of people living in any neighborhood, rich or poor?

Also, how are we to understand that final sentence: "For those like Aliya, pregnancy offers the promise of relational intimacy at a time few other emotional resources are available." What do the authors mean when they say "few other emotional resources are available" to these women?

Many of the women here also clearly love their children and are happy to have had them:

> While older and wiser parents and kin may—and do—encourage the young to wait, to "live their lives" first, many young women come to see parenthood as the point at which they can really start living. When Pepper Ann's mother learned she was planning to get pregnant at fifteen, she tried to put an end to her daughter's scheme. Now forty-seven, this African American mother of two grown children and a twelve-year-old remembers vividly how her mother wanted her to get a diploma first and "live her life." "But to me," she explains, "that [baby] *was* life!" (35)

How are we to understand this statement? "That baby *was* life."

### 3. "Trust"

The authors discuss "trust" in poor communities and suggest it is often hard to find:

> Trust among residents of poor communities is astonishingly low—so low that most mothers we spoke with said they have no close friends, and many even distrust close kin. The social isolation that is the common experience of those who live in poverty is heightened for adolescents, whose relationships with parents are strained by the developmental need to forge an independent identity. The "relational poverty" that ensues can create a compelling desire to give and receive love. Who better to do so with, some figure, than a child they can call their own? Pamela, a white middle-aged mother of seven children, ranging in age from fourteen to twenty-eight, reflects, "I think [I got pregnant] mainly because I wanted to be loved. I went through my childhood without it. Somehow, I knew that. . . I would grow up and have kids, and it was something that was *mine*. Nobody could take it away from me. It was something that would *love* me. I would be able to love it unconditionally." (34)

Edin and Kefalas introduce two important terms here: "social isolation" and "relational poverty." What kinds of conditions do these phrases describe? Is there any reason why researchers would find more social isolation and relational poverty in poor communities? What kinds of conditions might lead to social isolation and relational poverty?

Furthermore, Edin and Kefalas report that many mothers believe that motherhood had "saved" them:

> The redemptive stories our mothers tell speak to the primacy of the mothering role, how it can become virtually the only source of identity and meaning in a young woman's life. There is an odd logic to the statements

mothers made when we asked them to imagine life without children: "I'd be dead or in jail," "I'd still be out partying," "I'd be messed up on drugs," or "I'd be nowhere at all." These mothers, we discovered, almost never see children as bringing them hardship; instead, they manage to credit virtually every bit of good in their lives to the fact they have children—they believe motherhood has "saved" them. (11)

Is this surprising to you in any way? How can a small child born into poverty "save" someone? Why do these women need to be "saved"?

### 4. "Outsiders"

Edin and Kefalas note that "outsiders"—a term we are familiar with from our reading of Ruth Benedict—often do not understand why poor women make the choices they do:

> Whereas outsiders generally view childbearing in such circumstances as irresponsible and self-destructive, within the social milieu of these down-and-out neighborhoods the norms work in reverse, and the choice to have a child despite the obstacles that lie ahead is a compelling demonstration of a young woman's maturity and high moral stature. Pregnancy offers her a unique chance to demonstrate these virtues to her family and friends and the community at large. (47–48)

The authors also discuss what they regard as important differences between poor communities and more affluent ones:

> Middle-class beliefs about the right way to start a family are conditioned by a social context that provides huge economic rewards for those who are willing to wait to have children until a decade or more after attaining sexual maturity. For a white college-bound adolescent raised on Philadelphia's affluent Main Line, each year of postponed childbearing will likely lead to higher lifetime earnings. In fact, if she can hold out until her mid-thirties, she'll likely earn twice as much as if she'd had a child right out of college. Just imagine how her economic prospects would plummet if she brought a pregnancy to term at fifteen! From this privileged vantage point, a disadvantaged young woman's willingness to bear a child well before she is of legal age is beyond comprehension. (48)

Given what we know about how cultures work from our reading of Ruth Benedict, what can we say about this "privileged vantage point"? Why should bearing children well before a woman is of legal age be "beyond comprehension" to more affluent "outsiders" not living in poor urban communities?

And is there any way we can relate Edin and Kefalas's statement about "social context" to this idea of "privileged vantage point": "Putting motherhood first makes sense in a social context where the achievements that middle-class youth see as their birthright are little more than pipe dreams: Children offer a tangible source of meaning, while other avenues for gaining social esteem and personal satisfaction appear vague and tenuous" (49).

What is this "social context"? Why do other "avenues of gaining social esteem and personal satisfaction appear vague and tenuous"? What would those other avenues be? What is the difference between a "birthright" and a "pipe dream"?

## 5. Review of Research and Conclusions

Finally, Edin and Kefalas review the current research on this subject (197–213) and place their own work within this ongoing scholarly conversation. They mention three current theorists by name:

1. Nobel prize-winning economist Gary Becker's book, *Treatise on the Family*.

2. Charles Murray's *Losing Ground*.

3. William Julius Wilson's *The Truly Disadvantaged*.

How do each of these authors explain "the retreat from marriage" and the "huge changes in family formation that are so vividly illustrated in the lives of Mahkiya, Deena, Dominique, Jen and the other 158 women we spoke with" (197)?

What do Edin and Kefalas see as the strengths and weaknesses of their arguments?

Edin and Kefalas then go on to summarize what they've learned from their research and situate these conclusions within the context of existing knowledge on this subject. What are their primary conclusions? What are the important factors that Edin and Kefalas identify at play here that help us understand why these changes in family formation have occurred?

I recommend reading these pages carefully because the authors are condensing and synthesizing many years of work down to a few pages of conclusions and wisdom. Everything they've worked for is represented on these pages. So I recommend paying careful attention to them. This is a good test for you: a strong college-level reader should be able to summarize this material accurately. Can you?

# APPENDIX 3
## *"Only Quotations" Reading Guide*

## "RICH MAN, POOR MAN" READING GUIDE!

To help you get deeper into these readings, I've put together this reading guide. It's designed to help guide you to read and think about key passages. Enjoy!

### A. Key quotes from Milton Friedman's "Free to Choose"

1. ". . . millions of people streamed across the Atlantic, and a smaller number across the Pacific, driven by misery and tyranny and attracted by the promise of freedom and affluence. When they arrived, they did not find streets paved with gold; they did not find an easy life. They did find freedom and opportunity to make the most of their talents. Through hard work, ingenuity, thrift, and luck, most of them succeeded in realizing enough of their hopes and dreams to encourage friends and relatives to join them." (1)

2. "To Smith and Jefferson, government's role was as an umpire, not a participant." (4)

3. ". . . the Depression was widely interpreted as a failure of free market capitalism. That myth lead the public to join the intellectuals in a changed view of the relative responsibilities of individuals and the government. Emphasis on the responsibility of the individual for his own fate was replaced by emphasis on the individual as a pawn buffeted by forces beyond his control. The view that the government's role is to serve as an umpire to prevent individuals from coercing one another was replaced by the view that government's role is to serve as a parent charged with the duty of coercing some to aid others. These views have dominated developments in the United States during the past half-century." (5)

4. "Even the strongest supporters of the welfare and paternal state agree that the results have been disappointing." (5)

DOI: 10.7330/9780874219449.c013

5. "The experience of recent years—slowing growth and declining productivity—raises doubts whether private ingenuity can continue to overcome the deadening effects of government control if we continue to grant ever more power to government, to authorize a 'new class' of civil servants to spend ever larger fractions of our income supposedly on our behalf." (6)

6. ". . . there is a growing recognition of the dangers of big government." (7)

7. "The amount and kind of each resource each of us owns is partly the result of chance, partly of choice by ourselves and others. Chance determines our genes and through them affects our physical and mental capacities. Chance determines the kind of family and cultural environment into which we are born and as a result our opportunities to develop our physical and mental capacity. Chance determines also other resources we may inherit from our parents and other benefactors." (21–22)

8. "In every society, however it is organized, there is always dissatisfaction with the distribution of income. All of us find it hard to understand why we should receive less than others who seem no more deserving—or why we should be receiving more than so many others whose needs seem as great and whose deserts seem no less." (22)

## B. Key quotes from Herbert Gans's "The Uses of Poverty"

1. "Associating poverty with positive functions seems at first glance to be unimaginable." (1)

2. "Clearly, then, poverty and the poor may well satisfy a number of positive functions for many nonpoor groups in American society." (2)

3. "First, the existence of poverty ensures that society's 'dirty work' will be done." (2)

4. "Thirteenth, the role of the poor in upholding conventional norms . . . also has a significant political function. An economy based on the ideology of laissez faire requires a deprived population that is allegedly unwilling to work or that can be considered inferior because it must accept charity or welfare in order to survive. Not only does the alleged moral deviancy of the poor reduce the moral pressure on the present political economy to eliminate poverty but socialist alternatives can be made to look quite unattractive if those who will benefit most from them can be described as lazy, spendthrift, dishonest and promiscuous." (4)

5. "In sum, then, many of the functions served by the poor could be replaced if poverty were eliminated, but almost always at higher costs to others, particularly more affluent others. Consequently, a functional analysis must conclude that poverty persists not only because it fulfills a number of positive functions but also because many of the functional alternatives to poverty would be quite dysfunctional for the more affluent members of society." (6)

### C. Key quotes from John Cassidy's "Relatively Deprived"

1. "The epidemiological studies don't explain how relative deprivation damages people's health; they simply suggest that there is a connection. One possibility is that subordination leads to stress, which damages the body's immune system."

2. "Poor health may be the most dramatic consequence of relative deprivation, but there are more subtle effects as well. Although many poor families own appliances once associated with rich households, such as color televisions and dishwashers, they live in a society in which many families also possess DVD players, cell phones, desktop computers, broadband Internet connections, powerful game consoles, S.U.V.s, health-club memberships, and vacation homes. Without access to these goods, children from poor families may lack skills—such as how to surf the Web for help-wanted ads—that could enhance their prospects in the job market. In other words, relative deprivation may limit a person's capacity for social achievement. As Sen put it, 'Being relatively poor in a rich country can be a great capability handicap, even when one's absolute income is high in terms of world standards.'"

3. "Research by Tom Hertz, an economist at American University, shows that a child whose parents are in the bottom fifth of the income distribution has only a six-per-cent chance of attaining an average yearly income in the top fifth. Most people who start out relatively poor stay relatively poor."

### D. Key quotes from Dr. Martin Luther King's Nobel Lecture (December 11, 1964)

1. "Why should there be hunger and privation in any land, in any city, at any table when man has the resources and the scientific know-how to provide all mankind with the basic necessities of life?"

2. "Even deserts can be irrigated and top soil can be replaced. We cannot complain of a lack of land, for there are twenty-five million square miles of tillable land, of which we are using less than seven million. We have amazing knowledge of vitamins, nutrition, the chemistry of food, and the versatility of atoms. There is no deficit in human resources; the deficit is in human will."

3. "The well-off and the secure have too often become indifferent and oblivious to the poverty and deprivation in their midst. The poor in our countries have been shut out of our minds, and driven from the mainstream of our societies, because we have allowed them to become invisible. Just as nonviolence exposed the ugliness of racial injustice, so must the infection and sickness of poverty be exposed and healed—not only its symptoms but its basic causes. This, too, will be a fierce struggle, but we must not be afraid to pursue the remedy no matter how formidable the task."

4. "Ultimately a great nation is a compassionate nation."

5. "No individual or nation can be great if it does not have a concern for 'the least of these.' Deeply etched in the fiber of our religious tradition is the conviction that men are made in the image of God and that they are souls of infinite metaphysical value, the heirs of a legacy of dignity and worth. If we feel this as a profound moral fact, we cannot be content to see men hungry, to see men victimized with starvation and ill health when we have the means to help them. The wealthy nations must go all out to bridge the gulf between the rich minority and the poor majority."

6. "In the final analysis, the rich must not ignore the poor because both rich and poor are tied in a single garment of destiny. All life is interrelated, and all men are interdependent. The agony of the poor diminishes the rich, and the salvation of the poor enlarges the rich. We are inevitably our brothers' keeper because of the interrelated structure of reality."

# APPENDIX 4
## Sample Self-Authorship Essay

This artifact was written by Victoria, a student in my English 93 class during her first semester in college. This assignment is designed to promote listening and reflection, and is also designed with the work of Baxter Magolda in mind to help promote self-authorship. This is an element that I often build into one of my major writing assignments each semester. Victoria's essay here is in response to the "Where I Live and What I Live For" assignment that I listed in Chapter 5. Here is Victoria's essay:

### "WHERE I LIVE AND WHAT I LIVE FOR"

*Throughout my life I have seen people who seem generally happy, positive people. I have both been inspired and confused by these people. Why are they so happy? What do they have that I don't? Is it knowledge? Genetics? Or is it a choice? Even when trials come into their lives they remain calm and look on the bright side of things. They are the people who are interested in receiving advice—taking the meat and leaving the bones. These people are the ones who have lost, learned, pondered and achieved in life. They jump with confidence at any golden opportunity and let their wisdom and on-going beliefs and knowledge direct them—rather than their emotions. These people are the kinds of individuals who are interested in the things of life, and aren't afraid of change—who know who they are, where they're going and what they live for. I believe there have been these kinds of people others should look up to—the kind Shirley Jackson, David Foster Wallace, and Jonathan Haidt all describe and summarize throughout their own stories and revelations.*

> *"When you determine what you want, you have made the most important decision in your life. You have to know what you want in order to attain it"—Douglass Lourtan*

*My core values related to a lot of what Jackson, Wallace, and Haidt talk about in their writing, which I believe is to do what you love, and do it passionately. God, family, friends, my education and reaching out to help people in need all are my core values in my life, to name a few, but most important. When I read*

DOI: 10.7330/9780874219449.c014

these three authors' opinions, revelations, findings and persuasions in their pieces I find myself saying "Amen!" with them, to what they are saying that is so important and crucial in this life. One must think about where they currently are in life and where they are going. After reading these three stories I asked myself, What am I living for? What are my goals? What is my passion? New perspectives, interests and concerns have rose up inside me, and my motivation for living my life successfully has indeed grown.

"The Lottery" by Shirley Jackson struck me at first as an odd, but deep story about townspeople who were basically picking papers out of a black box. However, I believe Jackson encourages her readers to think beyond the surface of what she is really conveying to us. To understand Jackson's thought process and interpretation more effectively I asked myself, "What did this black box stand for? And why was it bad? What was the stress of this black box?

I think "The Lottery" takes place in a small town village where everyone knows each other and where gossip is found at almost every doorstep—for conversation sake and boredom. The writer seems to imply that the people of "The Lottery" seem to share the same belief system and practices in life.

The details in this story that especially lend vividness to the story are Jackson's description of the black box, and the black spot on the fatal slip of paper. "The black box grew shabbier each year; by now it was no longer completely black but splintered badly along one side to show the original wood color, and in some places faded or stained" (151). The black box to me represents the village as a whole, confusion, and pain. The community gets shabbier and more splintered as more of their family members get chosen. The black dot on the slip of paper indicated who was to get stoned in the town . . . this year. This was a tradition clearly passed down from many generations taking into consideration the conversion of wood chips to paper, and the enforcement of men picking out of the box rather than women. "The original paraphernalia for the lottery had been lost long ago and the black box now resting on the stool had been put into use even before Old Man Warner, the oldest man in town, was born" (150). If you were to ask one of these townspeople why they were even continuing this tradition and what it represented, I'm secure in saying that they couldn't tell you. These people are carrying down this un-moral tradition because it's always been practiced. Every year they lose more hope and get more work out just like the black box, but no one speaks out against the tradition or attempts to "upset it." Why live for something if you don't know what that something is or why you're doing it? Because of people's insecurity and timidness of this sacred tradition numerous people have been killed—all for what cause?

I believe Jackson is trying to convey to her readers the importance of knowing what it is you're doing in life, and to ask yourself, Are there things in my life that I'm doing that I have forgotten the meaning of? Are they worthwhile? We as *humans tend to lose sight of the truly important and crucial things in life, usually the simpler things in life. Most people tend to follow rather than lead, and before we follow anyone or anything, we should ask ourselves why and for what cause?*

*On the other spectrum, considering authors and stories, here is David Foster Wallace, everyone—a down to earth, honest, intellectual and well studied man who may indeed have some truth to what he says. Speeches are a totally different way of reaching an audience, and I believe David Foster Wallace's 2005 Kenyon College Commencement Address reached not only the class of 2005, but also readers throughout the years. Wallace uses various forms of implying to his readers that "your mind can either be your master or your servant, it depends on how you use it, and what you choose to think upon." He uses irony, humor, and honesty to convey his point clearly, with examples—such as the fish being ignorant about what he was swimming in (water).*

*Referring back to Wallace's original story of the fish in the water, you must keep reminding yourself, "this is water, this is water," revealing over and over again the truth of your mind life, and your education. So just as Wallace says, "What the hell is water anyway?" Water is the obvious, it is what surrounds you. "Probably the most dangerous things about an academic education—at least in my own case—is that it enables my tendency to over-intellectualize stuff, to get lost in abstract argument inside my head, paying attention to what is going on inside me" (4). Wallace is initially speaking of water, or we as humans look further and try to figure things out that are farther ahead than what we really need to know and pay attention to. In other words, we're trying to dig deeper and we actually need to look at what's right in front of us—the simple, current, and the* present. *Our knowledge comes from what we're doing, mistakes from where we've been, other people around us, and the hope of where we want to be. It's almost like someone keeps bending down to pick a pencil off the floor and they keep hitting their head on the desk, the pencil is on the desk . . . it never fell.*

*When Wallace refers to our "default setting" he is describing our self-centeredness as human beings, believing that each one of us in our own minds is the center of the universe and everything revolves around us. Everything a person does is seen through their eyes and perspective—from what they eat, wear, listen to, watch, and words they choose to speak, etc. "Other people's thoughts and feelings have to be communicated to you somehow, but your own are so immediate, urgent, real" (3).*

*What Wallace is saying is true when you think about it. When we are born, we are "set" into our default setting—everything is seen and experienced through ourselves. So the question is, is this wrong? And do we, as humans need to be taught how to think? I believe people do need to adjust their default settings somewhat and try to see through the lens of others and on a neutral level. Also, I think people do need to be taught how to think—to choose what* kind of knowledge to attain for themselves and what to do with the knowledge that is given to them.

I'm going to be honest with you. When Wallace began to get into the every day routine of, "an average adult day—getting up to your challenging, white-collar, college graduate job," I began to get nervous and ask myself where is he going with this? But I realized soon after how he was making a point of either thinking or living one way, by irking your way through life, or actually using your brain to your benefit showing it how to think, using the skills you've learned, and begin to be successful and happy. "This I submit is the freedom of real education, of learning how to be well-adjusted. You get to consciously decide what has meaning and what doesn't."

"You get to decide what to worship" (8). Ultimately what you decide to worship is what you decide to think upon, your knowledge. Whatever has meaning and depth to you, whatever is real and unbreakable, you can make that your number one. Whatever doesn't have meaning in this life to you—you can decide not to worship.

Although many readers may get caught up and confused with the details of Wallace's speech, I think when it comes down to it, his advice goes as far as thinking about what you're currently doing (just as Jackson encourages), to figure out who you are in this big pool of water, and to make your own choices based on the life you want to lead. A life that is going to lead to success, happiness, and wisdom.

Along with Jackson and Wallace, Haidt recognizes the importance of a person's direction in life, knowledge, and happiness. Inside this book you find explanations for being internally happy. Yes internally happy. The difference between letting your surroundings and circumstances determine your happiness, or deciding to be happy from within, which will later affect those circumstances, for good.

Haidt used imagery, quotes, and lots of evidence to explain inner happiness with one's self. Haidt refers to human beings like hamsters on a wheel saying, "Always wanting more than we have, we run and run and run, like hamsters on a wheel." Haidt's statement to me is very true, though it may be harsh to some. An example of wanting more refers back to Haidt's earlier example of a king in Jerusalem who basically had everything he could ever want or need, but still he was not happy with the "abundance" of his life.

An example that has stood throughout time that I often see is when single people say they'll only be happy when they get married, then when they are married they only want children; when they have children they can't wait for them to leave the nest, and so on. These are all awesome and natural things to desire but I think Haidt is trying to get the point across that if it was internal happiness to begin with we could equally enjoy every blessing and positive thing that came our way. Even though it is hard to practice, enjoying what you have in front of you at *the moment is key to living life happily. If you always wish for more, you'll never be satisfied with what you have.*

*Do you think one can achieve happiness through a formula? Well, Haidt does. Does H = S + C +V really lead people to genuine happiness within themselves? "One of the most important ideas in positive psychology is what Lyubomirsky, Sheldon, Schkade and Seligman call the happiness formula. H is the level of happiness that you can actually experience. It is determined by your biological set point (S) plus the conditions of your life (C) plus the voluntary activities (V) you do." The conditions of your lifestyle can be altered as well as the voluntary activities that you choose to do. Haidt seems to believe that if your biological set point, you're fully supplied with everything you need including food, shelter and clothing, and you have some attachments to other people (social) are met, it is within your grasp to receive and choose complete and effortless happiness for life.*

*All three pieces have very similar persuasions and thoughts, to enlighten their readers about living a happy and successful life. Jackson, Wallace, and Haidt all question their readers, "Where are you? And what are you living for?" When reading each story consecutively I began to realize the significance of what each author was "speaking about" in their writing, underneath the surface and on top. "The Lottery," David Foster Wallace's Commencement Speech, and The Happiness Hypothesis" are all tied together with a great big knot—knowing what you're doing in life, where you're heading, and what you're living for. Ultimately, the happiness you can attain through basic need and a* well-adjusted lens.

## DISCUSSION

One of Victoria's strengths as a writer, it seems to me, is her ability to listen. I think we see significant evidence of that skill in this essay. She uses quotes effectively and thoughtfully, and she appears to be working in good faith to engage the ideas she finds in these readings. She also exhibits patience with the readings, and doesn't appear to be in any rush to declare definitively on the complex questions these readings invite students to consider. Although "The Lottery" seems to puzzle her a bit, I see her patiently attempting to piece together data from the story, much like a detective, alert to important clues and details—precisely what we want student readers to be doing. I think we see this at play, for example, as she attempts to puzzle out the meaning of "the black box." Note here her patience and attention to detail:

> The details in this story that especially lend vividness to the story are
> Jackson's description of the black box, and the black spot on the fatal slip
> of paper. "The black box grew shabbier each year; by now it was no longer
> completely black but splintered badly along one side to show the original

wood color, and in some places faded or stained' (151). The black box to me represents the village as a whole, confusion, and pain. The community gets shabbier and more splintered as more of their family members get chosen. The black dot on the slip of paper indicated who was to get stoned in the town . . . this year. This was a tradition clearly passed down from many generations taking into consideration the conversion of wood chips to paper, and the enforcement of men picking out of the box rather than women.

This is a habit of mind and a quality of her writing practice that we see manifest throughout Victoria's essay. In an argumentative essay, of course, declaring definitively on complex questions would be a required move, as Graff and Birkenstein might say. It is my suggestion here, however, that such moves shortcut and work actively against careful reading and thinking. In some ways, Victoria is still an emerging writer, but I think this curricular focus on listening has provided her with an important opportunity to engage these readings thoughtfully and to proceed as a writer with caution, balance, and restraint—all essential hallmarks of good reading, writing, and thinking.

Victoria appears to be on surer ground when she turns her attention to Wallace, and I think she gets to the heart of the Wallace piece effectively here: "Wallace uses various forms of implying to his readers that 'your mind can either be your master or your servant, it depends on how you use it, and what you choose to think upon.' He uses irony, humor, and honesty to convey his point clearly, with examples—such as the fish being ignorant about what he was swimming in (water)."

She clearly understands the operative metaphor of "water" that Wallace is using, and I think we see her engaging this metaphor thoughtfully as she discusses it:

> So just as Wallace says, "What the hell is water anyway?" Water is the obvious, it is what surrounds you. "Probably the most dangerous things about an academic education—at least in my own case—is that it enables my tendency to over-intellectualize stuff, to get lost in abstract argument inside my head, paying attention to what is going on inside me" (4). Wallace is initially speaking of water, these fish, or we as humans look further and try to figure things out that are farther ahead than what we really need to know and pay attention to. In other words, we're trying to dig deeper and actually need to look at what's right in front of us—the simple, current, and *the present*.

The use of italics here to emphasize an important idea is noteworthy, it seems to me, and suggests a mature level of engagement and sophistication. Clearly, this writer is attempting to carefully engage and think through Wallace's ideas.

I also think Victoria summarizes some of the major ideas in the Wallace piece effectively, and she also has a nice metacognitive moment here:

> What Wallace is saying is true when you think about it. When we are born, we are "set" into our default setting—everything is seen and experienced through ourselves. So the question is, is this wrong? And do we, as humans need to be taught how to think? I believe people do need to adjust their default settings somewhat and try to see through the lens of others and on a neutral level. Also, I think people do need to be taught how to think—to choose what kind of knowledge to attain for themselves and what to do with the knowledge that is given to them.

This is precisely the kind of "thinking about thinking" that learning theorists suggest is a hallmark of higher order cognitive development. I designed this unit to promote this kind of development, and I think we see this student writer beginning to respond in appropriate ways to that important challenge.

Victoria also creates her own metaphor here to comment on one of Wallace's key ideas. Here she is purposefully and skillfully echoing one of Wallace's central tropes (a metaphor related to "water") and making her point in much the way Wallace himself does: "Our knowledge comes from what we're doing, mistakes from where we've been, other people around us, and the hope of where we want to be. It's almost like someone keeps bending down to pick a pencil off the floor and they keep hitting their head on the desk, the pencil is on the desk . . . it never fell." As a teacher, I loved seeing this.

I think Victoria also uses quotes effectively. I was particularly impressed, for example, with this section of her essay:

> But I realized soon after how he was making a point of either thinking or living one way, by irking your way through life, or actually using your brain to your benefit showing it how to think, using the skills you've learned, and begin to be successful and happy. "This I submit is the freedom of real education, of learning how to be well-adjusted. You get to consciously decide what has meaning and what doesn't."

I think we also see expressed here an emerging sense of provisionality and interminancy. Two instances of this are these comments about the chapters from Haidt's book, *The Happiness Hypothesis*:

> 1. "Haidt used imagery, quotes, and lots of evidence to explain inner happiness with one's self. Haidt refers to human beings like hamsters on a wheel saying, 'Always wanting more than we have, we run and run and run, like hamsters on a wheel.' Haidt's statement to me is very true, though it may be harsh to some."

2. "Haidt makes some important distinctions here regarding conditions, distinguishing between conditions that are not within our control and those that are."

Overall, there is more complexity that Victoria might have opened up here, but I am nonetheless happy to see her responding to the readings attentively and engaging the ideas patiently and thoughtfully.

Finally, we should note that there are many kinds of personal writing, and it seems to me that writing assignments can legitimately and productively seek to affirm both "an expressivist, autobiographical self whose autonomy creates coherence out of inchoate experience and a socially constructed self who is always already constrained by the conventions of discourse" (Hindeman 2001, 89). I think we see that dynamic at play in this essay in positive ways. For example, there are a number of places in this essay where Victoria turns *toward* the relation of the individual to the social world, and begins to posit an *historically- and locally-contingent sense of self.* A number of comments within her essay make that clear:

- The black dot on the slip of paper indicated who was to get stoned in the town . . . this year. This was a tradition clearly passed down from many generations taking into consideration the conversion of wood chips to paper, and the enforcement of men picking out of the box rather than women. "The original paraphernalia for the lottery had been lost long ago and the black box now resting on the stool had been put into use even before Old Man Warner, the oldest man in town, was born" (150). If you were to ask one of these townspeople why there were even continuing this tradition and what it represented, I'm secure in saying that they couldn't tell you. These people are carrying down this un-moral tradition because it's always been practiced. Every year they lose more hope and get more work out just like the black box, but no one speaks out against the tradition or attempts to "upset it." Why live for something if you don't know what that something is or why you're doing it?

- I believe people do need to adjust their default settings somewhat and try to see through the lens of others and on a neutral level.

I think we see evidence here that Victoria is beginning to see the world in a way that "assumes complexity as a general state." This assignment was designed to encourage that development.

# APPENDIX 5
## Sample First-Year Composition *"Patterns of Culture"* Essay

This artifact was authored by Robert, a student in my FYC class in 2012. As I hope readers will see, this is a very "mindful" essay. We see manifestations of flexibility, an embrace of "creative uncertainty" as a way to "stay open to experience," creation of new categories ("once distinctions are created, they take on a life of their own" [Langer 1989,11]), openness to new information, and awareness of more than one perspective.

Here is the assignment Robert is responding to:

### Patterns of Culture

*For this unit, we will be reading the first chapter from a classic book about culture by Ruth Benedict, Patterns of Culture. In this famous book, Benedict defines what culture is and how it works. She has a number of fascinating things to say about culture, including this: "The life history of the individual is first and foremost an accommodation to the patterns and standards traditionally handed down in his community" (2–3). For this project, we will be exploring this fascinating claim.*

*The remaining chapters of Benedict's book are case studies of widely different cultures. We will be reading our own case study—a sociological study of women living in a poor community in Philadelphia conducted by Kathryn Edin and Maria Kefalas. They report what they learned from this work in their widely-acclaimed book, Promises I Can Keep. We will be using Benedict's ideas as we read Edin and Kefalas to see what we can learn about the way culture works from this case study and to see if Benedict's many claims about culture are, indeed, valid.*

*I would like the focus of your essay to be on "listening" to these writers and then reflecting on what they have to tell us, rather than on formulating a thesis and supporting it.*

*You may organize your essay in response to these readings however you wish, and you are invited to discuss any issues in these readings that you think are important. Feel free to be creative, use personal experience and observation, etc. Essays should be at least 1500 words in length. Please quote at least twice from*

DOI: 10.7330/9780874219449.c015

*each of these readings in your essay, and please use MLA format to document your sources.*

Here is Robert's essay:

## Blurred by Our Own Realities

*What is reality? Is it possible that "reality" may be in the eye of the beholder? Someone that once acted as a mentor to me would say that "perception is reality." What he meant was that if someone perceives things to be a certain way, to them, that is "their" reality. As anthropologist Ruth Benedict says in her book Patterns of Culture, " . . . we must live within the framework of mine and thine that our own culture institutionalizes" (10). Could it be, though, that our own realities sometimes keep us from seeing things as they truly are, versus how we may perceive them to be? Unfortunately, I think that more often than not, this is the case. As Benedict noted "No man ever looks at the world with pristine eyes. He sees it edited by a definite set of customs and institutions and ways of thinking" (2). For all of us as humans to live in a world of peace and understanding with each other, we need to remove the veil of perceptive reality to see things as clearly as possible. "But we have failed to understand the relativity of cultural habits, and we remain debarred from much profit and enjoyment in our human relations with peoples of different standards, and untrustworthy in our dealings with them" (Benedict 11).*

*In order for us to see things clearly, I think it is first important to understand what it might be that prevents us from doing so in the first place. Why do we develop these different realities within the same world? "The life history of the individual is first and foremost an accommodation to the patterns and standards handed down in his community" (Benedict 2). Within different communities of people, there is a prevailing culture that typically forces us to see things in a particular way. "It is the old distinction of the in-group and the out-group . . ." (Benedict 10). Our culture has developed within each of us a belief system of what may be considered proper and what is not. In order for us to see things clearly with "pristine" eyes, we must be conscious of the altered perceptions our own cultures (as well as the cultures of others) have created. "There has never been a time when civilization stood more in need of individuals who are genuinely culture-conscious, who can see objectively the socially conditioned behavior of other peoples without fear and recrimination" (Benedict 10).*

*The cultural conditioning of each person ultimately leads them to do things which others, with a different set of cultural conditioning, may not be able to understand or empathize with. It is precisely this lack of understanding that leaves us in a world of wars and conflict, ultimately preventing us from living in our ideal world of compassion and understanding. Specifically, in our nation, it would seem that this problem could be more prevalent than anywhere else on earth. Over time we have developed a belief system founded on the idea that our way is the best and perhaps only way. A problem that is reflected by our own imperialistic government and general ignorance to other cultures of the world. We police the world, in the name of justice, forcing many of our own ideas and beliefs onto other people. Even right now as I write, within our nation, people are strongly divided by profoundly differing political perspectives and class wars. These divides are mostly the result of a failure to see things from others' perspectives. As author Harper Lee wrote "You never really understand a person until you consider things from his point of view."*

*Cultural differences don't just vary by geography, race, and demographics, they also vary across time. As Benedict observes, "when we look back even a generation we realize the extent to which revision has taken place, sometimes in our most intimate behavior" (10). There are many examples of cultural changes over time, but few that serve as prime an example as non-marital childbirth. Fittingly, this is where we have chosen to test our theory of Benedict's claim that we see things "edited by a definite set of customs and institutions and ways of thinking" (2).*

*Despite the fact that I myself am a white, middle-aged, middle-class male, exploring the issues of poor single mothers within impoverished inner city areas did not leave me short of emotionally charged opinions on the matter. After all, everything I have learned and observed within my own culture has embedded the dangers of parenting children at a young age, especially outside of a sound marital structure. The significant danger of opportunity costs in prolonging or stopping school, limited career paths due to the intense commitments of raising another person, etc. All of which has led me to view their situation from what Edin and Kefalas term a "privileged vantage point" (48). In this context, the intense emotional opinions (which appear to me more like common knowledge) serve only to further confuse my understanding of how these young women could possibly make such foolish decisions. "From this privileged vantage point, a disadvantaged young woman's willingness to bear a child well before she is of legal age is beyond comprehension" (Edin and Kefalas 48).*

*In their study, Edin and Kefalas related much of the reasoning and acceptance for the actions of these young single mothers to cultural differences. However, the follow-up question is what specifically within their culture was the direct cause for the trends. As with many complex societal issues there were a number of variables that ultimately influenced such decisions. However, the authors find a couple of key reasons which had been created by their economic conditions and social standing. The first reasoning was what the authors termed "relational poverty" or a lack of trusting, well established relationships. This was what ultimately led to a desire or "hunger" to be loved. As the authors observed, "Young women also hunger for the love and intimacy they can provide . . . pregnancy offers the promise of relational intimacy at a time few other emotional resources are available" (Edin and Kefalas 34). The other main reason for these decisions comes from a lack of opportunity cost. When a middle-class teen gets pregnant, she typically realizes the opportunity cost of giving up a college education and successful career, but when a poor young woman gets pregnant she sees many of those things as little more than a distant dream. She views her odds of having that life path as others may view winning the lottery (Edin and Kefalas 48).*

*Of course the aforementioned was reason enough for me to empathize with their decisions given their conditions. However, I really wasn't truly convinced and still felt as though these women were making foolish decisions (even if maybe they just didn't know any better). The real wrench in my own effort to break through my bias came later in their conclusive findings when the authors seemed to cleverly try and slide in this observation:*

> *This is not to say that the poor believe having children outside of marriage is the right way, or even the best way, to go about things—more than eight in ten tell survey researchers they believe that people who want children should get married first. They are also even more likely than those in the middle class to say they believe that a child raised by two parents is better off than a child reared by one. Their responses show that poor mothers also believe that children born and raised within marital unions generally do better than those who are not. (Edin and Kefalas 208)*

*I must've read this passage 15 times. I was so emotionally charged over the irony of why they would continue to have children outside of marriage with partners who are so unlikely to stay. I couldn't believe that the authors had the nerve to put this paragraph of text in their book without a very convincing explanation for why these women hypocritically go against precisely those things they believe to be so important. Then I realized that in my dazed raging fit of madness, I had highlighted the above passage so darkly I didn't notice the reasoning and explanation that immediately followed which ultimately provided me with the mother of all epiphanies:*

> *However, these abstractions are largely irrelevant to their lives. Poor women must calculate the potential risks and rewards of the actual partnerships available to them and, given their uncertain future prospects, take a "wait and see" attitude toward the relationships with the men who father their children. From their point of view, this approach makes enormous sense, as the men in the neighborhood partner pool—the only men they can reasonably attract, given their own disadvantaged place in the marriage market—are of fairly uniformly low quality. How does a poor woman like Deena sort the losers from the winners except by relying on the test of time? How else can she know which one her new boyfriend Sean will prove to be?" (Edin and Kefalas 208–9)*

*So, in all of my raging emotional confusion, I simply never bothered to consider the simplest explanation of all for why this whole poor single women childrearing trend may be materializing in the first place; they have no choice. Rather than soil the sanctity of marriage by rolling the dice with less than quality partners who are seldom employed and often involved with drinking, drugs, infidelity, etc. . . . These women simply choose the most accessible, realistic purpose creating path before them (motherhood) in spite of the lack of quality partners available to them. Then they simply elect a "wait and see" approach to determine if their John Doe is equally fit for the task of being a reliable, loving parent and spouse. Alas!!!*

*The previous reactionary roller coaster to the studies of Edin and Kefalas acts as a great example of the struggling and frustration I encountered when trying to see things clearly from someone else's perspective. It's one thing to theoretically discuss putting aside our preconceived notions and beliefs but entirely a different endeavor when we set out to actually do so. Conclusively, in my own experiment to test Benedict's claim, that each of us views the world through our own filtered lens, proved to be truer than I originally had expected. This lesson has taught me that being conscious of our own biases and views of the world allows us to begin to see things from others' perspectives. However, the deep, embedded nature of some of our beliefs makes the task of actually placing ourselves in others shoes figuratively, much more difficult a task then it may appear. The only way to realize the full benefits of seeing things from another's perspective is through a genuine effort to seek to understand and reflectively analyze things from a completely different approach than we may normally use. That being said, as demonstrated by my own efforts, determination and a genuine investment in truly trying to see things from someone else's perspective can lead to enlightenment and a better understanding of the world in which we live.*

## WORKS CITED

Benedict, Ruth. [1934] 2005. Patterns of Culture. New York: First Mariner Books. Print.

Edin, Kathryn, and Maria Kefalas. 2005. Promises I Can Keep. Los Angeles: University of California Press. Print.

# ACKNOWLEDGMENTS

There are few things that we say to one another over the course of a lifetime more important than "thank you." There is great power and magic in these words. So it is with sincere gratitude that I offer these brief words of thanks to the people who helped make this book possible.

My heartfelt thanks to my great editor, Michael Spooner, and the editorial staff at Utah State University Press. My deep thanks to the anonymous field reviewers at USUP. Your detailed responses to various drafts of this book have made it what it is.

My colleagues at Manchester Community College, where I have taught writing now for over twenty-five years, especially my good friends in the English Department, who make it a pleasure to come to work each day. Thank you, David, Kathy, Lois Coleman, Jeanine, Mariana, Michael, Kaarina, James, Kim, Wanda, Diana, Ken, Donna, Tanya, Lois Ryan, Gail, Steve, Rae, Linsey, Alina, Lisa, Andrew, and Steven.

Our remarkable college president, Gena Glickman. My good friends Andrew Paterna, Grace Talaga, George Ducharme, Pat Beeman, Deborah Simmons, David Nielsen, Duncan Harris, Bettylou Sandy, Brenda St. Peter, Julie and Wes Larkin, Michelle and Jeanne Nickerson, Kwan Jang Nim Bogdanski, Sa Bom Nim Duethorn, and Griz.

My grand old friends and extended family, Dan, Dennis, and Molly.

My great teachers at Mohegan Community College in Norwich, Connecticut, where this journey began many lifetimes ago: John Basinger, Jim Coleman, Jim Wright, and John Perch.

My friend and frequent collaborator, Howard Tinberg.

My friends and colleagues in the profession and at NCTE and TYCA, including Sheridan Blau, Jeff Sommers, Mark Reynolds, Kathi Yancey, John Schilb, Ed White, John Pekins, Muriel Harris, Cheryl Hogue Smith, David Jolliffe, Holly Hassel, Kelly Ritter, Leslie Roberts, Jody Millward, Sterling Warner, Lois Powers, Lawrence McDoniel, Joanne Giordano, Jeffrey Klausman, Frost McLaughlin, Miriam Moore, Yufeng Zhang, Mike Rose, Christie Toth, and Christine Vassett. A special thanks to Kurt Austin at NCTE for believing in that first book, *What Is "College-Level" Writing?*

My students, of course, especially my English 93 students, who have taught me so much. All the great student leaders I've had the privilege of working with as an advisor to our college's chapter of Phi Theta Kappa, the international honor society for community, junior, and technical colleges.

And to the people who I have lost who would have been delighted by this book. These include my wonderful father and mother, Donald and Barbara Sullivan. And my life-long mentor, Victor Kaplan, a writer and professor at Eastern Connecticut State University, who taught me how to write.

And finally my wife, Susan, and my children, Bonnie Rose and Nicholas, without whom none of this would have been possible.

# REFERENCES

Achieve, Inc. 2007a. *Aligned Expectations? A Closer Look at College Admissions and Placement Tests.* Washington, DC: Achieve.

Achieve, Inc. 2007b. *Closing the Expectations Gap 2007: An Annual 50-State Progress Report on the Alignment of High School Policies with the Demands of College and Work.* Washington, DC: Achieve.

Achieve, Inc. 2013. *Closing the Expectations Gap 2013: An Annual 50-State Progress Report on the Alignment of High School Policies with the Demands of College and Work.* Washington, DC: Achieve.

Ambrose, Susan A., Michael Bridges, Michele DiPietro, Marsha Lovett, and Marie Norman. 2010. *How Learning Works: Seven Research-Based Principles for Smart Teaching.* San Francisco: Jossey-Bass.

American College Testing Program [ACT]. 2006. *Reading between the Lines: What the ACT Reveals about College Readiness in Reading.* Iowa City: ACT.

American College Testing Program [ACT]. 2010. *The Condition of College and Career Readiness 2010.* Iowa City: ACT.

Anderman, Eric M., and Lynley Hicks Anderman. 2010. *Classroom Motivation.* Upper Saddle River, NJ: Pearson.

Association of American Colleges and Universities. 2007. *College Learning for the New Global Century.* Washington, DC: AAC&U.

Astin, Alexander. 1997. *What Matters in College? Four Critical Years Revisited.* San Francisco: Jossey-Bass.

Astin, Alexander. 1997. "Liberal Education and Democracy: The Case for Pragmatism." In *Education and Democracy: Re-Imagining Liberal Learning in America,* ed. Robert Orrill, 207–24. New York: College Board.

Atwell, Nancie. 1998. *In the Middle.* 2nd ed. Portsmouth, NH: Boynton Cook.

Atwell, Nancie. 2007. *The Reading Zone.* New York: Scholastic.

Bain, Ken. 2004. *What the Best College Teachers Do.* Cambridge, MA: Harvard University Press.

Banchero, Stephanie. 2010. "Scores Stagnate at High Schools." *The Wall Street Journal,* August 16.

Bandura, Albert. 1997. *Self-Efficacy: The Exercise of Control.* New York: Worth.

Bargh, John. 1997. "The Automaticity of Everyday Life." In *The Automaticity of Everyday Life: Advances in Social Cognition,* vol. 10. ed. R. S. Wyer, Jr., 1–61. Mahwah, NJ: Lawrence Erlbaum Associates.

Bargh, John, and T. L. Chartrand. 1999. "The Unbearable Automaticity of Being." *American Psychologist* 54 (7): 462–79. http://dx.doi.org/10.1037/0003-066X.54.7.462.

Bartholomae, David, and Anthony Petrosky, eds. 2005. *Ways of Reading.* 7th ed. Boston: Bedford St. Martin's.

Baxter Magolda, Marcia. 1992. *Knowing and Reasoning in College: Gender-Related Patterns in Students' Intellectual Development.* San Francisco: Jossey-Bass.

Baxter Magolda, Marcia. 2001. *Making Their Own Way: Narratives for Transforming Higher Education to Promote Self-Development.* Sterling, VA: Stylus.

Bazerman, Charles. 1988. *Shaping Written Knowledge: The Genre and Activity of the Experimental Article in Science.* Madison: University of Wisconsin Press.

DOI: 10.7330/9780874219449.c016

Bean, John C. 2011. *Engaging Ideas: The Professor's Guide to Integrating Writing, Critical Thinking, and Active Learning in the Classroom.* 2nd ed. San Francisco: Jossey-Bass.

Beaufort, Anne. 2007. *College Writing and Beyond: A New Framework for University Writing Instruction.* Logan: Utah State University Press.

Belanoff, Pat. 2001. "Silence: Reflection, Literacy, Learning, and Teaching." *College Composition and Communication* 52 (3): 399–428.

Belenky, Mary, Blythe Clinchy, Nancy Goldberger, and Jill Tarule. 1997. *Women's Ways of Knowing: The Development of Self, Voice, and Mind.* 10th anniversary ed. New York: Basic.

Benedict, Ruth. (Original work published 1934) 2005. *Patterns of Culture.* Boston: Houghton Mifflin.

Bereiter, Carl. 1995. "A Dispositional View of Transfer." In *Teaching for Transfer: Fostering Generalization in Learning*, ed. Anne McKeough, Judy Lupart, and Anthony Marini, 21–34. Mahwah, NJ: Erlbaum.

Berlin, James. 1982. "Contemporary Composition: The Major Pedagogical Theories." *College English* 44 (8): 765–77. http://dx.doi.org/10.2307/377329.

Berlin, James. 1987. *Rhetoric and Reality: Writing Instruction in American Colleges, 1900–1985.* Carbondale: Southern Illinois University Press.

Berlin, James. 2005. "Rhetoric and Ideology in the Writing Class." In *Teaching Composition: Background Readings*, 2nd ed., ed. T. R. Johnson, 19–38. Boston: Bedford St. Martin's.

Bernard-Donals, Michael, Lee Ann Carroll, and Doug Hunt. 2004. "Truth and Method: What Goes On in Writing Classes, and How Do We Know?" *College English* 66 (3): 335–43. http://dx.doi.org/10.2307/4140752.

Berthoff, Ann. 1981. "Learning the Uses of Chaos." In *The Making of Meaning: Metaphors, Models and Maxims for Writing Teachers*, 68–72. Portsmouth, NH: Heinemann.

Bizzell, Patricia. 1984. "William Perry and Liberal Education." In *Academic Discourse and Critical Consciousness*, 153–63. Pittsburgh: University of Pittsburgh Press.

Bizzell, Patricia. 1986. "What Happens When Basic Writers Come to College?" *College Composition and Communication* 37: 294–301.

Blackwell, Lisa, Kali Trzesniewski, and Carol Sorich Dweck. 2007. "Implicit Theories of Intelligence Predict Achievement Across an Adolescent Transition: A Longitudinal Study and an Intervention." *Child Development* 78 (1): 246–63. http://dx.doi.org/10.1111/j.1467-8624.2007.00995.x.

Bloom, Lynne Z. 1999. "The Essay Canon." *College English* 61 (4): 401–30. http://dx.doi.org/10.2307/378920.

Board of Directors of the Association of American Colleges and Universities. 2004. *Our Students' Best Work: A Framework for Accountability Worthy of Our Mission.* Washington, DC: AACU.

Bowen, William, Martin Kurzweil, and Eugene Tobin. 2005. *Equity and Excellence in American Higher Education.* Charlottesville: University of Virginia Press.

Brand, Alice. 1987. "The Why of Cognition: Emotion and the Writing Process." *College Composition and Communication* 38 (4): 436–43.

Bransford, John. D., Ann L. Brown, and Rodney R. Cocking, eds. 2000. *How People Learn: Brain, Mind, Experience, and School.* Washington, DC: National Academy Press.

Breneman, D. W., and W. N. Haarlow. 1998. "Remediation in Higher Education: A Symposium Featuring Remedial Education: Costs and Consequences." *Fordham Report* 2 (9): 1–22.

Brent, Doug. 1998. "Rogerian Rhetoric." In *Theorizing Composition: A Critical Sourcebook of Theory and Scholarship in Contemporary Composition Studies*, ed. Mary Kennedy, 263–65. Westport, CT: Greenwood.

Brent, Doug. 2012. "Crossing Boundaries: Co-op Students Relearning to Write." *College Composition and Communication* 63 (4): 558–92.

Brodkey, Linda. 1995. "Writing Permitted in Designated Areas Only." In *Higher Education Under Fire*, ed. Michael Berube and Cary Nelson, 214–37. New York: Routledge.

Bruffee, Kenneth. 1984. "Collaborative Learning and the Conversation of Mankind." *College English* 46 (7): 635–52. http://dx.doi.org/10.2307/376924.

Bruffee, Kenneth. 1999. *Collaborative Learning: Higher Education, Interdependence, and the Authority of Knowledge.* 2nd ed. Baltimore: John Hopkins University Press.

Burnham, Christopher. 1986. "The Perry Scheme and the Teaching of Writing." *Rhetoric Review* 4 (2): 152–58. http://dx.doi.org/10.1080/07350198609359117.

Burnham, Christopher. 1992. "Crumbling Metaphors: Integrating Heart and Brain through Structured Journals." *College Composition and Communication* 43 (4): 508–18.

Caldwell, David, Jeanine DeRusha, Gail Stanton-Hammond, Steve Straight, and Patrick Sullivan. 2011. "An Outcomes Assessment Project: Basic Writing and Essay Structure." *TETYC* 38 (4): 365–78.

Capossela, Toni-Lee, ed. 1993. *The Critical Writing Workshop: Designing Writing Assignments to Foster Critical Thinking.* Portsmouth, NH: Boynton Cook.

Carter, Michael. 1990. "The Idea of Expertise: An Exploration of Cognitive and Social Dimensions of Writing." *College Composition and Communication* 41 (3): 265–86.

Clinchy, Blythe McVicker. 2000. "Toward a More Connected Vision of Higher Education." In *Teaching to Promote Intellectual and Personal Maturity: Incorporating Students' Worldviews and Identities into the Learning Process,* edited by Marcia Baxter Magolda, 27–35. San Francisco: Jossey-Bass.

Code, Lorraine. 1991. *What Can She Know? Feminist Theory and the Construction of Knowledge.* Ithaca, NY: Cornell University Press.

Common Core State Standards Initiative. 2010. *Common Core State Standards for English Language Arts & Literacy in History/Social Studies, Science, and Technical Subjects.* Washington, DC: National Governors Association and Council of Chief State School Officers.

Colvin, Geoff. 2008. *Talent in Overrated.* New York: Penguin.

Costa, Arthur L., and Bena Kallick, eds. 2008. *Learning and Leading with Habits of Mind.* Alexandria: Association for Supervision and Curriculum Development.

Costa, Arthur L., and Bena Kallick, eds. 2009. *Habits of Mind across the Curriculum: Practical and Creative Strategies for Teachers.* Alexandria: Association for Supervision and Curriculum Development.

Costa, Arthur L., and Bena Kallick. 2013. *Dispositions: Reframing Teaching and Learning.* Thousand Oaks: Corwin.

Council of Writing Program Administrators. 2000. *WPA Outcomes Statement for First-Year Composition.* Council of Writing Programs Administrators.

Council of Writing Program Administrators. 2011. *Framework for Success in Post-Secondary Writing.* Urbana, IL: National Council of Teachers of English, and National Writing Project.

Covey, Stephen. 1990. *The 7 Habits of Highly Effective People.* New York: Simon and Schuster.

Csikszentmihalyi, Mihaly. 1996. *Creativity: Flow and the Psychology of Discovery and Invention.* New York: Harper Collins.

Curtis, Marcia, and Anne Herrington. 2003. "Writing Development in the College Years: By Whose Definition?" *College Composition and Communication* 55 (1): 69–90.

Damasio, Antonio R. 1994. *Descartes' Error: Emotion, Reason, and the Human Brain.* New York: Penguin.

Damasio, Antonio R. 2003. *Looking for Spinoza: Joy, Sorrow, and the Feeling Brain.* New York: Harcourt.

Darling-Hammond, Linda. 2010. *The Flat World and Education: How America's Commitment to Equity Will Determine Our Future.* New York: Teachers College Press.

Davidson, Richard, and Anne Harrington, eds. 2001. *Visions of Compassion: Western Scientists and Tibetan Buddhists Examine Human Nature.* New York: Oxford University Press.

DeBenedictus, Deb. 2007. "Sustained Silent Reading: Making Adaptations." *Voices from the Middle* 14 (3): 29–37.

Deci, Edward L., and Richard Flaste. 1996. *Why We Do What We Do: Understanding Self-Motivation.* New York: Penguin.

Deci, Edward L., Richard Koestner, and Richard M. Ryan. 1999. "A Meta-Analytic Review of Experiments Examining the Effects of Extrinsic Rewards on Intrinsic Motivation." *Psychological Bulletin* 125 (6): 627–68. http://dx.doi.org/10.1037/0033-2909.125.6.627.

Deci, Edward L., and Richard M. Ryan. 1985. *Intrinsic Motivation and Self-Determination in Human Behavior.* New York: Plenum.

Deci, Edward L., and Richard M. Ryan, eds. 2005. *Handbook of Self-Determination Research.* Rochester, NY: University of Rochester Press.

Dewey, John. 1997. *How We Think.* Mineola: Dover.

Doidge, Norman. 2007. *The Brain That Changes Itself.* New York: Penguin.

Doskoch, Peter. 2005. "The Winning Edge." *Psychology Today* (Nov/Dec).

Dreyfus, Stuart E., and Hubert Dreyfus. 1980. *A Five-Stage Model of the Mental Activities Involved in Directed Skill Acquisition.* Washington, DC: Storming Media; http://www.dtic.mil/cgi-bin/GetTRDoc?AD=ADA084551&Location=U2&doc=GetTRDoc.pdf. Accessed August 24, 2012.

Dreyfus, Stuart E., and Hubert Dreyfus. 1992. *Mind over Machine.* New York: Free Press.

Duckworth, Angela Lee, and Lauren Eskreis-Winkler. 2013. "True Grit." *Observer* 26 (4).

Duckworth, Angela, Christopher Peterson, Michael Matthews, and Dennis Kelly. 2007. "Grit: Perseverance and Passion for Long-Term Goals." *Journal of Personality and Social Psychology* 92 (6): 1087–101. http://dx.doi.org/10.1037/0022-3514.92.6.1087.

Duckworth, Angela, and Martin E.P. Seligman. 2005. "Self-discipline Outdoes IQ in Predicting Academic Performance of Adolescents." *Psychological Science* 16 (12): 939–44. http://dx.doi.org/10.1111/j.1467-9280.2005.01641.x.

Duncan, Greg J., and Richard J. Murnane, eds. 2011. *Whither Opportunity? Rising Inequality, Schools, and Children's Life Chances.* New York: Russell Sage.

Dweck, Carol. 2007. *Mindset: The New Psychology of Success.* New York: Ballantine.

Eisner, Elliot W. 2004. *The Arts and the Creation of Mind.* New Haven, CT: Yale University Press.

Elbow, Peter. 1973. *Writing Without Teachers.* New York: Oxford University Press.

Elbow, Peter. 1996. "Writing Assessment in the 21st Century: A Utopian View." In *Composition in the Twenty-First Century: Crisis and Change,* ed. Lynn Z. Bloom, Donald A. Daiker, and Edward M. White, 83–100. Carbondale: Southern Illinois University Press.

Elbow, Peter. 2008. "Coming to See Myself as a Vernacular Intellectual: Remarks at the 2007 CCCC General Session on Receiving the Exemplar Award." *College Composition and Communication* 59 (3): 519–24.

Elbow, Peter. 2012. *Vernacular Eloquence: What Speech Can Bring to Writing.* New York: Oxford University Press.

Elliot, Andrew J., and Carol Dweck. 2007. *The Handbook of Competence and Motivation.* New York: Guilford.

Engle, Randi A., Diane P. Lam, Xenia S. Meyer, and Sarah E. Nix. 2012. "How Does Expansive Framing Promote Transfer? Several Proposed Explanations and a Research Agenda for Investigating Them." *Educational Psychologist* 47 (3): 215–31. http://dx.doi.org/10.1080/00461520.2012.695678.

Engle, Randi A., Phi D. Nguyen, and Adam Mendelson. 2011. "The Influence of Framing on Transfer: Initial Evidence from a Tutoring Experiment." *Instructional Science* 39 (5): 603–28. http://dx.doi.org/10.1007/s11251-010-9145-2.

Eubanks, Philip, and John D. Schaeffer. 2008. "A Kind Word for Bullshit: The Problem of Academic Writing." *College Composition and Communication* 59 (3): 372–88.

Evans, Nancy, Deanna S. Forney, and Florence Guido-DiBrito. 1998. *Student Development in College: Theory, Research, and Practice.* San Francisco: Jossey-Bass.

Facione, Peter. 1990. "Critical Thinking: A Statement of Expert Consensus for Purposes of Educational Assessment and Instruction." [The Delphi Report Executive

Summary: Research Findings and Recommendations Prepared for the Committee on Pre-College Philosophy of the American Philosophical Association.] (ERIC Document Reproduction Service No. ED315423).

Facione, Peter, Carol Giancarlo, Noreen Facione, and Joanne Gainen. 1995. "The Disposition Toward Critical Thinking." *Journal of General Education* 44 (1): 1–25.

Faigley, Lester. 1986. "Competing Theories of Process: A Critique and a Proposal." *College English* 48 (6): 527–42. http://dx.doi.org/10.2307/376707.

Flower, Linda. 1979. "Writer-Based Prose: A Cognitive Basis for Problems in Writing." *College English* 41 (1): 19–37. http://dx.doi.org/10.2307/376357.

Fort, Keith. 1971. "Form, Authority, and the Critical Essay." *College English* 32 (6): 629–39. http://dx.doi.org/10.2307/374316.

Freedman, Aviva. 1995. "The What, Where, When, Why, and How of Classroom Genres." *Petraglia* 121–44.

Freedman, Aviva, and Christine Adam. 1996. "Learning to Write Professionally: 'Situated Learning' and the Transition from University to Professional Discourse." *Journal of Business and Technical Communication* 10 (4): 395–427. http://dx.doi.org/10.1177/1050651996010004001.

Frey, Olivia. 1990. "Beyond Literary Darwinism: Women's Voices and Critical Discourse." *College English* 52 (5): 507–26. http://dx.doi.org/10.2307/377539.

Friedman, Thomas L., and Michael Mandelbaum. 2011. *That Used to Be Us: How America Fell Behind in the World It Invented and How We Can Come Back*. New York: Farrar, Straus and Giroux. http://dx.doi.org/10.3410/f.

Fulkerson, Richard. 2005. "Composition at the Turn of the Twenty-First Century." *College Composition and Communication* 54 (6): 654–87.

Gallagher, Kelly. 2009. *Readicide: How Schools Are Killing Reading and What You Can Do About It*. Portland, ME: Stenhouse.

Gannett, Cinthia. 1992. *Gender and the Journal*. Albany: State University of New York Press.

Gardner, Howard. 1993. *Frames of Mind: The Theory of Multiple Intelligences*. 10th Anniversary edition. New York: Basic Books.

Gardner, Howard. 2006. *Multiple Intelligences: New Horizons in Theory and Practice*. New York: Basic.

Gilligan, Carol. 1982. *A Different Voice: Psychological Theory and Women's Development*. Cambridge, MA: Harvard University Press.

Gioia, Dana. 2007. "Preface." In *To Read or Not to Read: A Question of National Consequence*, 5–6. Washington, DC: National Endowment for the Arts.

Glaser, E. M. 1985. "Critical Thinking: Educating for Responsible Citizenship in a Democracy: National Forum." *Phi Kappa Phi Journal* 6: 24–7.

Glenn, Cheryl. 2004. *Unspoken: A Rhetoric of Silence*. Carbondale: Southern Illinois University Press.

Glenn, Cheryl, and Krista Ratcliffe, eds. 2011. *Silence and Listening as Rhetorical Arts*. Carbondale: Southern Illinois University Press.

Goleman, Daniel. 2005. *Emotional Intelligence: Why It Can Matter More Than IQ*. 10th Anniversary edition. New York: Bantam.

Graff, Gerald, and Cathy Birkenstein. 2006. *"They Say/I Say: The Moves That Matter in Academic Writing*. New York: Norton.

Halasek, Kay. 1999. *A Pedagogy of Possibility: Bakhtinian Perspectives on Composition Studies*. Carbondale: Southern Illinois University Press.

Hansen, Kristine. 2012. "The Composition Marketplace: Shopping for Credit versus Learning to Write." In *College Credit for Writing in High School: The "Taking Care of" Business*, ed. Kristine Hansen and Christine R. Farris, 1–39. Urbana, IL: NCTE.

Harris, Joseph. 1997. *A Teaching Subject: Composition since 1966*. Upper Saddle River, NJ: Prentice.

Haskins, Ron, and Isabel Sawhill. 2009. *Creating an Opportunity Society*. Washington, DC: Brookings Institution Press.

Hassel, Holly, and Joanne Baird Giordano. 2009. "Transfer Institutions, Transfer of Knowledge: The Development of Rhetorical Adaptability and Underprepared Writers." *Teaching English in the Two-Year College* 37 (1): 24–40.

Haswell, Richard. 1991. *Gaining Ground in College: Tales of Development and Interpretation*. Dallas: Southern Methodist University Press.

Haswell, Richard. 2000. "Documenting Improvement in College Writing: A Longitudinal Approach." *Written Communication* 17: 307–52.

Healy, Jane M. (Original work published 1990) 1999. *Endangered Minds: Why Children Don't Think—And What We Can Do About It*. New York: Simon and Schuster.

Heilker, Paul. 1996. *The Essay: Theory and Pedagogy for an Active Form*. Urbana, IL: NCTE.

Heilker, Paul. 2001. "Official Feasts and Carnivals: Student Writing and Public Ritual." *TETYC* 29 (1): 77–84.

Hetherington, E. Mavis, and John Kelly. 2002. *For Better or for Worse: Divorce Reconsidered*. New York: Norton.

Hillocks, George. 1995. *Teaching Writing as Reflective Practice*. New York: Teachers College Press.

Hillocks, George. 2002. *The Testing Trap: How State Writing Assessments Control Learning*. New York: Teachers College Press.

Hillocks, George. 2010. "Teaching Argument for Critical Thinking and Writing: An Introduction." *English Journal* 99 (6): 24–32.

Hindman, Jane E. 2001. "Making Writing Matter: Using 'the Personal' to Recover[y] an Essential[ist] Tension in Academic Discourse." *College English* 64 (1): 88–108.

Hirst, Paul. 1973. "Liberal Education and the Nature of Knowledge." In *Philosophy of Education*, ed. R. S. Peters, 87–111. New York: Oxford University Press.

Hoffman, Alice. 2006. "The Perfect Family." In *Interactions: A Thematic Reader*, 6th ed., ed. Ann Moseley and Jeanette Harris, 134–36. Boston: Houghton Mifflin. [Originally published as "Provider." *The New York Times*, 1 November 1992: A7.]

Hunt, Doug. 2002. *Misunderstanding the Assignment: Teenage Students, College Writing, and the Pains of Growth*. Portsmouth, NH: Boynton/Cook.

Johnson, Kristine. 2013. "Beyond Standards: Disciplinary and National Perspectives on Habits of Mind." *College Composition and Communication* 64 (3): 517–41.

Jolliffe, David A. 2007. "Review Essay: Learning to Read as Continuing Education." *College Composition and Communication* 58 (3): 470–94.

Jolliffe, David A. 2010. "Advanced Placement English and College Composition: Can't We All Get Along?" In *What Is "College-Level" Writing?* Volume 2: *Assignments, Readings, and Student Writing Samples*, ed. Patrick Sullivan, Howard Tinberg, and Sheridan Blau, 57–76. Urbana, IL: NCTE.

Jolliffe, David A., and Allison Harl. 2008. "Texts of Our Institutional Lives: Studying the 'Reading Transition' from High School to College: What Are Our Students Reading and Why?" *College English* 70 (6): 599–607.

Jones, Elizabeth, et al. 1995. *National Assessment of College Student Learning: Identifying College Graduates' Essential Skills in Writing, Speech and Listening, and Critical Thinking*. (NCES No. 95-001). Washington, DC: U.S. Government Printing Office.

Jung, Julie. 2011. "Reflective Writing's Synechodochic Imperative: Process Descriptions Redescribed." *College English* 73 (6): 628–47.

Kahneman, Daniel. 2011. *Thinking, Fast and Slow*. New York: Farrar, Straus, and Giroux.

Kaufman, James C., and Robert J. Sternberg, eds. 2006. *The International Handbook of Creativity*. Cambridge: Cambridge University Press.

Kaufman, James C., and Robert J. Sternberg. 2010. *The Cambridge Handbook of Creativity*. Cambridge: Cambridge University Press.

Kegan, Robert. 1994. *In Over Our Heads: The Mental Demands of Modern Life*. Cambridge, MA: Harvard University Press.

King, Patricia, and Karen Strohm Kitchener. 1994. *Developing Reflective Judgment.* San Francisco: Jossey-Bass.

Kirsch, Gesa E. 2009. "From Introspection to Action: Connecting Spirituality and Civic Engagement." *CCC* 60 (4): W1–W15.

Kirsch, Gesa E., Faye Spencer Maor, Lance Massey, Lee Nickoson-Massey, and Mary P. Sheridan-Rabideau, eds. 2003. *Feminism and Composition: A Critical Sourcebook.* Boston: Bedford St. Martin's.

Kohn, Alfie. 1993. *Punished by Rewards: The Trouble with Gold Stars, Incentive Plans, A's, Praise, and Other Bribes.* Boston: Houghton Mifflin.

Kohn, Alfie. 2000. *The Case against Standardized Testing: Raising the Scores, Ruining the Schools.* Portsmouth, NH: Heinemann.

Koretz, Daniel. 2008. *Measuring Up: What Educational Testing Really Tells Us.* Cambridge, MA: Harvard University Press.

Krashen, Stephen D. 2004. *The Power of Reading: Insights from the Research.* 2nd ed. Westport, CT: Libraries Unlimited.

Kurfiss, Joanne G. 1988. *Critical Thinking: Theory, Research, Practice, and Possibilities.* ASHE-ERIC/Higher Education Research Report vol. 17, no. 2. Washington, DC: ERIC.

Lamb, Catherine. 1991. "Beyond Argument in Feminist Composition." *College English* 42 (1): 11–24.

Langer, Ellen J. 1989. *Mindfulness.* Cambridge, MA: Perseus.

Langer, Ellen J. 1997. *The Power of Mindful Learning.* Cambridge, MA: Perseus.

Langer, Judith A., and Arthur N. Applebee. 1988. *How Writing Shapes Thinking.* Madison: University of Wisconsin Press.

Larsen, Lindsay. 2010. "Disappearing into the World of Books." In *What Is "College-Level" Writing?* Volume 2: *Assignments, Readings, and Student Writing Samples,* ed. Patrick Sullivan, Howard Tinberg, and Sheridan Blau. Urbana, IL: NCTE. 280–92.

Lazere, Donald. 2009. "Review: Stanley Fish's Tightrope Act." *College English* 71 (5): 528–37.

Levinas, Emmanuel. 2006. *Humanism of the Other.* Trans. Nidra Poller. Urbana: University of Illinois Press.

Lindblom, Ken, ed. 2010. *English Journal.* Special Issue: Motivating Students. 100 (1).

Lindquist, Julie. 2004. "Class Affects, Classroom Affectations: Working through the Paradoxes of Strategic Empathy." *College English* 67 (2): 187–209. http://dx.doi.org/10.2307/4140717.

Lujan, Alfredo. 2010. "The Salem Witch Trials: Voice(s)." In *What Is "College-Level" Writing?* Volume 2, ed. Patrick Sullivan, Howard Tinberg, and Sheridan Blau, 41–57. Urbana, IL: NCTE.

Lunsford, Andrea, and Karen Lunsford. 2008. "'Mistakes Are a Fact of Life': A National Comparative Study." *College Composition and Communication* 59 (4): 781–806.

Lyotard, Jean-François. 1988. *Perigrinations: Law, Form, Event.* New York: Columbia University Press.

Mack, Maynard. 1993. *Everybody's Shakespeare.* Lincoln: University of Nebraska Press.

Maliszewski, Casey. 2010. "Home Schooled." In *What Is "College-Level" Writing?* Volume 2: *Assignments, Readings, and Student Writing Samples,* edited by Patrick Sullivan, Howard Tinberg, and Sheridan Blau, 257–66. Urbana, IL: NCTE.

Manning, G. L., and M. Manning. 1984. "What Models of Recreational Reading Make a Difference?" *Reading World* 23 (4): 375–80. http://dx.doi.org/10.1080/19388078 409557787.

Marini, Anthony, and Randy Genereaux. 1995. "The Challenge of Teaching for Transfer." In *Teaching for Transfer: Fostering Generalization in Learning,* ed. Anne MacKeough, Judy Lee Lupart, and Anthony Marini, 1–20. Mahwah, NJ: Erlbaum.

Marius, Richard. 1992. "Composition Studies." In *Redrawing the Boundaries: The Transformation of English and American Literary Studies,* ed. Stephen Greenblatt and Giles Gunn, 466–81. New York: MLA.

Massey, Douglas S. 2007. *Categorically Unequal: The American Stratification System.* New York: Russell Sage.

McCormick, Kathleen. 1994. *The Culture of Reading and the Teaching of English.* Manchester, UK: Manchester University Press.

Melzer, Dan. 2009. "Writing Assignments across the Curriculum: A National Study of College Writing." *College Composition and Communication* 61 (2): 378.

Meyer, Jan H.F., Ray Land, and Caroline Baillie, eds. 2010. *Threshold Concepts and Transformational Learning.* Rotterdam, Netherlands: Sense.

Meyer, Sheree L. 1993. "Refusing to Play the Confidence Game: The Illusion of Mastery in the Reading/Writing of Texts." *College English* 55 (1): 46–63. http://dx.doi.org/10.2307/378364.

Miller, Donalyn. 2009. *The Book Whisperer: Awakening the Inner Reader in Every Child.* San Francisco: Jossey-Bass.

Miller, Donalyn. 2013. *Reading in the Wild: The Book Whisperer's Keys to Cultivating Lifelong Reading Habits.* San Francisco: Jossey-Bass.

Morrow, Nancy. 1997. "The Role of Reading in the Composition Classroom." *JAC* 17 (3).

Mosley, Milka Mustenikova. 2006. "The Truth about High School English." In *What Is "College-Level" Writing?* ed. Patrick Sullivan and Howard Tinberg, 58–68. Urbana, IL: NCTE.

National Center on Education and the Economy. 2013. *What Does It Really Mean to Be College and Work Ready?* Washington, DC: NCEE.

National Commission on Writing in America's Schools and Colleges. 2003. *The Neglected "R": The Need for a Writing Revolution.* Princeton, NJ: College Board.

National Council of Teachers of English. 2007. Adolescent Literacy: An NCTE Policy Research Brief." http://www.ncte.org/library/NCTEfiles/Resources/Magazine/Chron0907AdLitBrief.pdf.

National Endowment for the Arts. 2007. *To Read or Not to Read: A Question of National Consequence.* Washington, DC: National Endowment for the Arts.

Nussbaum, Martha. 2001. *Upheavals of Thought.* Cambridge: Cambridge University Press. http://dx.doi.org/10.1017/CBO9780511840715.

Oliver, Mary. 2005. "Mockingbirds." In *New and Selected Poems: Volume Two.*, 154–55. Boston: Beacon.

Olson, Gary A. 1995. "Resisting a Discourse of Mastery: A Conversation with Jean-François Lyotard." In *Women Writing Culture*, ed. Gary A. Olson and Elizabeth Hirsh, 169–92. Albany: State University of New York Press.

Olson, Gary A. 1999. "Toward a Post-Process Composition: Abandoning the Rhetoric of Assertion." In *Post-Process Theory: Beyond the Writing-Process Paradigm*, ed. Thomas Kent, 7–15. Carbondale: Southern Illinois University Press.

Pascarella, Ernest T., and Patrick T. Terenzini. 2005. *How College Affects Students*, vol. 2: *A Third Decade of Research.* San Francisco: Jossey-Bass.

Perkins, David N., and Gavriel Salomon. 2012. "Knowledge to Go: A Motivational and Dispositional View of Transfer." *Educational Psychologist* 47 (3): 248–58. http://dx.doi.org/10.1080/00461520.2012.693354.

Perlstein, Linda. 2007. *Tested: One American School Struggles to Make the Grade.* New York: Holt.

Perry, William. (1968, 1970) 1999. *Forms of Ethical and Intellectual Development in the College Years: A Scheme.* San Francisco: Jossey-Bass.

Peterson, Christopher, and Martin E.P. Seligman. 2004. *Character Strengths and Virtues: A Handbook and Classification.* New York: Oxford University Press.

Petraglia, Joseph, ed. 1995. *Reconceiving Writing, Rethinking Writing Instruction.* Mahwah, NJ: Lawrence Erlbaum.

Pink, Daniel. 2009. *Drive: The Surprising Truth about What Motivates Us.* New York: Riverhead. http://dx.doi.org/10.4271/2009-01-1609.

Qualley, Donna. 1997. *Turns of Thought: Teaching Composition as Reflexive Inquiry.* Portsmouth, NH: Boynton Cook.

Ratcliffe, Krista. 2005. *Rhetorical Listening: Identification, Gender, Whiteness.* Carbondale: Southern Illinois University Press.

Ravitch, Diane. 2010. *The Death and Life of the Great American School System: How Testing and Choice Are Undermining Education.* New York: Basic.

Ripley, Amanda. 2013. *The Smartest Kids in the World: And How They Got That Way.* New York: Simon and Schuster.

Ritchhart, Ron. 2002. *Intellectual Character.* San Francisco: Jossey-Bass.

Roberts, Judith C., and Keith A. Roberts. 2008. "Deep Reading, Cost/Benefit, and the Construction of Meaning: Enhancing Reading Comprehension and Deep Learning in Sociology Courses." *Teaching Sociology* 36 (2): 125–40.

Robillard, Amy E. 2003. "It's Time for Class: Toward a More Complex Pedagogy of Narrative." *College English* 66 (1): 74–92. http://dx.doi.org/10.2307/3594235.

Robinson, Ken. 2011. *Out of Our Minds: Learning to be Creative.* Revised and updated ed. West Sussex, UK: Capstone.

Rogers, Carl R. 1961. "Dealing with Breakdowns in Communication—Interpersonal and Intergroup" [Formerly: "Communication: Its Blocking and its Facilitation."] In *On Becoming a Person,* 329–37. Boston: Houghton Mifflin.

Rothstein, Richard. 2004. *Class and Schools: Using Social, Economic, and Educational Reform to Close the Black-White Achievement Gap.* Washington, DC: Economic Policy Institute.

Rothstein, Richard, Rebecca Jacobsen, and Tamara Wilder. 2008. *Grading Education: Getting Accountability Right.* Washington, DC: Economic Policy Institute.

Russell, David. 2002. *Writing in the Academic Disciplines: A Curricular History.* 2nd ed. Carbondale: Southern Illinois University Press.

Ryan, Richard M., and Cynthia L. Powelson. 1991. "Autonomy and Relatedness as Fundamental to Motivation and Education." *Journal of Experimental Education* 60: 49–66.

Ryan, Richard M., V. Mims, and Richard Koestner. 1983. "Relation of Reward Contingency and Interpersonal Context to Intrinsic Motivation: A Review and Test Using Cognitive Evaluation Theory." *Journal of Personality and Social Psychology* 45: 736–50.

Sacks, Peter. 1999. *Standardized Minds: The High Price of America's Testing Culture and What We Can Do about It.* Cambridge, MA: Perseus.

Sahlberg, Pasi. 2011. *Finnish Lessons: What Can the World Learn from Educational Change in Finland?* New York: Teachers College Press.

Salvatori, Mariolina. 1996. "Conversations with Texts: Reading in the Teaching of Composition." *College English* 58 (4): 440–54. http://dx.doi.org/10.2307/378854.

Salvatori, Mariolina, and Patricia Donahue. 2005. *The Elements (and Pleasures) of Difficulty.* New York: Pearson Longman.

Saxon, D. Patrick, and Hunter R. Boylan. 2001. "The Cost of Remedial Education in Higher Education." *Journal of Developmental Education* 25 (2): 2–8.

Scardamalia, Marlene, and Carl Bereiter. 2006. "Knowledge Building: Theory, Pedagogy, and Technology." In *Cambridge Handbook of the Learning Sciences,* ed. K. Sawyer, 97–118. New York: Cambridge University Press.

Scherff, Lisa, and Carolyn Piazza. 2005. "The More Things Change, the More They Stay the Same: A Survey of High School Students' Writing Experiences." *Research in the Teaching of English* 39 (3): 271–304.

Schon, Donald A. 1983. *The Reflective Practitioner: How Professionals Think in Action.* New York: Basic.

Schon, Donald A. 1987. *Educating the Reflective Practitioner: Toward a New Design for Teaching and Learning in the Professions.* San Francisco: Jossey-Bass.

Seabury, Marcia Bundy. 1991. "Critical Thinking via the Abstraction Ladder." *English Journal* 80 (2): 44–49. http://dx.doi.org/10.2307/818752.

Sedaris, David. 2004. "Us and Them." In *Dress Your Family in Corduroy and Denim*, 3–12. New York: Little, Brown.

Seo, Byung-In. 2007. "Defending the Five-Paragraph Essay." *English Journal* 97 (2): 15–6.

Smit, David W. 2004. *The End of Composition Studies*. Carbondale: Southern Illinois University Press.

Smith, Kerri. 2006. "Speaking My Mind: In Defense of the Five-Paragraph Essay." *English Journal* 95 (4): 16–7. http://dx.doi.org/10.2307/30047081.

Smith, Michael W., and Jeffery D. Wilhelm. 2002. *Reading Don't Fix No Chevys: Literacy in the Lives of Young Men*. Portsmouth, NH: Heinemann.

Soliday, Mary. 2002. *The Politics of Remediation*. Pittsburgh: University of Pittsburgh Press.

Soliday, Mary. 2004. "Reading Student Writing with Anthropologists: Stance and Judgment in College Writing." *College Composition and Communication* 56 (1): 72–93.

Soliday, Mary. 2011. *Everyday Genres: Writing Assignments across the Disciplines*. Carbondale: Southern Illinois University Press.

Sommers, Nancy. 1980. "Revision Strategies of Student Writers and Experienced Adult Writers." *College Composition and Communication* 31 (4): 378–88.

Sommers, Nancy. 1982. "Responding to Student Writing." *College Composition and Communication* 33 (2): 148–56.

Sommers, Nancy, and Laura Saltz. 2004. "The Novice as Expert: Writing the Freshman Year." *College Composition and Communication* 56 (1): 124–49.

Sternberg, Robert. 1999. *Handbook of Creativity*. New York: Cambridge University Press.

Sternberg, Robert. 2007. *Wisdom, Intelligence, and Creativity Synthesized*. Cambridge: Cambridge University Press.

Sternberg, Robert, and Todd I. Lubart. 1995. *Defying the Crowd: Cultivating Creativity in a Culture of Conformity*. New York: Free Press.

Sternglass, Marilyn. 1997. *Time to Know Them: A Longitudinal Study of Writing and Learning at the College Level*. Mahwah, NJ: Lawrence Erlbaum Associates.

Strong American Schools. 2008. *Diploma to Nowhere*. Washington, DC: Strong American Schools.

Sullivan, Patrick. 2005. "Cultural Narratives about Success and the Material Conditions of Class at the Community College." *Teaching English in the Two-Year College* 33 (2): 142–60.

Sullivan, Patrick. 2010. "What Can We Learn About 'College-Level' Writing From Basic Writing Students? The Importance of Reading." In *What Is "College-Level" Writing?* Volume 2: *Assignments, Readings, and Student Writing Samples*, edited by Patrick Sullivan, Howard Tinberg, and Sheridan Blau, 233–53. Urbana, IL: NCTE.

Sullivan, Patrick, and Howard Tinberg, eds. 2006. *What Is "College-Level" Writing?* Urbana, IL: NCTE.

Sullivan, Patrick, Howard Tinberg, and Sheridan Blau, eds. 2010. *What Is "College-Level" Writing?* Volume 2: *Assignments, Readings, and Student Writing Samples*. Urbana, IL: NCTE.

Summerfield, Judith, and Philip Anderson. 2012. "A Framework Adrift." *College English* 74 (6): 544–47.

Taczak, Kara, and William H. Thelin. 2009. "(Re)Envisioning the Divide: The Impact of College Courses on High School Students." *Teaching English in the Two-Year College* 37 (1): 7–23.

Tannen, Deborah. 1999. *The Argument Culture: Stopping America's War of Words*. New York: Ballantine.

Tishman, Shari, David N. Perkins, and Eileen Jay. 1994. *The Thinking Classroom: Learning and Teaching in a Culture of Thinking*. Boston: Allyn & Bacon.

Tough, Paul. 2012. *How Children Succeed: Grit, Curiosity, and the Hidden Power of Character*. Boston: Houghton Mifflin Harcourt.

Tremmel, Michelle. 2011. "What to Make of the Five-Paragraph Theme: History of the Genre and Implications." *Teaching English in the Two-Year College* 39 (1): 29–42.

United States Department of Education. 2006. *A Test of Leadership: Charting the Future of U.S. Higher Education.* Washington, DC: U.S. Department of Education. http://www2. ed.gov/about/bdscomm/list/hiedfuture/reports/pre-pub-report.pdf

United States Department of Education, National Center for Education Statistics. 2010. Profile of Undergraduate Students: 2007–08. Table 6.2: Percentage of first- and second-year undergraduates who reported ever taking a remedial course after high school graduation.

United States Department of Education, National Center for Education Statistics. 2011. *The Condition of Education 2010.* Washington, DC: U.S. Department of Education.

United States Department of Education, National Center for Education Statistics. 2013. *2011–12 National Postsecondary Student Aid Study* (NPSAS:12). Washington, DC: NCES.

United States Department of Education, National Center for Education Statistics. 2014. *The Condition of Education 2014.* Washington, DC: U.S. Department of Education.

Venezia, Andrea, Michael Kirst, and Anthony Antonio. 2003. *Betraying the College Dream: How Disconnected K–12 and Postsecondary Education Systems Undermine Student Aspirations.* Final Policy Report from Stanford University's Bridge Project.

Vygotsky, L. S. 1978. *Mind in Society: The Development of Higher Psychological Processes.* Ed. Michael Cole, Vera John-Steiner, Sylvia Scribner, and Ellen Souberman. Cambridge, MA: Harvard University Press.

Wagner, Tony. 2008. *The Global Achievement Gap.* New York: Basic.

Wardle, Elizabeth. 2009. "'Mutt Genres' and the Goal of FYC: Can We Help Students Write the Genres of the University?" *College Composition and Communication* 60 (4): 765–89.

Weimer, Maryellen. 2013. *Learner-Centered Teaching: Five Key Changes to Practice.* San Francisco: Jossey-Bass.

White, Edward M. 2010. "My Five-Paragraph-Theme Theme." In *What Is "College-Level" Writing?* Volume 2: *Assignments, Readings, and Student Writing Samples,* edited by Patrick Sullivan, Howard Tinberg, and Sheridan Blau, 137–41. Urbana, IL: NCTE.

Wiggins, Grant, and Jay McTighe. 2005. *Understanding by Design.* Expanded 2nd ed. Alexandria: Association for Supervision & Curriculum Development.

Williams, Raymond. 1977. *Marxism and Literature.* New York: Oxford University Press.

Willingham, Daniel T. 2009. *Why Don't Students Like School: A Cognitive Scientist Answers Questions about How the Mind Works and What It Means for the Classroom.* San Francisco: Jossey-Bass.

Wilson, William Julius. 1996. *When Work Disappears: The World of the New Urban Poor.* New York: Vintage.

Wineburg, Sam. 2001. "Historical Thinking and Other Unnatural Acts." In *Historical Thinking,* 3–27. Philadelphia: Temple University Press.

Winsor, Dorothy. 2000. "Ordering Work: Blue Collar Literacy and the Political Nature of Genre." *Written Communication* 17 (2): 155–84. http://dx.doi.org/10.1177/074108830 0017002001.

Wolvin, Andrew D., ed. 2010. *Listening and Human Communication in the 21st Century.* Hoboken, NJ: Wiley-Blackwell. http://dx.doi.org/10.1002/9781444314908.

Wolvin, Andrew, and Carolyn Gwynn Coakley. 1996. *Listening.* 5th ed. Boston: McGraw-Hill.

Worthy, Jo, Margo Turner, and Megan Moorman. 1998. "The Precarious Place of Self-Selected Reading." *Language Arts* 75 (4): 296–304.

Yancey, Kathleen Blake. 1998. *Reflection in the Writing Classroom.* Logan: Utah State University Press.

Yancey, Kathleen Blake. 2009. "2008 NCTE Presidential Address: The Impulse to Compose and the Age of Composition." *Research in the Teaching of English* 43 (3): 316–38.

Yancey, Kathleen Blake, Liane Robertson, and Kara Taczak. 2014. *Writing across Contexts: Transfer, Composition, and Sites of Writing.* Logan, UT: Utah State University Press.

Yancey, Kathleen Blake, and Michael Spooner. 1998. "A Single Good Mind: Collaboration, Cooperation, and the Writing Self." *College Composition and Communication* 49 (1): 45–62.

Zeiger, William. 1985. "The Exploratory Essay: Enfranchising the Spirit of Inquiry in College Composition." *College English* 47 (5): 454–66. http://dx.doi.org/10.2307/376877.

# ABOUT THE AUTHOR

PATRICK SULLIVAN teaches English at Manchester Community College in Manchester, Connecticut. He believes deeply in the community college mission, and has greatly enjoyed his many years teaching at MCC. His scholarly work has appeared in *Teaching English in the Two-Year College, Academe, College English, College Composition and Communication, Journal of Developmental English, Community College Journal of Research and Practice,* and *The Journal of Adolescent and Adult Literacy.* He is also the editor, with Howard Tinberg, of *What is College-Level Writing?* (NCTE 2006) and, with Howard Tinberg and Sheridan Blau, of *What is College-Level Writing? Volume 2: Assignments, Readings, and Student Writing Samples* (NCTE 2010). In 2011, he received TYCA's Nell Ann Pickett Award for service to the two-year college.

# INDEX